Everyday Adjustments
in Havana

Lexington Studies on Cuba

Series Editor: John M. Kirk, Dalhousie University
and Mervyn Bain, University of Aberdeen

This series will publish texts on all aspects of Cuba, focusing on the post-1959 period. It seeks to be truly interdisciplinary, with studies of all aspects of contemporary Cuba—from foreign policy to culture, sociology, to economics. The series is particularly interested in broad, comprehensive topics (such as women in Cuba, economic challenges, human rights, the role of the media, etc.). All ideological positions are welcomed, with solid academic quality being the defining criterion. In exceptional circumstances, edited collections will be considered, but the main focus is on high-quality, original, and provocative monographs and innovative scholarship.

Recent Titles in This Series

Everyday Adjustments in Havana: Economic Reforms, Mobility, and Emerging Inequalities
By Hope Bastian

Cuba's Gay Revolution: Normalizing Sexual Diversity Through a Health-Based Approach
By Emily J. Kirk

Everyday Adjustments in Havana

Economic Reforms, Mobility, and Emerging Inequalities

Hope Bastian

LEXINGTON BOOKS
Lanham • Boulder • New York • London

Published by Lexington Books
An imprint of The Rowman & Littlefield Publishing Group, Inc.
4501 Forbes Boulevard, Suite 200, Lanham, Maryland 20706
www.rowman.com

Unit A, Whitacre Mews, 26-34 Stannary Street, London SE11 4AB

British Library Cataloguing in Publication Information Available

Library of Congress Cataloging-in-Publication Data

Names: Bastian, Hope, author.
Title: Everyday adjustments in Havana : economic reforms, mobility, and
    emerging inequalities / Hope Bastian.
Description: Lanham : Lexington Books, [2018] | Series: Lexington studies on
    Cuba | Includes bibliographical references and index.
Identifiers: LCCN 2018016327 (print) | LCCN 2018017342 (ebook)
Subjects: LCSH: Havana (Cuba)—Social conditions—21st century. | Havana
    (Cuba)—Economic conditions—21st century. | Havana
    (Cuba)—Civilization—21st century. | Havana (Cuba)—History.
Classification: LCC HN210.H33 (ebook) | LCC HN210.H33 B37 2018 (print) | DDC
    306.097291/23—dc23
LC record available at https://lccn.loc.gov/2018016327

ISBN: 978-1-4985-7109-8 (cloth : alk. paper)
ISBN: 978-1-4985-7111-1 (pbk. : alk. paper)
ISBN: 978-1-4985-7110-4 (electronic)

To my parents, Joyce and Jeff Bastian

Contents

List of Figures and Tables

FIGURES

TABLES

Acknowledgments

This journey has been a long one and so is the list of people who have helped me along the path, without whom this book would have never been written. I am deeply grateful to everyone who shared their life stories with me to help me understand different parts of Cuba's history and present.

First, I'd like to express my most sincere gratitude for the people I have worked closely with in Havana over the years. Since 2004, when I came to live in Cuba for the first time, I have been privileged to collaborate with the Centro Memorial Martin Luther King where I have learned so much from the Suárez family, the great translators and people on the logistics teams, members of the *Redes*, and Cubans from all over the country who I have participated in workshops with at the center.

My research in Havana was sponsored by the Instituto Cubano de Investigación Cultural "Juan Marinello" (ICIC). Thanks to the vision of Fernando Martínez Heredia and Elena Socarrás, the Juan Marinello has been an important institution for the development of cultural anthropology in Cuba. I was lucky to have the support of friends and colleagues, Henry Heredia, Rodrigo Espina, and Yisel Rivero Baxter, while doing my field research, and to participate over the years in events with an amazing group of researchers including Hamlet López, Yeisa Sarduy, Niurka Pérez, Ana Vera Estrada, and Carlos Venegas. I am grateful to have shared my time in the field with fellow cultural anthropologist Maya Berry and ethnomusicologist Ruthie Meadows.

At the Centro de Investigaciones Psicológicas y Sociológicas (CIPS), I have learned so much from the legacy of Mayra Espina and Lilia Núñez Moreno, members of the original Social Structure Research Group, and Enrique Gómez Cabezas who has continued their work. At the beginning of my research, I enjoyed conversations with Daybel Pañellas at the University of Havana about our common research interests and am proud to cite her work and that of her students in this book. My knowledge of the city of Havana and housing owes a great debt to Ricardo Núñez, Mario Coyula, Marta Garcialaso, Gina Rey, and Ruslan Muñoz.

Casa de las Américas has been another home for me in Havana. Working with Professors Marta Núñez, Manuel Yepe, Barbara Danzie, Jorge Mario Sánchez, Rafael Hernández, Enrique Beldarraín, Susana Haug, Gustavo Arcos, Yulexis Almeida, Victor Fowler, Carlos (Kako) Escalona, Susel Gutierrez, and Patricia Motola has taught my students so much, and me even more.

At the Consortium for Advanced Studies Abroad (CASA) and Brown University I am lucky to have Rainer Schultz, Kendall Brostuen, Evelyn Hu-DeHart, Esther Whitfield, Jennifer Lambe, and Daniel Rodríguez as colleagues. Over the years the insightful questions asked by my students in study abroad programs at American University, CIEE, and CASA have helped to sharpen my thinking about Cuba and figure out how to explain Cuba's complexities and contradictions. At the Colegio San Geronimo in Old Havana, colleagues Myriam Padrón and Michael Sánchez have helped me understand the dynamics and norms of Cuban higher education and become the teacher I am today. I am proud to be a member of the faculty in this program founded by Eusebio Leal Spengler.

I am also indebted to my European social anthropologist colleagues, María Padrón Hernández and Heidi Härkönen, whose great theses inspired me to finish mine; to all the academics who study Cuba and whom I have had the pleasure to share with in Havana; and to those who have inspired me from afar: Denni Blum, Karen Dubinsky, Susan Lord, John Kirk, Anna Cristina Pertierra, Hanna Garth, Laurie Fredrik, Devyn Spence Benson, Elise Andaya and Sarah Blue. Thanks also to the Pioneers: Mona Rosendahl, Nadine Fernandez, and Jill Hamberg.

Thanks are also due to the faculty at American University and Guilford College, especially Brett Williams, Phil Brenner, David Vine, and to fellow students Ashanté Reese, Matt Thomann, Ted Samuel, Nikki Lane, Joowon Park, Jennifer Grubbs, Erin Moriarity Harrelson, Nell Haynes, Elijah Edelman, Audrey Cooper, Julie Maldonado, and Naomi Steiner. I am truly grateful for the ways in which each have shaped me and the academic path I have taken.

In the US we say that "No man is an island" and in Havana people often say that "Your neighbors are your closest family." I am lucky to have had the best neighbors in the world: Ana and Duzán, and Magdalena and Rolando. I am blessed as well by my life-long friends Fenna Mandolang, Sara Leitman, Melissa Onyango-Robshaw, and Zoe Kelly, who accompanied me from afar on the journey.

My deepest love and gratitude to my family: my mom, Joyce Bastian, my dad, Jeff Bastian, for a lifetime of unconditional love and support. My mother, the Comma Queen, is my most dedicated reader and editor and has read this book at every stage of its development. Any missing commas, however, are strictly my own omissions. Living in Cuba takes a stateside support team and they have been the best team imaginable. I am also grateful to my sister, Laura Bastian, and the love of my nieces Mila, Ally, and Sasha who make me so proud to be their Auntie Hopi.

My heartfelt thanks to my extended families in Cuba, the people who have loved me and cared for me as family over the years in Havana: Baby and family; Jorge, Rosa Nieves and Jorgito; Mariluz and Eduardo; Katy, Mariblanca, Eduardo, Elizabeth, Monica, and Alberto; Jova and Silvia; and Kirenia and the F/friends of Havana Monthly Meeting.

And last, but never least, my partner *en todo*, my wife Dachelys Valdés Moreno.

Introduction

Understanding Inequality in Cuba

On July 26, 2007, in his first speech as acting President, Raúl Castro asked Cubans to speak out about the changes they felt the country needed. The motto of the current revolutionary period was unveiled that day: "Revolution means a sense of our moment in history, it means changing all that ought to be changed" (Castro Ruz, 2007). Since 2010, Cuban President Raúl Castro and the Cuban Communist Party have begun a process that they call the "updating" of the nation's social and economic system. In November 2010, the Cuban Communist Party unveiled a draft of its new five-year plan for reorienting the priorities of the state's new economic and social policies (Morris 2014, 36). These "Guidelines of Economic and Social Policy of the Party and the Revolution" have served as the blueprint for new policies that have shrunk the role of the state in the Cuban domestic economy, and opened new spaces of labor and consumption. As the *Guidelines* are gradually implemented, new logics of distribution and value are becoming increasingly important in everyday life and inequalities are becoming more visible.

Before the Revolution, Cuba was an extremely unequal society. In 1953, 40 percent of Cuba's population received only 6.5 percent of direct income while the richest 5 percent received 26.5 percent of the income (Brundenius 1989, 167). After the 1959 Revolution, state policies designed to redistribute wealth and reduce inequalities were extremely successful. A wave of new laws and reforms aimed to eliminate the widespread social and regional inequalities, malnutrition, unemployment, and poverty which had characterized pre-revolutionary society. This first period from 1959–71 was characterized by radical social transformations, a radical reorganization of the pre-revolutionary class structure, and generalized upward social mobility. A second period of revolution, from the 1970s to 1989, was characterized by the consolidation and reproduction of a new Socialist social structure. As the result of Revolutionary reforms, by the mid-1980s, many widespread social and regional inequalities so common before 1959 had been largely eliminated (Burchardt 2002, 57). By 1986, the poorest 40 percent of the Cuban population received 26 percent of the country's income and the top 5 percent only 10.1 percent (Brundenius 1989, 167).

The post-Soviet economic crisis of the 1990s, known as the "Special Period" in Cuba, began a period of economic re-stratification, characterized by generalized downward mobility and the emergence of new routes of selective upward social mobility. Anthropological research on gender and household reproduction in Cuba in the 1990s has explored the gendered effects of the crisis and first wave of economic reforms on Cuban households. This research describes some of the survival strategies and consumption practices that became the norm in Havana in the period preceding my study.

During the Special Period, economic inequalities began to reemerge in Cuba. Today there are two currencies in circulation in Cuba: the "hard currency" CUC (approximately $.87 USD= 1 CUC), and the "soft" CUP/Cuban peso (24 CUP=1 CUC). The CUC is a currency that can be freely converted to dollars or euros at hotels, banks, and easily accessible government-run money changing establishments, *Casas de Cambio,* or *CADECAs*, which are located throughout the island. People with access to remittances can change these foreign currencies into CUCs to make purchases in government run "dollar stores." State salaries are paid in CUP. Items in the ration book, bus fares, street food, and limited consumer products are sold in CUP, but it's necessary to have access to CUC for a growing number of daily necessities.

As a result of the 1990s crisis and reforms, by the early 2000s a new system of social and economic stratification had formed. One of the most visible economic cleavages was between people with access to hard currency (CUC) and those attempting to make ends meet on peso salaries (CUP) from state jobs (Togores González 2007).[1]

When compared with many other countries, the scale of difference between the top and bottom of Cuban society may not seem extreme. Cuban poverty has been called a "poverty with protections," as Cuba's "have-nots" enjoy free health care, education, and a social safety net (or the expectation of one) uncommon elsewhere in the region (Ferriol 2004, 179). But despite these guarantees, the differences that exist are particularly jarring given the Revolution's historical commitment to egalitarian social policies. In the period of economic structural adjustments which began in 2010, the consolidation and naturalization of the economic differences are a sign of a crisis of values and a clash of ideologies.

This book explores inequalities and stratification in late socialist Cuba and how macro forces affect everyday lives in Havana households. Changes in social structure in urban Havana from 2008–2015 have made the inequalities that began to reemerge in Cuban society in the 1990s increasingly visible. In order to understand stratification in contemporary Havana, I argue that, rather than looking solely at inequalities in income and the gap between those who have access to CUC and those who do not, it is also important to consider how distinct configurations of capitals (social capital, cultural/political capital [revolutionary cultural capital], and economic capital) structure opportunities for mobility, access to consumption, and power. I use ethnographic data to show how Havana households are adjusting to the adjustments of the economic system by making decisions about their participation in the state and emerging sectors.

When I proposed this research in 2012, media outside of Cuba were framing the rapid restructuring of the Cuban economic and social system since Raúl Castro assumed the presidency in 2008 as an unqualified success story. They pointed hopefully to reforms that increased self-employment and legalized property sales as the beginning of a happy ending to socialism. But, on the island, things often looked and felt differently. Paired with massive layoffs, the policy which allows Cubans to work for themselves was a double-edged sword.

Multigenerational households are common in Havana as a result of housing shortages, and the soaring prices in the housing market after private sales were legalized signaled that this was unlikely to change. The overwhelming uncertainty and anxiety that accompanied the announced changes were rarely mentioned in the foreign press' narratives. Herein lies the urgent need for anthropological research that shows how economic restructuring and growing social inequalities affect people's everyday lives, which can inform policymakers seeking to target social policy to maintain equity.

One of the strengths of the anthropology of post-socialisms has been its ability to challenge neoliberal transition narratives (Burawoy and Verdery 1999; Berdahl, Bunzl, and Lampland 2000). Anthropologists, in their insistence on recognizing the agency of people living in post-socialist countries and exploring "how extra-local economic, political, and social processes intersect with the individual lives of people in the community," have powerfully debunked the idea that all post-socialist societies follow the same steps in an inevitable transition to neoliberal capitalist modernity and have shown that one-size-fits-all economic predictions are inherently faulty (Berdahl, Bunzl, and Lampland 2000, 5). Anthropologists have shown that "post-socialist moral and value systems, when merged with Western ideas, create unpredictable outcomes" (Buyandelgeriyn 2008, 240). As changes continue in Cuba, the new economic system that develops will be unique, influenced by local norms of culture, kinship, and community.

By documenting an important moment in contemporary Cuban history, this book challenges the dominant narratives of transition and assures that the voices and experiences of people in Havana can be heard. Before the 2014 announcement that diplomatic relations between the US and Cuba would be reestablished, information about daily life in Cuba was particularly hard to access due to United States policies which limited US citizens' ability to visit the island. Even today, when cheap flights and expensive packaged tours make Havana much more accessible to US visitors, often getting out of the tourist bubble is difficult, especially for people without language skills to interact directly with Cubans from different walks of life. Stuck in the tourist bubble, even those who manage to make it to the island return with little more information of what is going in the country than the opinions of those they come in contact with who work in the tourism/service industry, itself a privileged sector of the Cuban economy.

People in the US are curious about the changes in Cuba, especially after the death of leader Fidel Castro. Ethnography offers a rare opportunity to break the information blockade, sharing information about life in Cuba and how different social groups in Cuba are experiencing rapidly changing realities with readers in the United States and internationally. Anthropological literature on Cuba that, since the 1990s, has interrogated the effects of economic crisis and reforms on Cuban society and culture and frequently focuses on basic consumption and the everyday challenges of meeting basic needs in a dual economy characterized by increasing inequalities, as well as describing how Cubans are dealing with economic changes and the introduction of neoliberal policies on the island. For pioneering research on basic consumption in Cuba, see Del Real and Pertierra 2008; Pertierra 2008; Garth 2009; Pearson 1997; Porter 2008; Ritter 2005; Sacchetti 2009; Weinreb 2009; Wilson 2009b, 2009a. For writing on how Cuban households deal with changes in economic policy, see Andaya 2009; Brotherton 2005, 2008, 2011; Burchardt 2002; Pearson 1997; Pertierra 2008; Powell 2008. Among recent ethnographies, Weinreb (2009) explicitly looks at class, focusing her study on upper-class Cubans' unrealized consumer desires. However, Cuba today, more than five years into the reforms begun by President Raúl Castro, is already very different from the early 2000s.

My research, in the midst of the wave of economic restructuring following the guidelines, examines social stratification and the diversification of social relations in Cuba to address basic anthropological questions of how state policy changes affect everyday lives on the local scale. The current process of "updating" the country's economic and social system is changing the structures of opportunity created in Cuba after the 1959 Revolution. In light of these changes, how do individuals and families in Havana change their everyday practices and in the way they relate to the labor market to accommodate these new realities? How are responses to recent changes shaped by gender and generational cohorts?

Raúl Castro assumed the presidency in 2008, and many of the reforms were announced between 2010 and 2013. As a result of these reforms, opportunities for mobility and structures of social stratification are changing quickly in Havana and economic difference are becoming more obvious. In this book, I explain how different types of capital (economic, social, and political/cultural) are decisive in access to mobility, consumption, and power in contemporary Havana, and I describe what social structure looks like in Havana today.

This introduction explains my positionality and background as a researcher in Havana during this period, discusses the challenges of "doing Anthropology" and Social Sciences in Cuba, describes the research methods used, and provides summaries of each of the subsequent chapters of the book.

MY POSITIONALITY: BLURRING THE EMIC/ETIC IN HAVANA

When I was seventeen years old I fell in love with the utopian vision of the Cuban Revolution. Despite growing up in Florida, I wasn't really aware of Cuba until I took a class in US Foreign Policy at Tallahassee Community College. I learned in that class about US interventions that hadn't been mentioned in my high school history textbooks: Honduras, Guatemala, Nicaragua... the list seemed endless. Then there was Cuba. It seemed that somehow that little island had been able to achieve the sovereignty that so many other nations had tried and failed to achieve. I was inspired and intrigued: How had Cuba been able to succeed when so many other countries had failed? What was the secret to Cuba's resistance? How had the Revolution been able to survive? I felt like I needed to understand this if I were to have any hope in fighting for justice in my country.

As a teenager I spent long afternoons in the university library reading everything that I could get my hands on about Cuba, and in August 2000, I visited the Eastern Cuban province of Holguín for two weeks. In 2002, I spent a semester in Havana through a study abroad program at the University of Havana (FLACSO), and after college, I returned to Havana to work for Witness for Peace, a US NGO dedicated to changing US policy towards Latin America. I lived in the Marianao neighborhood from September 2004–May 2005 as a Witness for Peace International Team member, working with the Martin Luther King Memorial Center, a Cuban NGO. In May 2005, as a result of a tightening of US travel restrictions, faith-based organizations like Witness for Peace were denied license renewals and I had to leave Cuba.

In February 2008, I returned to Havana to work as an editor for a public health journal. When I returned, I found the city full of optimism. Beautiful new articulated busses plied Havana's streets and there were other visible signs that improvements in the country's macroeconomic indicators were being invested in rebuilding the country's infrastructure. A couple weeks after my return, Raúl Castro was elected President of the Cuban Council of State and Council of Ministers. Later that year when Cupid struck, I did what most young Cubans do in the context of Havana's extreme housing shortage: I moved in with my in-laws. In my new home, I learned much more than I bargained for about life in Cuba and the question that had driven my hunger to learn more about Cuba since the beginning, "How did Cuba survive?," began to change slightly to "How do Cubans survive?" and most pressingly, "How can we survive on my partner's public health salary?" Immediately, before beginning graduate school, I lived in Cuba for eighteen months with my partner and extended family.

After completing my first two years of graduate studies in the US, I returned to Havana in the summer of 2011 to do preliminary dissertation research with a grant from the Tinker Foundation. In that time, I made more contacts in Cuban academia, and became familiar with recent Cuban social science literature in my area of interest. From August to December of 2011, I led American University's undergraduate study abroad program through the Casa de las Américas. During that semester, I got to know Lilia Núñez Moreno, a Cuban sociologist who has studied class and social inequalities since 1978 at the Center for Psychological and Sociological Research (CIPS) [*Centro de Investigaciones Psicológicas y Sociológicas*].

I returned to Cuba from August–December 2012 to collaborate as a research associate at the Juan Marinello Institute for Research and Development of Cuban Culture [*El Instituto Cubano de Investigación Cultural Juan Marinello*]. At the Juan Marinello I did a project on cultural consumption among Cuban youth and explored the effects of the economic crisis and reforms on young people's social participation and consumption practices. I also continued to collaborate with the Social Structure Research Group at CIPS.

In February 2013, I began eighteen months of formal dissertation research funded by the National Science Foundation Doctoral Dissertation Improvement Grant with a research visa provided by the Juan Marinello Institute. I continued my research part-time through 2014 and 2015 while organizing study abroad programs for US students and teaching at the University of Havana.

Participant Observation in Cuban Academia: Some Challenges of "Doing Anthropology" and Social Science Research in Cuba

When I arrived in Cuba to begin my field research I quickly realized that the research questions I was interested in were quite controversial, especially since I was a foreigner from the US. From abroad it had been difficult to locate published studies on inequalities in Cuba in international journals, but on the island I met Cuban colleagues at public lectures, book presentations, and post-graduate workshops who were doing fascinating work and found a thriving community of scholars. I learned about many studies on inequalities that had been commissioned directly by different state agencies or policy makers and, as a result, many of the reports were classified, the researchers were not allowed to publish the results, or were only allowed to do so decades later.

I tried to find work within local research institutions that were doing fascinating work in areas related to my research and was welcomed by Cuban colleagues. On several occasions I came close to being offered appointments as a researcher and faculty member, but in the end, because I am from the US, my appointment did not proceed. It seemed that no one wanted to be the one to take ultimate responsibility for having hired me, a US citizen, to work on such a sensitive research subject. In other research centers, the research agenda was set directly by the Council of State [*Consejo de Estado*] and they could not have a US citizen, even an Anthropologist trained in methods needed by the project team, participating in such sensitive projects. I watched Cuban colleagues take on similar projects with institutional support and often the grass looked greener on the other side. But it took me awhile to learn that there are many challenges to doing social science research in Cuba, no matter who you are, or where you are positioned. In a society in which the state is positioned as the defender of social, economic, gender, and racial equality, some actors felt that collecting information about inequalities was a threat which could possibly provide ammunition to the enemy and discredit the Revolution.

Working alone made the work more difficult and isolating. It was frustrating to know that, as I was trying to study the impacts of recent policy changes, across town my Cuban colleagues were doing the same, but the sensitive politicized nature of the research and my identity as a US citizen meant that we could only collaborate from a distance, or informally. For a US anthropologist coming from an academic culture which values connections with, and learning from, local academics in our field sites, it was frustrating to not be able to have closer connections.

As an anthropologist of Cuba living on the island, I share with my Cuban neighbors and friends "a sense of lost utopia" (Tanuma 2007, 48). Approaching the current reality, Cubans on the island often adopt an ironic stance which Ruth Behar (2000) calls "post utopian irony." We laugh at the same jokes, they from their position as formerly committed "insiders," and I as a committed "outsider," a stance common to many non-Cuban anthropologists who, through participant observation and anthropological thinking, end up dismantling their original presumptions and ethics (Tanuma 2007, 49).

As Tanuma observes, like studies of many other post-communist societies, writing about Cuba "can be broken down into two groups, one who writes seriously in a straightforward voice as if still a committed insider and another who writes ironically as an observing outsider. The former is critical of the introduction of the capitalist economy, whereas the latter is critical of the enduring socialist legacy"(Tanuma 2007, 52). For true outsiders, it is easy to criticize the Cuban Revolution and the Cuban state, joining common cause with dissidents and exiles who aim to change Cuba's leadership and its political, economic, and social system. For both committed outsiders and committed insiders, it can be difficult to distance ourselves from the other group and have critiques accepted as constructive and supportive ones.

Like many anthropologists, I went into the field looking for alternatives and answers to take back home, but in the process, my definition of the home changed. I don't want to produce research that could "feed the enemy" or make Cuba look bad. It is precisely my commitment to the values promoted by the Revolution that continues to convince me of the importance of doing critical research to support the social project of the Cuban Revolution. Like many of the Cuban social scientists I have met, I believe that if we (those committed to the project) don't ask the hard questions, how else are we to understand the society in which we live and the injustices around us while also addressing them? Although controversial, my subject of research is not dissident or made with the intention to support exile views or undermine the Cuban state or the revolutionary social project.

My interest in this research was originally to participate in academic discussions with my Cuban peers, not primarily to explain Cuba to outsiders. But, as the Obama administration advanced the process of normalization of US-Cuban relations, the number of visitors from the US grew exponentially. Over the last couple of years, I have been called on frequently to speak to groups of US visitors about life in Cuba and share my experiences living here as a US anthropologist. These experiences convinced me that, although I feel called to research to contribute new knowledge to Cuban academia, my shifting position as an insider/outsider is unique and has something to contribute to academic debates outside the island as well.

Seeing how interested US visitors are in understanding daily life in Cuba inspired me to write this book to share the lives and stories of the Cubans who have taught me so much in my fieldwork. With the recent changes in travel regulations made by President Trump, fewer US Americans may be able to visit the island, making this book all the more important as a way to teach those outside the island about daily life in Havana, and the frustrations, joys and complexities Cubans face as they adjust to changing political and economic circumstances.

RESEARCH METHODS

Participant Observation

Participant observation was the most important method that I used in my research. I moved several times during the period of my research (2011–2016), which allowed me to observe everyday life in different Havana neighborhoods: Vedado (2011, 2012, 2015, 2016), Centro Habana (2013), and Playa (2014). In the neighborhoods where I lived, I attended periodic *Asamblea de Rendición de Cuentas* meetings held by the neighborhood delegates to the Municipal People's Power Assembly. Municipal delegates directly elected by residents are required to hold yearly public accountability meetings to give voters/neighbors the chance to identify local problems to be addressed by the local government and report back to voters on local issues identified by neighbors the year before. I also attended events organized by my CDR (*Comité de Defensa de la Revolución*) and usually arrived early and stayed late at meetings to participate in informal conversations about the subjects of the called meetings. From 2011–2015, I took fieldnotes from participant observation at beauty parlors, bodegas (especially from the long lines the days when chicken was distributed), neighborhood primary care physician's offices [*Médico de la familia*], policlinics and hospital waiting rooms, public parks, bus stops, the campus of the University of Havana, social events, church gatherings, and dinner-table conversations.

Waiting in line is an important part of life in Havana and, while in the beginning I tried to avoid the lines, I quickly realized that the worst lines are the best places for doing research! Cubans are generally not shy in striking up conversation and when the line can't be avoided, conversing with the people around you is the best defense against the mind-numbing wait. After waiting for two hours to buy potatoes one morning in Centro Habana I had come to know the complete life history of the people before and after me in line: how they came to the neighborhood, their work history, their salaries, their children's recent problems, recent rumors or jokes they had heard, their takes on current events, life in the neighborhood, and the future of the country. I realized that rather than being an endeavor that took my time away from my research, waiting in line in Havana was actually an extremely fruitful research method (and at the end I also had a shopping bag of much coveted potatoes to show for my efforts!)

During my time in the field, I regularly attended academic spaces like the Último Jueves debates organized by Temas, Cuba's premier cultural studies journal, class lectures with Cuban professors taught to my US undergraduate students, and public academic talks, workshops and conferences. During the fall semesters 2011–2012 these courses were taught to American University students and during the Summer and Fall 2014 to CIEE students, and short term groups from a number of US universities. These academic events helped me identify local experts and review research being done by researchers on the island and abroad about historical changes in the configuration of social structure in the revolutionary period. In order to understand stratification in contemporary Cuba, I also met with several local experts on the subject, including Mayra Espina, Lilia Núñez, María del Carmen Zabala, Daybel Pañellas Álvarez, and Enrique Gómez Cabezas.

In order to be generally informed about what was going on around me in Havana, I subscribed to Cuban daily newspapers, *Granma* and *Juventud Rebelde*, and regularly watched Mesa Redonda, and the nightly 8:00 pm news broadcasts on *Cubavisión,* as well as reading weekly news updates published by Cuba Central (Center for Democracy in the Americas). I also attended important cultural events like presentations by Cuban comedians, plays staged by Cuban theatre companies, and Havana's yearly International Festival of New Latin American Cinema. Insights from my fieldnotes of these observations have informed all aspects of this book.

Informal Interviews

Participant observation often resulted in the formation of longer-term relationships with people who I interacted with regularly in informal interviews. These informal interviews provided me with significant amounts of information that are present in all chapters of the book. During my fieldwork, there were more than seventy people with whom I interacted regularly in my research. Often conversations with these individuals would introduce me to new ideas that I would explore further in more formal interviews. Our conversations helped connect me to different neighborhoods and understand life in Havana from many different perspectives. A list of these contacts with brief summaries of their household composition, profession, occupation, and place of residence is published in Appendix A.

Three-Part Interviews

In order to understand perceptions of social stratification and class, consumption practices, and cultural practices in contemporary Havana, I designed a three-part interview process that included an interview on Social Networks, one on Basic Consumption and Cultural Consumption, and a third that focused on the Social Stratification. In this stage of research, between 2012 and 2013, sixteen individuals participated in formal interviews.

Given the difficulties of doing social science research in Cuba, I quickly realized that it would be impossible to do random sampling. In order for people to feel comfortable talking to me in these structured interviews, I needed to contact them through trusted members of their social networks. These people could vouch for me and assure them that there were no risks in speaking honestly with me.

Since I depended on snowball sampling (or chain-referral method), it was not possible to build a completely representative sample. Instead, I consciously built a sample that was equally split by gender and included individuals from different municipalities of Havana. There is so much interest in academic circles and in the media about the new emerging private sector that I wanted to focus on the understudied majority of Havana's population who are tied to the state sector. I wanted to make sure that most of the interviewees were of working age (between mid-twenties to early fifties) and linked to the state sector through either work or study. The group included members with varying levels of different types of capital from diverse sources.

The first set of interviews focused on everyday consumption practices and collected detailed information about lifestyles of Cubans from different groups. They included sections on family composition, family life, housing conditions, relationships with neighbors, food sources, leisure practices, family budgets, and proxy measurements for household income.

In order to create more nuanced characterization of everyday life of Cubans in different social groups, and corroborate the characteristics of different social groups as described by people from outside the group, I combined the interviews with participant observation in spaces for consumption that are frequented by each social group. In the area of basic consumption I visited *La cuevita* (an underground market in San Miguel de Padrón), Mercado 114 (a wholesale agricultural market that had recently opened), Carlos III Street Stands, Neptuno Street Stands, Sears de Marianao, CUC stores selling basic food and consumer goods in Playa, Marianao, Plaza, and Centro Habana municipalities. I also visited trendy new leisure spaces, including private restaurants, cafeterias, and bars (*Espacios, El Madrigal, La Pachanga, Escaleras al Cielo, Humbolt 52, El cocinero, El chanchullero, El Arca de Noé, Burner Brothers*), 3D Cinemas (*ICAIC; Playa, Infanta Cine 3D*), and gyms: (State run: *Aramburu*, public parks with fitness programs, *Martí* and *Monte Barreto;* Private:*17 y E*). These strategies allowed me to identify new social groups not reported by the individuals I interviewed and began to collect ethnographic data about the social group that I call "Newly-satisfied Consumer-Citizens" in the Epilogue.

Finally, from 2012–2013, I did fourteen open-ended interviews with the same group of participants in which I asked them to talk to me about class in

Cuba and explain the social stratification system that they witnessed (two of the sixteen participants, one man and one woman, did not complete the social stratification interview). Respondents drew visual representations of "class structure" in Cuba, described the characteristics of the various social groups, placed themselves and their contacts within the structure, and discussed the relationships between the groups. These interviews also asked about the importance of different types of capital in Cuba. These sources were used to characterize contemporary social groups in Cuba and their relationships to each other after the Special Period. They also contributed to my understanding of the roots of economic and social inequalities and the processes by which they are being reproduced. These sources provided the data analyzed in chapter three: "Stratification, Income, and Cultural Consumption in Contemporary Cuba."

Work History Interviews

Because my sample in the three-part interviews was relatively young (the average age about thirty-one years old), I decided to also do work history interviews which I applied with a group of nine respondents in their fifties to seventies who had worked in different sectors of the economy. These interviewees included six women and three men who lived in six different municipalities and included two black Cubans and two internal immigrants (from Granma and Las Tunas provinces) who settled in Havana after the 1990s. This data was used in shaping chapter four: "'Adjusting to the Adjustment': Household Reproduction Strategies and New Economic Spaces in Havana, 2010–2015" and helped me explore generational differences in orientation towards work, motivation, and attitudes about different sectors of the economy.

Housing Market Research

During my field research in Havana studying social stratification and social networks in the context of Cuba's current economic restructuring, I began to observe that the newly re-created housing market in Havana was having a significant impact on economic stratification. Through participant observation in the nascent legal housing market, in outdoor public meet-ups between potential buyers and sellers, state housing offices where property listings are maintained, online real estate sites, and formal and informal interviews with buyers, sellers, real estate agents, notaries, and neighbors, I found that the re-creation of the Cuban housing market had created new economic opportunities for homeowners of valuable properties that formerly housed Havana's elite and upper middle classes. In December 2012 and January 2013, I also had the opportunity to observe two real estate transactions in Havana from beginning to end. This data was used to write chapter five: "The Rebirth of Real Estate: Reproducing Class Inequalities in Havana."

Research Protocols

Despite the fact that in my past experiences in Cuba I have never felt that my relationships with locals were subject to surveillance, I followed a strict protocol designed to mitigate risks. I performed all of the interviews in private spaces or locations chosen by the person being interviewed and never used recording devices in public unless it was indicated by the person I was recording that such usage was appropriate and without social risks. I conducted all interviews in Spanish. As approved by my university's Institutional Review Board, consent was obtained orally for formal or recorded interviews, protecting respondent's identities by leaving no paper trail connecting us.

Throughout the course of the project, and in the publication of my results, I have assigned research participants pseudonyms to protect their identity. I explained this to all participants with the hope that they would feel more comfortable with sharing their opinions and personal stories honestly. Some individuals, however, preferred that I use their real names and in these cases their wishes were respected.

SUMMARY OF CHAPTERS

In the first chapter, I compare and contrast the reforms associated with the 2011 *Guidelines for Economic and Social Policy* with the economic reforms of the 1990s. This discussion of the economic crises and social transformations in the last 25 years in Cuba prepares readers to understand the impacts of the reforms which took place on the island during the time of my research. The current economic reforms, and the process of "Updating" Cuba's economic model from 2010–present have altered the social structure which took form after the 1990s economic crisis and affected processes of social mobility. The remaining chapters of the book contribute in different ways to describing the effects of these changes on Havana households and social stratification today.

In chapter two, I use Bourdieu's ideas about configurations of economic, political, and social capital to explore the how dominant configurations of these types of capital changed after the Revolution to give birth to a system in which a type of capital, which I call *revolutionary cultural capital*, was dominant in the social field and determined access to social mobility, consumption opportunities, and power. From there, I look at how these Cuban logics of social stratification have changed: in the late 1980s, right before the Special Period crisis, in the period that coincided with Perestroika in the USSR; in the 1990s, during Cuba's Special Period crisis; and again after 2010, bringing about a new logic of social stratification.

Chapter three draws on interviews from 2012 and 2013 with working-age adults associated with the state sector from a geographically diverse cross section of Havana neighborhoods to characterize the structures of stratification that had become the new "normal" in Cuba at the end of the first wave of crisis and reforms of the Special Period. I introduce a composite map of social structure in Havana in 2013, based on the maps that my interviewees drew to describe social stratification. Through the words of José and Rosa, two interviewees from families with low levels of economic capital, but high levels of social capital and revolutionary cultural capital, I continue to explore social stratification and the interactions between groups with different configurations of capitals.

In chapter four, I provide a brief summary of how recently implemented public policies based on the Guidelines have reconfigured the labor market in Cuba since 2010, and explore how Cuban households today are adjusting to structural adjustments being made to the Cuban economy by changing the way that they relate to the new labor market. The chapter continues the tradition of anthropological scholarship on social reproduction in Cuba from the household perspective by showing how current changes affect social reproduction in Havana households and how urban households are experimenting with emerging sectors of the economy as state discourses toward self-employment [*trabajo por cuenta propia* or TCP] and self-employed workers [*cuentapropistas*] and the emerging the private sector have shifted. Through these stories, I look at how people in Havana feel about moving into previously stigmatized economic spaces and what they see as the advantages and disadvantages of working in each space, as well as exploring how generation influences the meaning people give to their insertion in the labor market.

In chapter five, I look at how the re-creation of a real estate market in November 2011, in response to Guideline 297, has allowed the descendants of pre-revolutionary and revolutionary elites to use the capital in their homes to reestablish themselves at the top of an emerging socioeconomic hierarchy in Cuba. On the other hand, those who benefited from state-built housing in the 1970s and 1980s, find that their homes are not assets that can be harnessed to take advantage of new opportunities in the emerging economy. Rather than contributing to solving the serious housing shortages experienced by Havana families, the new housing market has concentrated valuable properties in small social networks and limited the local housing stock. Foreigners and Cubans who have lived and worked abroad snatch up second homes, invest to improve living conditions of their relatives on the island, and remodel rentals to service the booming tourist market. Housing prices in central areas of Havana are now significantly higher than previous black-market prices, and out of reach for most local residents in need of housing. Local residents are displaced into peripheral areas of the city to make room for businesses catering to foreign visitors and the new local economic elites, and short term vacation rentals for foreign tourists.

In the Epilogue, I look at contemporary Havana and how the social structure of Cuba's "Post-Soviet normal," circa 2012–13, is being modified as the impacts of recent changes in state policy become clearer. I describe three new social groups that have gained importance in the Cuban field as a result of changes in state policies from 2011–present: circular migrants, employers and employees, and "Newly Satisfied Consumer-Citizens."

The current economic reforms and the process of "updating" Cuba's economic model signal the beginning of a new period of changes in Cuba's social structure. In this new period, the logics of stratification and social structure, which took form after the 1990s economic crisis, are being transformed. In the Conclusion, I return to the fundamental questions of the book to provide some final thoughts on social stratification in Cuba and the contribution of long-term ethnographic research in offering insights on how new state policies are changing structures of opportunities for social mobility and consumption in Havana.

NOTE

1. Other names for the CUC: Cuban convertible *pesos, divisa, chavitos, fula, dólares, pesos.* CUP: Moneda Nacional (MN), Cuban *pesos, pesos.* During the time of my research, an increasing number of state stores, which sell products in CUCs, began to accept both CUC and CUP for purchases. Cash registers were reprogrammed to accept both currencies, and prices on store shelves in many stores reflect both prices. In May 2016, there was a rumor that the CUC-CUP conversion rate would be changed as part of the process of revaluing the CUP and eventually eliminating the CUC. The rumor took on such power that it had to be officially refuted in state media. A previous rumor in March 2014 took on similar dimensions.

Chapter One

The Political and Social
Context of Contemporary Cuba

When I began this research there were two "befores" in the Cuban imaginary: the first "before" is "Before the Revolution." According to this narrative, Cuba was a profoundly unequal place and marked by racial segregation. Class and geography mostly limited access to quality health care and education to Havana. The population lived under a dictatorship that brutally repressed those fighting to make the country a more just place. The stories about this "before" are told by members of the older generation who experienced first-hand what life was like back then and repeated by their children who have grown up on these stories. By telling these stories, the storytellers remind themselves and their listeners that things were once much worse "before the Revolution," but by coming together they were able to change their reality and improve their lives.

The second "before" in the Cuban imaginary is the "Before the Special Period," the long economic crisis which started in the 1990s with the fall of the Soviet Union. Stories of life before the start of the Special Period paint Cuba as a land of plenty: food, consumer goods, and transportation were plentiful. Prices were controlled and subsidized by the state. The average salary was enough, not only to make ends meet, but also to indulge in the occasional luxury, put away money for a rainy day, or enjoy a nice family vacation. Education and service to the Revolution/community were key routes to social mobility. As a result of the Revolution, access to health care and education, as well as athletics and culture, came to be seen by the population as basic human rights. The Revolutionary State took on an expanded role in guaranteeing these rights, as well as guaranteeing equal access to basic consumer needs for all households.

The state assumed a larger role in socializing the provision of services which had previously been provided by women as unpaid laborers in their

1

own households. This allowed many women to integrate more completely into the public sphere, first as students and later as professionals: doctors, teachers, lawyers, judges, scientists, and technicians. Sometimes, to those who came of age in the worst years of the 1990s economic crisis, the stories about this utopian "before" seem like the surreal and mythical stuff of dreams. By telling these stories, Cubans remind each other of a moment of shared history in which things were better, and keep the hope alive that they could improve again.

HOW CUBA DEALT WITH THE LAST ECONOMIC CRISIS: THE "SPECIAL PERIOD" AND REFORMS OF THE 1990s

In the 1980s, Cuba had become dependent on trade with the Council of Mutual Economic Assistance (CMEA), the Soviet trading bloc, which in addition to paying above market prices for Cuban sugar, also provided low-interest loans to cover bilateral trade deficits (Domínguez, Pérez Villanueva, and Barberia 2004, 20). Total Soviet subsidies to Cuba between 1960–1990 averaged US $2.1 billion per year (Jatar-Hausmann 1999, 207). Most trade between the Soviet bloc and Cuba was through barter agreements: Cuba imported 95 percent of its fuel and lubricant needs, 80 percent of machinery and equipment, and 63 percent of foodstuffs through imports from the Soviet bloc (Jatar-Hausmann 1999, 207). The CMEA received 63 percent of Cuba's sugar exports, 73 percent of nickel exports and 95 percent of citrus exports (Jatar-Hausmann 1999, 207). Without this important trade partner, Cuba was suddenly alone and without access to international credit.[1] A full 85 percent of Cuba's foreign trade consisted of subsidized agreements with CMEA countries (González-Corzo 2010, 1). Much of this trade ceased after 1989 when Cuba had to pay for these imports with hard currency. Between 1989–1993, Cuba's export volume fell 47 percent while its import capacity fell by more than 70 percent (González-Corzo 2010, 1). The Cuban economy crumbled and "before" was over.

Between 1990–1993, Cuba's GDP lost more than 30 percent of its value (Domínguez, Pérez Villanueva, and Barberia 2004, 19). The crisis had an immediate effect in all aspects of daily life in Cuba: between 1990–1996, the caloric intake of the population fell by 27 percent. Public schools and the health system suffered from shortages of basic goods. Public transportation ground to a halt. About 50 percent of bus routes were eliminated, consolidated, or cutback due to lack of fuel (Pérez 2006, 294). It was common to wait for hours for a spot on an overcrowded bus to get to work, only to arrive and find that none of your coworkers had been successful on their commutes. Workers in construction and transportation were displaced to form part of the new self-employed labor pool (Segre 1997, 223). To address the collapse of Cuba's public transit systems, close to a million *Phoenix* and *Flying Pigeon* bicycles were imported from China and sold on installment plans for $60 pesos for students and $220 pesos for workers (Alepuz 1993 cited in Segre 1997, 223).

In the early 1990s, around 53 percent of Havana's labor force worked in the productive sphere. This changed quickly as shortages of raw materials and power outages forced close to half of factories to close (Segre 1997, 293). The lack of raw materials led to massive layoffs. In 1995, Pedro Ross, the president of the CTC reported that some 140,000 workers were on furlough waiting to be relocated (Reuters 1995).

As a result of the crisis, many basic services once provided by the government began to deteriorate, and households had to dedicate more time and energy to caring for themselves. Whereas "before" family members might stay with a sick relative at the hospital for sentimental reasons, after the Special Period it was necessary to have someone with you to supplement meals, draw water to flush the toilet, and help maintain the cleanliness of the room. Whereas, "before" children received morning and afternoon snacks and a substantial lunch at school, now parents packed their kids lunches to supplement the meager offerings provided by the school. "Before" school teachers were highly trained and experienced, but during the Special Period, many of these professionals left the classrooms to look for better paying work in the emerging sectors of economy. They were replaced with young teachers, just out of high school, trained to guide students through a series of recorded lessons on video cassette. Today, the education of younger members of the household depends more on the home-based educational efforts of the older generations than "before."

In the 1990s, the way that the Cuban government reacted to the economic crisis diverged from the steps prescribed by the Washington consensus. Most market economies would have responded to the external shock by devaluing their currency. A devalued currency would have decreased individual buying power, making the average citizen so poor that they would not be able to buy imported goods. New sky-high prices for imported goods would provide an incentive for local industry to produce similar goods, using cheapened local labor, and reap huge profits by pricing their goods lower than the imports. Cuba's cheapened labor source would also have been attractive to transnational corporations looking to lower labor costs to reap higher profits. In the 1990s, Cuba could have become a great location for a sweatshop.

But instead, Cuba took a different path, choosing to avoid the sudden devaluation of the currency. Between 1990–1993, the government took on a huge fiscal deficit, totaling 40 percent of the GDP in 1993, to maintain subsidies for basic household consumption, education, and health care, and the salaries of hundreds of thousands of individuals who were laid off when the lack of imported inputs and fuel caused the government to close many factories. To continue to finance this spending, the government, unable to depend on external sources, was left with no choice but to print more money. The situation quickly led to excess liquidity. Between 1990–1994, the number of pesos in circulation increased from 5,000,000,000 to 11.1 billion (Jatar-Hausman 1996:209). There was too much currency circulating in the market, chasing after a limited amount of goods to buy with that money.

Although they were not working, hundreds of thousands of laid-off workers continued to receive the same salaries. Prices stayed low as well, thanks to state subsidies. Even though imports had stopped, the government did not raise prices. Consumers with cash in hand quickly exhausted the existing supply of basic consumer goods in the formal market, and the government did not have the hard currency necessary to import more (Domínguez, Pérez Villanueva, and Barberia 2004, 24). From then on, households turned to the black market, where the rules of supply (extremely limited) and demand (extremely acute) led to rising prices and the erosion of the real buying power of the Cuban salary. From 1989–1997, the consumer price index increased, causing the average Cuban salary to lose 42 percent of its value (Togores González 1999; Valdés Carranza, Paz, and Rosales 2004, 181; Nerey and Brismart 1999; Ferriol, Quintana, and Pérez 1999).

The Cuban peso's value deteriorated so severely that by 1992, the average family needed twice its income to satisfy its basic needs. Vast sectors of the labor forces experienced downward mobility (Togores González 1999). This continues to be a serious problem more than 25 years later. Between 1989–1993, the value of the Cuban peso on the black market fell from $7 Cuban pesos per dollar to $120 (Domínguez, Pérez Villanueva, and Barberia 2004, 24). The value of the peso deteriorated so severely that the US dollar, despite the fact that it was illegal to possess at the time, became the new medium of exchange in black-market transactions.

First, the state tried to ameliorate the effects of the crisis through deficit spending and limited reforms, such as inviting foreign direct investment to help develop international tourism to bring in hard currency. In June of 1990, the Polit Bureau announced its willingness to accept foreign direct investment, especially in the development of a new international tourism industry. According to Jorge Domínguez, these measures have proven to be among the most important for the recovery of the Cuban economy since the early 1990s (2004:22). During the 1990s, tourism grew 20 percent annually, and Jesus M. Garcia Molina estimates that this activity generated, directly and indirectly, 300,000 jobs (Núñez Sarmiento 2010, 135).

After three years of these policies, the Cuban government decided that more structural changes were needed. Between 1993–1995, a series of economic reforms were implemented that changed the structure of labor, exchange, and consumption. The first of these measures was the legalization of the dollar in August 1993. The sugarcane harvest of 1993 was the worst in thirty years, diminishing any hopes for replenishing the country's critically low foreign exchange reserves (Jatar-Hausmann 1999). Ironically enough, the Cuban government didn't have to look far to find a source of foreign currency: due to rampant inflation and the subsequent devaluation of the Cuban peso, the US dollar had already become the de facto currency of exchange in the black market. A growing proportion of the population had access to dollars through work in the tourism sector or family remittances. It is estimated that between 1989–1996, about $3 million of remittances entered Cuba (CEPAL 1997:124 cited in Barberia 2004: 369). Because it was illegal to hold dollars until August 1993, they were used only in transactions on the black market, out of the reach of the government which desperately needed them to continue social spending and buy necessary imports. By legalizing the use of US dollars and opening a chain of stores in which otherwise scarce goods were sold in dollars at high markups (an average 240 percent on imported goods, and 170 percent on domestically produced goods), the government was able to capture the dollars circulating in the economy and help channel them towards national economic priorities such as reducing the deficit (Sánchez Egozcue 1998; Barberia 2004, 376).

The next reform, in September 1993, was the restructuring of large state farms into cooperatives and the legalization of certain types of self-employment. Unprofitable state farms were dissolved and reconstituted as semi-private collectives (Domínguez, Pérez Villanueva, and Barberia 2004, 24–5). More than two-thirds of the agricultural land in Cuba was redistributed to cooperatives or small individual farmers (Peters 2000, 3). In October 1994, the government opened agricultural markets where prices were ruled by market mechanisms. After filling their government production quotas, private farmers and members of state cooperatives could sell surpluses at market prices. These markets increased food availability and provided variety which was not available in other state markets, allowing families to supplement their consumption.

Food shortages were most acute in Havana and provincial capitals where families lacked land and/or knowledge to produce their own food. Higher market prices and lower taxes encouraged farmers to sell their products in the cities. The farmers' markets were so successful in increasing the food supply for urban families that black-market prices were immediately undercut: in Havana, the price of rice fell 75 percent; pork, 49 percent; and beans, 14 percent (Nova González in Peters 2000, 5).

In 1993, the Cuban government also expanded the private sector of the economy. Licenses were offered for self-employment in 112 different occupations, legalizing much of the work already being done in the informal sector. In the mid-1990s, the average *cuentapropista* [self-employed worker] earned about $135 CUC a month, compared to their previous state salary which, when changed from Cuban pesos to CUC, equaled about $10 CUC per month (Smith 1999, 51). In late 1995, at the height of licensed self-employment, 208,000 people worked as *cuentapropistas* (Smith 1999, 50). In 1997, the government opened industrial and craft markets, giving self-employed individuals a physical marketplace to sell their goods.

In 1998–1999 the government stopped issuing new licenses for *cuentapropistas* (Phillips 2007:315 note 9). Shortly after, the government introduced an income tax law subjecting *cuentapropistas* to high levels of taxation (Smith 1999, 50). The new taxation system had a large impact on the number of *cuentapropistas*. Smith reports that in 1997 there were only 150,000 workers still in the sector, a decline of 28 percent in less than two years (1998:50). Others report a similar trend: in 2000, about 160,000 Cubans, or 4 percent of the labor force, worked as *cuentapropistas* (Peters 2000, 375; Barberia 2004). Between 1996–2000 this number fell by about 25 percent as a result of attrition due to high taxation, competition, and regulatory enforcement (Peters 2000, 375; Barberia 2004).

The last of the economic reforms of the mid-1990s was the opening of a chain of exchange houses or CADECAs [*Casas de Cambio*], where individuals could exchange US dollars and other foreign currencies for the new Cuban convertible pesos or Cuban pesos at a floating exchange rate. In 1995, the Cuban government opened sixteen exchange houses as part of the CADECA system, and it expanded quickly, with more than 290 exchange offices across the country in 2002 (Banco Central de Cuba 2004 cited in Barberia 2004:370). The CADECA helped to restore Cubans' confidence in the value of the Cuban peso and its usefulness for domestic transactions improved. The exchanges gave the government another method to capture a greater portion of the foreign currency in circulation on the island. By 2000, the CADECA system was exchanging an average of US$20 million annually (CEPAL 2000:170 cited in Barberia 2004, 370).

NEOLIBERAL TOOLS IN THE
SERVICE OF SOCIALIST SOCIETY?

When these measures were adopted in the mid-1990s, the government explained that they did not signal a change in ideology or a renunciation of socialism, but a pragmatic adoption of certain market mechanisms as "necessary evils" in order to allow the Revolution to survive. After the collapse of the Soviet Union, the country found itself without strong allies in a world governed by the rules and logics of neoliberalism. The Cuban government began to experiment with quasi-neoliberal reforms as tools in the service of a socialist society which found itself threatened by hegemonic global capitalism.

The reforms of the 1990s were made to change structures to allow Cubans to fend for themselves since the state was no longer able to provide for them. Today, the state's chronic lack of resources has led it to redefine the ideal relationship between the state and the population: from providing everything equally to everybody regardless of need, to providing a social safety net to those who need it (Valdés Paz 2005; Powell 2008, 184). The goal has changed from guaranteeing total equality, towards a notion of defending fairness. Although, in other contexts, economic reforms which redefine the role of the state in this way would have been labeled as neoliberal, in Cuba this perception is not a part of public discourse. While sometimes utilizing the tools of neoliberal economic restructuring, the state continuously challenges transition narratives coming from abroad, which assume the inevitability of a return to capitalism on the island and a complete dismantling of the Socialist means of production.

The structural reforms of the 1990s were successful in increasing foreign investment and remittances, accounting for a slight economic recovery (Molina Díaz 2007). Cuba recuperated an average annual growth rate of 4.3 percent between 1994–2000 (Molina Díaz 2007, 3 & 6). Cuban economists consider that the economic measures adopted in the early 1990s were successful in avoiding the collapse of the Cuban economy, but they also recognize that the social costs have been high. The relief that comes with economic recovery has not been equally shared among the population. The Cuban peso recovered its value from a rate of $150 Cuban pesos to the dollar in 1993, to $20 pesos in 2000, to $26 pesos in 2003 and has been maintained relatively stable since (Valdés Carranza, Paz, and Rosales 2004, 181). In 2016, the exchange rate was $1 CUC to $25 CUP (buy) and $24 CUP to $1 CUC (sell).

The legalization of the dollar allowed the Cuban government to capture hard currency to finance continued subsidies and importations, but it did so at the cost of entrenching a monetary duality that led to social exclusion (González-Corzo 2010). In 1997, 50 percent of Cubans had access to hard currency, and by 2001, the number had grown to 62 percent of the population (Núñez Sarmiento 2010, 137).

RECOVERING (AND RELAPSE)

As the economy improved in the late 1990s and again in the mid-2000s, the government increased investment in public services, remodeling and updating equipment in schools and hospitals. The government used the new windfall to invest in large scale youth jobs programs in social work and opportunities for postsecondary education for young people who came of age during the worst years of the crisis. Many of these young people had dropped out. Instead of continuing to higher education or technical training, they had dedicated themselves to working in the informal sector or in the household (Mesa-Lago 2005).

Between 2001–2007, the Cuban economy grew rapidly, (with the exception of a small recession between 2001–2003 brought on by a drop in tourism after 9/11, a drop in international market prices for Cuban nickel and sugar exports, and bad weather). From 2004–7, Cuba's GDP increased at an annual average of 9.2 percent (Mesa-Lago 2010, 692). Cuba began a close relationship with Venezuela, in which it exchanged the services of Cuban doctors for Venezuelan petroleum. Of the 160,000 barrels per day in petroleum products that Cuba consumed, more than 50 percent came from Venezuela under preferential financing arrangements (Mesa-Lago 2010, 694).

Just as things looked like they were getting better, and Cuba had succeeded in leaving the Special Period behind once and for all, things got worse. In 2008, the price of Cuba's principal export products fell on the international market at the same time that the prices of oil and food soared. Between 2007–2010, the price of nickel dropped more than 60 percent (Palmer 2010). That fall, three hurricanes hit Cuba, affecting most of the island and causing $9.7 billion of damages in housing stock and lost food crops (Vidal Alejandro 2010). When Hurricane Gustav hit Cuba on August 31st as a Category 4 storm, it was considered the worst hurricane to hit the island in fifty years.

As recovery efforts began, Ike, a Category 3 storm, hit Eastern Cuba and over two days slowly made its way across the island, affecting 100 percent of the country. The third storm, Hurricane Paloma, hit in November 2008. The official preliminary report on damages of the first two storms were published in the Cuban daily newspaper, Granma, declared that "The country's economic, social and housing infrastructures had been devastated like never before" (Granma 2008). More than 514,875 homes were damaged, 91,254 of which were completely demolished and Susan McDade, Resident United Nations Coordinator in Cuba, estimated that 1.5 million people were left homeless by the storms (IPS 2008). Thousands of schools and hundreds of public health installations were damaged. The country's agricultural industry was hard hit.

I was living in Havana at the time, and went with a group of friends to Los Palacios, a small town in Pinar del Rio province where the storm had passed. The town was leveled. Many houses had been blown away, only the foundations remained, and we helped haul off rubble as families searched for their belongings among the wreckage. There was nothing green to be seen for miles. It was as if the wind had burned everything living. My friends were students in a master's degree program in Psychology studying how to use theatre to deal with trauma. So, after a full day of helping the families dig through the rubble, we provided entertainment in the evening by playing theatre games with the kids. Back in Havana, we shared the pictures of the damage. Early estimates put the extent of material damages at $5 billion.

Many Cubans feared that the storms could bring about another severe economic crisis. I shuddered as I heard people whisper that this might bring on "another Special Period" and repeat rumors that the Ministry of Armed Forces was tapping into its reserves. Rumors are an extremely important source of information for residents in Havana, as well as the anthropologist studying Cuban society. In Havana, this news source is jokingly referred to as "Radio Bemba"(Fat Lip Radio) (Dubinsky 2016, 158).

Cuba's new president Raúl Castro, who had been elected in February of 2008, inherited an economy again in crisis. Cuba's export partners were suffering from the effects of the world economic crisis. Venezuela, which accounted for 27 percent of Cuba's total trade volume suffered a drop in GDP which reduced demand for Cuban medical service exports (Mesa-Lago 2010, 695). Canada, the EU, and Russia, which made up another 25 percent of Cuba's trade volume also experienced declining GDPs (Mesa-Lago 2010, 695). As a result, revenue from tourist services in Cuba dropped by 11.1 percent in 2009 (Mesa-Lago 2010, 695). Cuba's imports from Canada, its second largest trading partner dropped 60 percent in 2009 (Palmer 2010). Imports from the US were also down 25 percent (Palmer 2010).

Cuba had to make up for the crops lost in the hurricanes by importing food (with less money to do it with, due to the fall in prices for Cuban exports). In 2008, imports reached 23.3 percent of GDP, the highest degree of dependence on imports in the decade 2009 (Mesa-Lago 2010, 694). Cuba dealt with the lack of access to international credit by simply not paying creditors for imports that had already been delivered, using that money to pay for more imports (Vidal Alejandro 2010). The country's external debt increased 15 percent in one year (Vidal Alejandro 2010). In that year, Cuba had the largest fiscal deficit in fourteen years (Vidal Alejandro 2010). The growth rate of Cuba's GDP decelerated to 1.4 percent in 2009 (Mesa-Lago 2010, 695). It seemed that the new president had no choice but to begin to cut the state budget to bring things back into balance.

THE NEW "BEFORE": ECONOMIC RESTRUCTURING FROM 2010–15: "CHANGE WHAT NEEDS TO BE CHANGED"

In September 2010, the Cuban Labor Federation [*Central de Trabajadores Cubanos*- CTC] announced that half a million state-sector workers would be laid off (Frank 2010a). A month later, the state began encouraging citizens to apply for business licenses to begin working in the non-state sector. These new small entrepreneurs could rent commercial space, hold licenses for more than one category, and hire employees, rather than being restricted to employing family members. The limit on the number of seats in private restaurants was raised from twelve to twenty, and later to fifty, and these restaurants were allowed to sell lobster, beef, and potatoes, which had previously only been supplied to state restaurants. Private individuals could also work as contractors for the state, open bank accounts in their business' name, and apply for bank loans (Frank 2013, 221).

Most significant for Cuba's social structure was that the new list of 178 occupations included 83 categories which could legally hire other employees (Café Fuerte 2013). Six months later, all license categories were allowed to hire employees (Frank 2013, 222). These measures began to transform what had been called, in the official discourse, *trabajo por cuenta propia* or *TCP* [self-employment] and *cuentapropistas* [self-employed workers] into a true *private sector* of small businesses, complete with investors, bosses, and workers. In this new private sector, employees' salaries and investors' dividends are significantly higher than in the state sector. Under new regulations, the small business owners who employed others, in addition to paying sales taxes, would also pay a labor tax and a 25 percent social security tax for each contracted worker (Frank 2013, 222). According to research by the Havana-based Center for Psychological and Sociological Research (CIPS) [*Centro de Investigaciones Psicológicas y Sociológicas*], in 2011, employees were only 10 percent of the total TCPers but by 2014, 20 percent of individuals with TCP licenses were salaried workers, employees of other TCPers. (Social Structure Research Group Results, PPT, slide fifteen, CIEE IFDS Course, June 2015.) In the Epilogue, I discuss the importance of this change, which divides the emerging TCP sector into a true private sector with distinct classes of employers and private employees.

By the time I came to Cuba in 2008, people who had licenses had held them for years and new licenses were generally not available. By 1994, only 22 percent of applications were being granted (Pérez Izquierdo 2004, 10). Despite the difficulty of securing business licenses, it often seemed like everyone I knew in Havana had some sort of side gig. Among my circle of friends and research participants, I could count a night watchman, a babysitter, a housecleaner, a computer fix-it whiz, and several bakers. There were others who resold stuff they pinched from work or things brought by family members abroad, and those who taught: homework help for middle-schoolers, dance lessons, and Spanish to foreigners. Their businesses were illegal because they didn't have the option of making them legal.

With these changes, business licenses, which for the last fifteen years had been so routinely denied that people had given up on even applying, were now being approved in less than a week. The doors to legal self-employment had been thrown wide open. For people already working in TCP without access to licenses, these new changes gave them the opportunity to legalize their activity. CIPS research suggests that 68 percent of newly licensed TCPers had been officially "unemployed" before taking out their licenses. Only 17 percent had been actively working in another position, and 15 percent were retirees before taking out their licenses (slide 10). However, it is likely that many of those who were officially "unemployed" were actually working without business licenses.

Suddenly, after years of doing business in the shadows, Cubans had to figure out how to deal with the changing rules. Many wondered if it was really necessary to get a license and decided to continue under the table. Everyone who continued as before wondered what the consequences would be. Now that going legal was an option, would the state crackdown even harder on those who refused to legalize? There were rumors that legions of inspectors had been trained and were busy looking for illegal businesses, trying to stop the bleeding of resources from state warehouses that supplied the black market that small entrepreneurs depended on. For others the new licenses were a relief. Even though profit margins would be lower with the new taxes and licensing fees, many people told me that they felt like it was worth it to no longer have the uncertainty and fear of getting caught hanging over their heads.

The new regulations to allow TCP were strict, and many TCPers complained that the new small businesses were being required to create sanitary conditions that the state did not even have in its own establishments. The sanitary codes based on international standards were tough, and some inspectors, hoping for bribes, were even tougher. One baker I interviewed in Playa had been making cakes for people in the neighborhood for years and decided to apply for a license. The health inspector asked for a bribe which she did not pay. Despite making multiple renovations to her kitchen to meet the health codes, she was never granted a license. Her sister-in-law, who made cakes in a different municipality, had better luck. After making the same required alterations, she was granted a license right away.

In Cuba it is extremely difficult to find accurate statistics. Often key data is maintained confidential and even the Statistical Yearbook published by the Cuban National Statistics Office [*Oficina Nacional de Estadísticas*- ONE] is often released with a lag time of a couple of years. In the meantime, researchers must mine media reports for data. ONE's 2012 Statistical Yearbook showed insignificant growth in TCP between 2008–2010 (from 141,600 to

147,400) (ONE 2012). However, the number of TCPers in the country has grown significantly since 2010. However, the largest growth in TCP expressed in the Yearbook statistics, from 147,400 to 391,500 workers, happens between two ONE data points (2010 and 2011) and is not further broken down by month.

Table 1.1. Number of TCPers in Cuba, 2008–2015

2008	2010	2011	2012	2013	2014	2015
141,600	147,400	391,500	404,600	424,300	483,400	499,000

Source: Anuario estadístico de Cuba, 2012 & 2015

Table 1.2. Increase in Number of TCPers in Cuba by Period

Period	Increase in TCPers
2008–2010	5,800
2010–11	**244,100**
2011–12	13,100
2012–13	19,700
2013–14	**59,100**
2014–15	15,600

Source: Anuario estadístico de Cuba, 2012 & 2015

In May 2017, the most recent numbers publicly available from ONE came from the 2015 Yearbook which listed 499,000 self-employed workers in the country (ONE 2015). According to Cuban press reports in May 2015, some 504,613 people were working in the non-state sector (CubaDebate 2015). In November 2016, Prensa Latina reported that three months earlier the number of self-employed workers in Cuba had reached 518,479 (Hernández 2013).

Disappearing State Supports and Subsidies

At the same time that the state opened up new opportunities for self-employment, it began to cut back on state subsidies. In his speech to the National Assembly of People's Power on August 1, 2010, Raúl Castro promised that "nobody will be left to their own fate and that, via the social security system, the socialist state will give the support needed to live a life of dignity to those people who are genuinely not in a position to work and who are the sole means of support for their families"(Castro Ruz 2010). This statement is not an afterthought, and was part of the same speech in which he declared "We have to erase forever the notion that Cuba is the only country in the world in which people can live without working." However, it remains to be seen what changes are being made in social policy in order to make equity a reality and protect vulnerable populations.

Every time the state says that they plan to do away with the ration book, it sends shivers of horror through those Cubans who depend on these subsidized goods. It appears that eliminating blanket social entitlement programs like the ration book and replacing them with targeted "equity" programs has the potential to save the state a substantial amount of foreign reserves, since such a high proportion of the goods distributed in this manner are imported. In the new eagerness to get rid of "unnecessary" subsidies, the ration book is often the first subsidy that comes to people's minds, because of its centrality in Cuban daily life.

For most Cubans working in the unrecovered state sector, the ration book is an unnecessary subsidy. The ration only provides a small portion of a family's monthly basic consumption. Before the changes in November 2009, which removed potatoes and chícharo beans, it only provided 36 percent of an individual's daily caloric intake, lasting an average of twelve days a month (Grogg 2009, 14). Nevertheless, the quota makes an important contribution to family food budgets. In 2009, without the ration book a family of four would pay $270.20 CUP more per month to maintain the same level of consumption, a significant sum in a country where most people earned $225–$450 CUP a month (IPS 2009).

After significant improvements between 2002–2006, state spending for social welfare deteriorated after 2008 (Mesa-Lago 2010). From 2008–2011, state spending for social welfare decreased by $386.2 million. By 2011, 399,568 fewer individuals were receiving these welfare benefits than in 2008 (ONEI 2012).

Table 1.3. **Numbers of Individuals Losing Social Welfare Benefits, 2008–2011**

	Change 2008–2011
Total Social Welfare Beneficiaries	–399,568 individuals
Households Protected by Social Welfare	–211,371
Social Welfare Beneficiaries by Type:	
Elderly	–81,767
People with Disabilities	–67,594
Mothers with Severely Disabled Children	–2,150
Home Care	–12,732

Source: Data published by ONEI, Anuario Estadístico 2012, "7.15 Main indicators of the social welfare system," Ministerio de Trabajo y Seguridad Social.

In my observations, with the exception of individuals with leadership positions in state ministries or the party apparatus [*dirigentes*], most people in Havana no longer have confidence that the state has the capacity to provide for their basic needs, or that the state will be able to develop the country in a way that will enable them to improve their lives by themselves. These finding are corroborated by Cuban studies of different social groups in Cuba between 2011–2015 by Social Psychologist, Daybel Pañellas Álvarez.

Since 2011, Pañellas Álvarez has written about social identities in Cuba among five socio-occupational groups: *campesinos*, the self-employed workers, *dirigentes*, intellectuals and laborers, as well as their perceptions of their groups and exogroups (Pañellas Álvarez 2015, 2013). I met with her early in my dissertation research because of our common interest in social networks. From 2013–2017, she has tutored an impressive number of undergraduate theses on social identities, social networks, social mobility and inequalities in Havana (Caballero 2013; Curbelo 2013; Del Llano 2013; Dujarric and Vázquez 2015; Torralbas and Rodríguez Alemañy 2011).

Pañellas Álvarez has found that the lack of trust in the state is true both of individuals working in the state sector, trying to live on low peso salaries, as well as small business people, who are fearful that they might lose their investments if state policy changes. Both groups are aware that Cuba's recent history has included a series of cycles of experimentation with private enterprise that have always been reverted. As a result, changes are often met with skepticism and mistrust that the current changes would stick (Henken 2004). For many, especially those in older generations who had lived through the reforms and reversals of earlier decades, investing what little capital they have in forming a new business was seen as extremely risky.

In one study she found that self-employed workers as a group expressed dissatisfaction in everyday life related to the "elements that people expected to be guaranteed or provided by the state: salary, basic needs, housing, recreation, transportation and working conditions"(Pañellas Álvarez 2015, 174). She found that only two occupational groups, leaders and laborers [*dirigentes and obreros*] focused on the basic achievements of the Revolution related to health care, education, internationalism, solidarity, sports, and culture (2015, 174).

The Approval of the Guidelines

So much is changing in Cuba today that now a third "before" has been added to the Cuban narrative. It is no longer just "Before the Revolution" and "Before the Special Period." We are now witnessing a third moment in which the word *Before* is used in a new way, to index a period which is neither pre-

1959 nor pre-1990s. The new *Before* is an un-clearly defined period that at times begins pre-2008 (before the Raúl Castro presidency), at others indexes pre-2011, before the approval and implementation of the new "Guidelines for Economic and Social Party of the Party and the Revolution," the Cuban Communist Party's plan for restructuring the state and determining the priorities for new economic and social policies.

From December 2010–February 2011, it seemed that everywhere one went there were meetings about the proposed Guidelines: they were analyzed in 163,079 meetings with 8,913,838 participants in base committees, workplaces, schools, and community meetings (Cuba 2011). In these meetings, 395,000 comments were registered (Sánchez Egozcue 2012). The proposed Guidelines were next discussed in the 7th Legislature's sessions from December 15–18, 2010. They were also discussed in a joint meeting of the Political Bureau, the Executive Committee of the Council of Ministers with the participation of the Secretaries of the Central Committee of the Cuban Communist Party and the cadres of the mass organizations, the Cuban Central Labor Union, and the Union of Young Communists [*Unión de Jóvenes Comunistas*] which took place on March 19 and 20, 2011 (Cuba 2011). The proposal was discussed by delegates to the Party Congress in their provinces before the Sixth Party Congress of the Cuban Communist Party met in Havana from April 8–10, 2011 to approve the Guidelines (Cuba 2011). A Commission for the Implementation and Development of the Guidelines was appointed which was required to give updates every six months to the National Assembly on their progress.

I lived in Cuba before the era of "Change everything that needs to be changed" began. It wasn't that things didn't change, or that life was static. I always made a point with foreign visitors of trying to debunk the myth of Cuba as an island "stuck in time." During the time of my fieldwork, every month a new reform, a new law, or new regulation was announced. Later, a Cuban economist explained to me that he saw this as proof of the measured and strategic way in which new policies were being gradually implemented to avoid "shock therapy." He told me that, for the first time, many Cuban economists were at the table as policies were being designed and knew what was coming next. However at the time, I, like many Cubans outside of these limited policy circles, experienced this as a barrage of new laws, resolutions and policies. These measures modified the revolutionary reforms made during the first five years of the Revolution. Between 2010–2013, every day there was a new proposal which was quickly approved, and most Cubans, despite their high education levels, were overwhelmed by daily problems of subsistence, leaving little time to search out and read the proposals (let alone study, reflect, or opine on them).

No matter how much things were changing structurally, for most urban residents daily life had stayed the same: salaries were too low to put food on the table and a growing percentage of Havana families lived in poverty and could not keep up with changes in economic policy or even the proposed new Labor Code (Zabala Argüelles 2015). To implement the Guidelines, 130 new policies were enacted, 344 new legal regulations were published, 55 existing regulations modified, and 684 eliminated (Castro Ruz 2016). It all happened so fast that there wasn't enough time to read and understand the changes being made. There was a sense that everything was changing, that the ground was shifting beneath our feet.

December 17, 2014

On December 17, 2014, everything changed (again), marking a new beginning in US-Cuban relations. That morning I went to the research center that hosted my research visa for a meeting. When I arrived a little before 10:00 a.m., I found the department secretary at her desk deep in a conversation with one of the staff people who worked upstairs in the director's office. I sat down on the couch and asked them to fill me in on the gossip that had them with such long faces.

"They have announced that Raúl will speak at noon about topics having to do with US-Cuban relations," Henry explained.[2] They were trying to guess what it might be. I was impressed that a special announcement was going to be made. This seemed unprecedented. "The end of the embargo?" I said jokingly, and they laughed as if that was an extreme impossibility. "Topics, plural" Henry said. "Whatever it is, it's more than one thing."

After a couple more minutes of speculating, the phone rang and the secretary took the call. When she hung up she informed us that the announcement was going to be about the Cuban Five.[3] The remaining three Cubans who were still in prison in the United States serving multiple life sentences had been returned to Cuba! We were surprised, but still a little incredulous. We would believe it when we heard it first-hand from Raúl. At the same time, we were relieved. Before the call we had known that something was coming, without any idea of whether what was coming would be positive or negative. Now with this rumor, we felt like we had enough information to get on with our workday until the noon speech by President Raúl Castro.

We went back to Henry's office to get started working. When we passed through the reception area again, there were already three or four coworkers lounging on the couches hanging out and killing time until the noon announcement. Four or five mismatched chairs had been brought in and lined up next to the black metal tube sofas with red vinyl cushions. Henry joked that one of the seats on the comfortable couches belonged to him as he had been the first person in the office that morning. The network administrator defended his place on the couch. "You might've been here, but did you ask for the *último*?" he asked. "I'm sorry if you didn't ask for the last person when you were here this morning it doesn't count," he joked to Henry.

After a bit of good-natured ribbing we went back to Henry's office to keep working until I realized that it was already a couple minutes past noon. When we returned to the reception area it was full of people and the speech had already begun. I didn't recognize many of the people in the room who looked to be mostly young researchers. There was one older woman in her 40s, with a girl wearing a middle school uniform. As Raúl spoke everyone was staring at the screen. My own attention was divided between wanting to take in every detail of the transmission and wanting to take in every detail of the faces of the people in the room and their reactions to whatever the announcement would be.

There was a lot of murmuring and responses to Raúl's speech in different moments. When he announced that the Cuban heroes had been released there were gasps which made it hard to hear what was being said. The group thought they heard only two names (of the remaining three) and several people asked "Only two of them were freed?" But no one had really heard it clearly. When the announcement was over we still weren't really sure if all three had been freed or just the two of them. After the announcement was over people stood up and began to talk among themselves.

At this time, I had become an ineffective observer. I was in shock. In addition to announcing that the remaining three Cuban prisoners had been freed, what most impacted me was the announcement that diplomatic relations were to be reestablished between Cuba and the United States! This was something that I never imagined that I would see in my lifetime and it had just happened! This was a complete game changer. Diplomatic relations would mean Cuba being taken off the terrorist list, it meant someday using US credit and debit cards in Cuba, it meant regular direct commercial flights to Havana, Postal Service, and telecommunications.

The announcement meant that the isolation of Cuba by the US could come to an end, and it created the hope that maintaining connections between me and my family and friends in the United States could become much easier. Of course, it also meant the same for the hundreds of thousands of Cubans with family on the other side. After more than fourteen years of maintaining friendships with Cubans, my government was no longer opposing this, nor would I have to struggle and continuously challenge US law to maintain those connections. It was as if the United States had declared a cease-fire in its decades-long war on Cuba. I couldn't believe it.

After Raúl's speech was over, most people in the office seemed content to go back to whatever it was that they were doing before the announcement, but about a dozen people stuck around the TV. A white young man in his twenties with long brown hair sitting in front of me suggested that we turn to *Telesur* to see if we could hear Obama's speech as well. When we changed the channel Obama was speaking.

The speech was dubbed into Spanish. Strangely, Obama sounded like "one of us," like my activist friends and colleagues in the US dedicated to fighting against the embargo. The words coming out of his mouth were our talking points and (of course) they sounded so sensible. "We've had this policy for more than fifty years and hasn't worked, it would be stupid to keep trying the same policy" he said. "There is a saying in Cuba "'*No es fácil'*…Life is hard for Cubans and it would be inhumane of us to continue a policy that is aimed at making life so difficult for Cubans that they want to rise up and change their government." Obama quoted Martí and said *"Somos todos americanos"* in the sense that people in Latin America mean it. Latin Americans often point out that the name "American" is not only the USA, but includes the rest of the continent. Obama recognized in his speech the obvious truth that all Latin Americans are also "Americans."

It was a speech which seemed to announce a radical shift in US policy, or at least in methodology. Obama seemed to suggest that the US was going to get out of the way and allow Cubans to decide their own future. At my most cynical, I recognize that if US policy towards Cuba changed with Obama, it was because the White House believed that it is in its best interest to do so. Perhaps they thought that by getting out of the way, the changes they would like to see take place in Cuba would be more likely to occur.

In the end, there was still a lot of language about "democracy promotion" in the US government's discourse, but I have to say that I felt that the speech was beautifully and strategically written. Cuba has always blamed the US aggressions and the US embargo for all the country's problems. Obama did what I have heard Cubans suggest for a very long time when they say "I wish that the embargo would end so it would become clear that the embargo is not the root of all our problems. The government would have no one else to blame things on and would have to recognize its own responsibility." By changing its policy, the US effectively "called the Cuban government's bluff." Obama appeared to be committed to doing everything he could possibly do within his powers as president to take away that pretext.

Obama elegantly laid down his sword and invited the Cuban people to do what they wanted to make their country what they wanted it to be. And he did it in a historical moment in which what many Cubans desired was economic stability, personal mobility, and security. For some, this freedom to take action is freedom to participate in social processes to make their communities better and fix their own problems, while for others, they just want the state out of their way so that they can have profitable small, medium, and maybe, someday, large businesses.

"Before the Americans Come"

December 17, 2014 introduced a new *before*: the *"Before the Americans come."* Tourism surged in Cuba after the December 17th announcements. European tourism surged with those who wanted to see Cuba before the Americans arrive in droves, ruining the imagined authenticity of the island. They came to see the "real" Cuba, before it was corrupted or polluted by Americans. Thanks to the US's travel restrictions, at this time, only European and Canadian tourists (and adventuresome Americans who flaunt these restrictions by travelling through third countries, hoping not to get caught) could travel as tourists to the island. In 2016, US tourism began joining them, driven by the desire to visit Cuba before it changed, before their own presence ruined the socialist authenticity and exceptionalism that they came to Cuba seeking.

For many Cubans living on the island, and their families abroad, this new *before* was associated with a frenzy of preparations. After December 17, 2014, some made investments to start new businesses before the onslaught of American tourists began to arrive in large numbers when travel restrictions were further eased in January 2015 and regular commercial flights to Havana resumed on November 28, 2016 (Baker 2015). Others worried that normalization would bring the repeal of the US immigration policies which offered unique opportunities for Cuban immigrants who entered the country without authorization. After December 2014, many Cubans, afraid that the Cuban Adjustment Act and the "Wet foot, Dry Foot policy" would soon be repealed, sold their properties. They took the cash and rushed to Ecuador and Mexico with the goal of making it to the US border. Under the exceptional "Wet foot, Dry Foot policy" Cuban citizens arriving to a US port of entry without a visa were paroled into the US and eligible under the Cuban Adjustment Act to apply for permanent residency on the one-year anniversary of their arrival.

In November 2015, the large numbers of Cubans travelling through Central America attempting to arrive to the US caused a crisis when four thousand were stranded in Costa Rica after being denied entry visas by the Nicaraguan government. Another 1,000 Cubans were stuck in Panama when Costa Rica decided to close its border to Cubans (Economist 2016). Eventually, the US assisted in negotiating an agreement with multiple Central American nations to facilitate the stranded Cubans' arrival to the US border (Leogrande 2015).

According to US border officials, the number of unauthorized Cubans arriving nearly doubled in fiscal year 2015, rising to 43,159 from 24,278 the previous year (Miroff 2015). The 2016 fiscal year saw 56,000 Cubans arrive, more than double the number two years before (Economist 2017). Despite the constant flow of Cuban migrants interested in securing US residency before the policies changed, it wasn't until January 12, 2017 that the US government announced that the twenty-two-year-old "Wet foot, dry foot" policy would immediately cease (Economist 2017). By that date, American visitors were already arriving to Cuba in record numbers. Direct flights between JFK and Havana were available for a little over $100 round trip. In the year that followed, the announcement of the normalization of relations, the number of US visitors grew by 77 percent (Trotta 2016).

CONCLUSION

Key to understanding life in contemporary Havana is capturing the instability which permeates everyday life in the capital. The image of an island "stuck in time" presented in the US media could not be further from the experience of many people in Havana who narrate their collective and personal histories as a series of historic transformations and everyday examples of heroic resilience. Everything is always changing in Cuba and most Havana residents have little advance notice of what changes will come next, or how permanent the changes might be. These conditions make it hard for people to make plans or prepare for the future. Just when one understands the rules, everything changes and a new "before" begins.

In the next chapter, I will explore how logics of social stratification have changed in Cuba in three periods: in the late 1980s, right before the Special Period (during Perestroika in USSR); in the 1990s, during Cuba's Special Period; and, again, after 2010, bringing about a new logic of social stratification. This history is key to helping US academics, students, and visitors to the island understand the dynamics of economic inequalities in contemporary Havana.

NOTES

1. In 1974, sugar prices on the international market spiked and Cuba took advantage of the windfall to diversify its trade relationships, expanding imports from Western Europe. Lured by the promise of easy credit due to the world glut of petrodollars, Cuba took on $4 billion of debt to increase imports from Western Europe, counting on continued high sugar prices to pay them back. Unfortunately, by 1978 sugar prices

returned to their normal levels and Cuba was left with an un-payable debt. By 1982, Cuba could no longer service its debt and, in 1986, Cuba declared a moratorium on debt payments (LeoGrande and Thomas 2002: 332). Cuba's inability to settle these debts has prevented the country from getting further international loans.

2. In Cuba, the historic revolutionary leaders, Raúl and Fidel Castro, Ernesto "Che" Guevara, and Camilo Cienfuegos, are referred to simply as Raúl, Fidel, Che and Camilo and I generally follow that convention in this text. As anthropologist Sachiko Tanuma notes, "the only Cubans who call them by their last names are people who are strongly against those figures. Thus, it makes me uncomfortable to use their last names" (2007, 61).

3. The Cuban Five were a small group of men who were known as national heroes in Cuba for serving the country as secret agents in the US where they had infiltrated Cuban-American groups planning terrorist attacks on Cuba. They were tried in Miami courts and sentenced to long sentences (Landau 2010).

Chapter Two

Changing Configurations of Capital and Logics of Stratification in Cuban Society

It was a hot mid-morning in June and I sat talking with Frank and his mother Lourdes on their large front porch, just a couple blocks away from Havana's famous Malecón. Nineteen-year-old Frank was completing his required social service after having graduated with a *Técnico Medio* degree in Computer Science and Lourdes, an engineer in her late forties, was not working outside the home. However, when I interviewed them in 2012, they had recently returned from spending a week at an all-inclusive beach resort in Varadero. They had also recently managed to make significant repairs to their detached single family home in a comfortable area of Vedado. I had just finished interviewing Frank about his social network and he invited his mother to join us for the section of the interview about the family's consumption practices, explaining that his mom was the one that took care of buying things in the household. When Lourdes joined in the conversation she told me that she felt they were doing well economically for the first time in years.

As the conversation developed, I realized that both Lourdes and Frank repeatedly referred to life "before" and "after," but this chronology did not map onto the collective narratives of "before" the Revolution or "before" the Special Period I was accustomed to hearing. They talked about their economic difficulties "before," when they were unable to sustain an acceptable level of consumption, or fix their house, and going to Varadero beach for the holidays was a distant dream that they had no hope of making come true. When I asked them what they meant when they referred to "before," they explained that for their family everything changed when Lourdes' father died. "We had all of these things [cars, houses] before my father's death, but since my father was so, so revolutionary, so communist, he would not allow us to do anything on the side. We couldn't rent the house because he wasn't going to allow it, I

23

think that my father died to show us the way, to be able to evolve, because he wasn't going to do it."

The mestizo, son of important landowners in Eastern Cuba, Lourdes' father, Felipe came to Havana to study medicine in the late 1950s and got swept up in the revolutionary movement. He was arrested several times for being associated with the Revolutionary Directorate. In 1957, after the March 13 attack, he was arrested, but his family was able to use their connections and money to get him out of jail and out of the country. They sent him to Spain to continue studying medicine safe from the Batista regime. After the 1959 "Triumph of the Revolution," he came back to Cuba and finished his medical degree in Havana. Although he would have been allowed to start his own private practice, he preferred to be a part of the public health system and was one of the founders of an important hospital in Vedado.

Lourdes began, "He got into this because..." She was silent for a few seconds before continuing. "Where do I start!? He became a revolutionary because, I imagine it's because he was young! He had that spirit of change, I don't know what reason he had, but it was not lack of food, you see. He didn't get involved because he was hungry."

Felipe's father (Lourdes's grandfather) was most definitely not a communist. He would try to discourage his son, and ask him why he was getting involved "In this communism stuff." "Don't you know that communists take everything away from you? The communists don't give you anything!" he told his son, but Felipe didn't pay much attention to his father. Lourdes remembers years later, in the hardest moments of the Special Period, when Felipe told her this story, he commented, "Turns out my father was right!"

Felipe was one of the few doctors that stayed after the Revolution. "Fidel took care of those few doctors because, if he didn't, they were going to leave as well. My father had certain privileges because he earned them with his work and his effort," Lourdes explained. He was put in charge of a specialty hospital and given a house. Even though he was now working for the state, rather than a private clinic, he continued to earn the same salary. Like Felipe, some members of the Cuban professional class who stayed in the country were given important positions in government ministries. Often high-level professionals and technicians were allowed to keep their pre-revolutionary salaries as a stimulus to make sure that they would not leave the country (Karl 1975, 33). These were known as "historic salaries" and most were eliminated in the mid-1970s after the Thirteenth Workers Congress in 1973 (Karl 1975, 37).[1]

"He was beyond revolutionary! Everything that they asked in this country and outside of this country he joined and participated," Lourdes explained. He participated in two international missions as a doctor. When he returned from his mission in Angola they wanted to give him a car, because back then all the doctors were given one when they returned from the mission but, since he already had a car, he turned it down. He explained that he didn't need two cars and that they should give it to someone else. Much later, when he returned from his second mission, the family was able to convince him to accept the car he was given because by then the family's car was on its last legs.

Although he could have earned much more if he had left Cuba, even in the hardest years he never talked about leaving Cuba. "He always liked to live here and he was very respected. He never asked for anything ever," Lourdes explained. "He was "the real deal," "on the straight and narrow." He was one of the ones that you have to take off your hat for because he was revolutionary and communist and he showed it with his actions. He was not one of those communists or those *dirigentes* today." Felipe's strong moral commitments to the Revolution were received by his daughter and grandson with a mix of awe, respect, and consternation.

By following the rules of revolutionary habitus, people like Felipe effectively secured their exclusion from the new economy. In a rapidly changing post-Soviet field, social capital has become more important in gaining access to resources than the embodied and institutionalized cultural capital invested in by the state and individuals since the beginning of the Revolution.

Since the onset of the crisis, living standards have "come to depend much more on informal networks" (Burchardt 2002, 62). During this period, access to economic capital undoubtedly can resolve many problems, but often access to economic capital alone is not enough. In order to have access to opportunities for consumption, it is necessary to both have, and be willing to use, social capital. When Felipe got sick, his daughter drew on his social networks to get help for him, something he never would have done because it seemed to him to be a violation of his values as a revolutionary to use his position for personal, rather than collective, benefit.

The Cuban public health system provides oxygen tanks, hospital type beds, and adult diapers to terminally ill patients, but, in practice, there are huge gaps in coverage and often families end up paying for these services in the black market, or using their contacts to assure that they are put on the top of the list for the services provided by the state. Felipe preferred to wait and have things come to him through the regular channels rather than use his position to get them. His daughter, who was faced with the responsibility of assuring the logistics necessary to care for her ailing father, used all means necessary.

"That's the way my grandfather was, he was dying, he was gasping for air, and you had to go help him because he would die, in fact he did die, without asking for help from anyone," Frank explained.

Lourdes told me that even when her father got sick he would never ask for anything and her mother was the same way. "He never asked for anything and I had to be really strong. I told him, 'If you don't ask, I will ask.'"

And that's just what she did. It didn't seem fair to her, "He fought a lot for this country, he did a lot for this revolution. He saved too many lives for him to die as a poor man. He deserved for them to take care of him," Lourdes said.

Things came to a head one day when she arrived home, exhausted from a day waiting in line after line, going to various hospitals trying to get the help she needed for her father without results. Lourdes was in bad shape, and she realized that if she continued hitting up against so many walls that she would end up making herself sick. She called an important *dirigente* in the country who was a close personal friend of her father. From that moment on, everything flowed. After that point, her father only lasted a couple more months.

As her father's daughter Lourdes had tried to everything in her power to get what she needed through official channels before she decided to ask for special help. Sometimes she regrets that she didn't ask for help earlier. "If I had done it from the very beginning, it would've been better. When I finally called that person, he reacted in an instant," she told me, snapping her fingers for emphasis. "Despite the fact that he had a lot of personal problems in his life to worry about, he was really great with my dad."

Lourdes' father raised her to never ask for anything. She learned from his example, but as she got older this began to cause more conflicts between the two of them.

"He had what he had because he earned it," she told me. "What they gave him he had because he earned it, not because he asked for it. If he had asked for or taken what he needed the family would have lived much more comfortably. We could have had much more, but he never allowed it." Sometimes they fought bitterly over this, but in the end she told me that she raised her son to respect him and adore him the way she did because he was so dedicated to them.

After Felipe passed away, his daughter and grandson felt freer to use the capital that they inherited from him to convert it into forms that could be used more readily, something that his communist values prevented him from doing. After Felipe died, Lourdes sold one of his two cars and swapped her father's huge crumbling house in Miramar for an elegant apartment in Vedado. The Miramar house was in such bad shape that she felt relieved to find a swap before it collapsed. Felipe hadn't been able to keep up maintenance because, in order to do so, he would have had to turn to the black market or use his contacts to obtain materials neither of which he felt were moral options.

Lourdes made money off the swap and started to rent out the new apartment, something that she tells me he never would have allowed. Renting out the apartment provided a new source of income for the household; the 500 CUC a month they earned allowed the family to fix the home where they live in Vedado and change their lifestyle. Lourdes used to drink coffee from the bodega before, but now she only drinks *Cubita* coffee or some other brand sold in CUC stores.

"So of course I'm not satisfied with the coffee from the bodega anymore, because life is taking me down this path and my necessities are growing," she explains. Frank chimes in and adds his two cents, "Progress can't be stopped!" Lourdes nods her head and agrees, "That's the way it is. Before, I didn't buy the good cheese because I didn't have money to buy good cheese. Now I have the money to buy good cheese and so I spend it buying good cheese. In the end we are still living thanks to him because everything that we have is because he left it."

Felipe's legacy continues to provide for his family with the properties that they have been able to convert into a source of economic capital. In addition, Felipe's long record of dedication to the Revolution has provided his daughter and grandson with other privileges in the form of social capital.

"Sometimes we have a difficult situation, some sort of problem, and I always, always resolve the problem because someone who knows him appears. . . . Our last name is pretty rare, and someone always says, 'But you know, I used to know someone with that last name,' and then there it is, he saves the day. If the last name doesn't come up, I bring it up" Lourdes says proudly.

French sociologist Pierre Bourdieu explains that capital is power and can be presented in three different forms: economic capital, which is "immediately and directly convertible into money and may be institutionalized in the form of property rights"; cultural capital, which is "convertible, on certain conditions, into economic capital and may be institutionalized in the form of educational qualifications"; and social capital, "made up of the social obligations ("connections"), which is convertible, in certain conditions, into economic capital" (Bourdieu 1986b).

In this chapter, I show how dominant configurations of economic, cultural, and social capital changed in the 1960s after the Revolution. These years witnessed the birth of a stratification system in which what I call *Revolutionary Cultural Capital* (a historically specific formation of the "right" type of political attitudes and cultural capital) opened opportunities for success in Cuba's Revolutionary society. Through the mid-1980s, revolutionary cultural capital was dominant in the social field and determined access to power, consumption, and opportunities. Next, I show how these Cuban socialist logics of social stratification have changed: in the late 1980s, right before the Special Period (during Perestroika in USSR); in the 1990s, during Cuba's Special

Period economic crisis; and today, in 2015, as a result of the current process of reform.

In defining the social "field," Bourdieu describes dominated and dominant positions that can be analyzed in terms of their distinct profiles of capital, or resources which actors accrue which help them to achieve positions of relative privilege within the field (Emirbayer 2005, 691). Bourdieu says that "the structure of the distribution of the different types and subtypes of capital at a given moment in time represents the immanent structure of the social world, that is, the set of constraints, inscribed in the very reality of that world, which govern its functioning in a durable way, determining the chances of success for practices"(Bourdieu 1986b).

Within a given field, actors with different amounts and combinations of capital struggle to have their constellation of capital recognized as legitimate by others. If they are successful, they win moral authority and power. Immediately after the military success of the Cuban Revolution, revolutionary social actors utilized de-legitimatizing strategies to call into question the morality of the economic capital of national and international powerbrokers in Cuba, and successfully, albeit perhaps temporarily, achieved the primacy of a new form of revolutionary cultural capital, a particular form of capital encouraged by the Revolutionary State.

Sociologist, Carolyn Hsu (2007), has looked at how institutions of social stratification were changed during the transition to market socialism in the city of Harbin, China. Hsu defines institutions as "the script social actors follow: they are 'the way that we do things,' and the constituent rules of society. The institutions of stratification are the sets of social practices which produce and reproduce inequality in a given society" (2007, 5). Stratification systems shape class structure and determine which social actors have access to power and resources.

Stratification systems are composed of three types of institutions (Grusky 2001, 3). The first types of institutions are those which determine the worth of various forms of capital: economic, social, human, cultural, and, in states with socialist political systems, political capital (which comes from party membership and ones' rank in the party hierarchy) (2007, 6). The second type of institution determines how much of each form of capital is allocated to different occupations and positions: this determines the hierarchy of occupations, as well as how much of each form of capital is required to enter (Grusky 2001, 3; 2007, 7). The third type of institution is the mechanisms that encourages or limits an individual's access to valued forms of capital, thereby limiting access to different positions. Practices which are sexist, racist, regionalist (urban/rural), and classist may exclude certain groups and favor the reproduction of structural inequalities (2007, 6).

In this chapter, I look at the first of these institutions to explore how the relative importance of different types of capital and the legitimacy of distinct configurations of capital have changed in three historical periods. The first change came immediately after the Revolution (late 1960–80s), the second at the beginning of the Special Period economic crisis (1990s), and they continue to be transformed today. In my study of changing capital configurations in these different historical periods, I look at the presence of three categories of capital: Bourdieu's economic capital and social capital, and Revolutionary Cultural Capital, my own term to describe a particular hybrid of political capital specific to socialist states that includes specific forms of cultural capital which were valued and promoted by the Cuban Revolution.

Revolutionary cultural capital dominated the Cuban field in the 1970s–1980s, where adherence and dedication to the socio-political project of the Revolution was valued above all other forms of capital. During the Special Period, the importance of revolutionary cultural capital began to decline, as economic and social capital began to play a dominant role in structuring social inequalities. Since the Special Period, uses of capital framed as illegitimate or morally suspect by the Revolution (the accumulation of economic capital or drawing on ones' personal social capital to resolve problems that cannot be resolved through formal channels available to all) have gradually become more socially accepted. During the Special Period, revolutionary cultural capital continued to circulate in dialectic coexistence with newer configurations of capitals specific to the new economic conditions in Cuba. In the wake of the recent wave of economic reforms, dominant configurations of capital are again being contested within the social field. Revolutionary Cultural Capital has lost its supremacy as the path to social mobility by providing access to opportunities for consumption, social status, and power.

AFTER THE REVOLUTION: CHANGING CAPITAL CONFIGURATIONS AND THE BIRTH OF *REVOLUTIONARY CULTURAL CAPITAL*

Immediately after the success of the Revolution in 1959, the state intervened to fight social inequalities by raising wages, reducing rents and utility rates, taxing imported luxury items, providing free universal health care and education, and expropriating large landholdings to give land to squatters, sharecroppers, and renters (Pérez 2006, 243). During this period, economic differences were reduced and not relevant in determining access to consumption. Through all of these reforms, the Revolutionary State struggled to subvert the prerevolutionary distribution, valuation, and hierarchy of different types of capital, working to build a more just society by "transform[ing] the field's system of authority...the very rules of the game according to which it ordinarily functions, to their benefit" (Emirbayer 2005, 693).

With a leveled playing field, access to cultural capital was no longer dependent on economic capital. New dominant configurations of capital stressed revolutionary cultural capital over economic capital, which had been dominant before the Revolution. In 1961, the Cuban literacy campaign had mobilized 271,000 people to provide basic literacy training throughout the island. This campaign was followed by others to help workers complete primary, middle, and high school and continue their education in state vocational schools and universities (Pérez 2006, 273). University enrollments expanded tenfold, as free higher education was opened to any qualified individual. Housing was provided for students from rural areas and students were given stipends to cover the costs of attendance. These revolutionary policies helped remove traditional barriers to education which opened the doors to occupational mobility.

As in many other socialist societies, education was a major mechanism through which members of the pre-revolutionary working class and peasants (and their children) previously excluded from paths to mobility, were able to move into positions as skilled technicians and professionals. These positions provided them with increased social status and salaries that provided a higher quality of life and opportunities to satisfy basic consumption that would have not been possible for them under the previous system.

Due to the massive out-migration of middle-class Cubans with professional and technical skills after the Revolution, there were jobs waiting for these new graduates. According to Lou Pérez, "approximately half of all teachers emigrated. Of an estimated total 85,000 professionals and technicians in Cuba, approximately 20,000 immigrated. More than 3,000 physicians out of a total of 6,000 and 700 dentists out of almost 2,000 parted. The senior medical faculty at the University of Havana was reduced from two hundred to seventeen . . . no less important was the flight of almost all of the 6,500 North American residents, many of whom had worked in important technical and managerial capacities in both the US and Cuban enterprises" (2006:261–262).

Women and people of color benefited disproportionately from this brain drain, overcoming economic, racial and gender barriers which had previously prevented occupational mobility from manual to intellectual labor (Blue 2010, 37). The extent of these transformations is clearly seen in the health care sector. In the 1950s, only 6 percent of Cuban doctors were women, but by 1990, 48 percent of doctors were female (Smith and Padula 1996, 57). By 1981, 31 percent of Cuban health workers were black or mulatto, close to their representation in the population at large (34%) (de la Fuente 2001, 309). Access to education gave these individuals the opportunity to move from physical labor to intellectual labor and assume more prestigious positions gaining higher social status.

A second common route to social mobility after the Revolution was through the military. After Batista had been defeated, the rebels came down from the Sierra Maestra Mountains of Eastern Cuba and made their way to Havana to take control of the government. Those who had been active in the rebel troops, or in the underground urban struggle, assumed important positions in the new Revolutionary State. While Fidel Castro and "Che" Guevara were college-educated professionals from upper middle class families, many of the other officials of the rebel army came from very humble backgrounds without formal education. To establish control of the most important functions of the state and its bureaucratic structure, the revolutionary leadership felt the need to replace corrupt officials, loyal to the previous government, with people who were loyal to the Revolution. There was a large migration from Eastern Cuba of men (and their families) who were brought to the capital to assume positions in state ministries.

In assigning leadership for important tasks, political loyalties and trustworthiness (political capital) often mattered more than one's professional, technical, or academic background. A gifted military strategist trained as a medical doctor, in 1959, Che Guevara was named the head of the Cuban National Bank and Minister of Industry.

The great social experiment that the Revolution proposed was a "Cuba for the Cubans" which could only be built with the participation of all. Those who did not participate in the new social experiment risked being seen as anti-revolutionary or identified as part of an anti-social element possibly even linked to the US government. In order to be a good Cuban citizen, one must be "integrated" into the revolutionary process [*integrado*]. A person who was "integrated" was a person who participated in the process of social transformations that began in the country after the Revolution took power. Many of these social projects required mass participation to be achieved.

Regular Cuban citizens of all walks of life were called on to participate in neighborhood chapters of the Federation of Cuban Women (*la Federación de Mujeres Cubanas*-FMC) to help integrate women into the revolutionary campaigns. They formed local neighborhood watches on every block to protect against counter-revolutionary activities (*Comité de Defensa de la Revolución*-CDR). Within a year of its founding the CDRs had 800,000 members (Pérez 1998, 251). Cubans were expected to volunteer to cut sugar cane, harvest coffee and potatoes, or plant trees to meet the state's agricultural goals. They were also expected to donate blood, to teach literacy and allow their children to go off to the countryside for months to teach illiterate *campesinos* how to read. They were expected to take up arms to defend the country in case of US invasion. Cubans from all walks of life received military training, and by 1961, almost 300,000 Cubans had joined the civilian militia to be ready to defend the country from attacks (Pérez 1998, 251). In rural areas, about 100,000 small farmers and peasants were organized into the National Association of Small Farmers [*Associación Nacional de Agricultores Pequeños*-ANAP] (Pérez 1998, 251).

It was possible to be seen as a "good revolutionary" even if one had not been a part of the underground urban guerrilla or gone to the Sierra Maestra to fight in the mountains. The Revolution called for the creation of a *hombre nuevo*, a new man ruled by a new moral code "motivated not by expectation of personal gain but by the prospects of collective advancement...disciplined, highly motivated, and hard-working" (Pérez 2006, 259). A person who was integrated was expected to always "take a step forward" [*dar el paso al frente*] and volunteer when help was needed, willing to go wherever the Revolution needed them.

Being a good Cuban citizen meant being a good revolutionary. It was through these experiences and processes of mass participation that revolutionary cultural capital became embodied and institutionalized. According to Bourdieu, capital becomes embodied and institutionalized when it is gained through "a labor of inculcation and assimilation,[which] costs time, time which must be invested personally by the investor and... converted into an integral part of the person, into a habitus, effective in guaranteeing material and symbolic profits for its possessors" (Bourdieu 1986a, 48–49). The word *citizen* fell out of use during this period and was replaced by the word *compañero* (comrade). Claims to access to goods, services and opportunities were no longer made on the basis of citizenship, but on the basis of one's revolutionary integration, being a true *compañero* or *integrado.*

Revolutionary cultural capital became more legitimate than economic capital in determining social mobility and access to resources. As salaries for low wage workers increased, the economic differences associated with salaries of workers in different occupations were not significant. The state subsidized cultural production by providing regular salaries to artists, and made the consumption of objectified cultural capital affordable and accessible to all. Cultural forms respected as "highbrow culture" before the Revolution, such as ballet, were made available at low prices to popular audiences. Within the Cuban theatre establishment, the formation of the New Theatre movement brought theatre to rural areas and the voices of *campesinos* [rural people] to the stage (Frederik 2012, 21, 57). Attendance at theatre events increased 1,000 percent from 1958–1965, reaching one million annually (Martin 1994).

Given the levels of economic equality and state subsidies for education and cultural consumption and production, economic capital was not an important indicator of access to opportunity. The most important resources were distributed not based on economic capital, but universally to all. A ration system, installed in 1962, guaranteed minimum consumption for all. The ration system prevented prices on basic goods from soaring based on supply and demand and also prevented those with higher incomes from stockpiling goods and leaving others without.

When there were significant differences in access to goods and services, it was an individual's commitment to the Revolution and successful adoption of a new revolutionary habitus which provided the advantage. Revolutionary cultural capital was rewarded with access to consumer goods and was distributed based on the recommendations of union and party officials (Pérez 2006, 269). In the 1970s, material incentives were linked to work outcomes, and consumer goods like motorcycles, cars, televisions, washing machines, refrigerators, and bicycles were distributed through the workplace to "outstanding workers"(Pérez 2006, 269). According to Pérez, in 1973, 100,000 television sets were distributed to vanguard workers through labor assemblies on the recommendation of party and union officials (Perez 1998: 269).

THE SPECIAL PERIOD: EMERGING IMPORTANCE OF ECONOMIC AND SOCIAL CAPITAL

After the fall of the Soviet Union, the severe economic crisis known as the Special Period began. The first phase of neoliberal restructuring in response to the crisis brought about the uneven distribution of economic capital and a reconfiguration of relative importance of the different types of capital. As a result of the crisis and the subsequent strengthening of the US embargo, the Cuban state no longer had the resources to guarantee equality and distribute goods/services based on revolutionary cultural capital. Cubans were forced to turn to the black market, where economic and social capital became the basis on which resources were accessed and distributed. Before the Special Period "the only requirement was that you put the needs of your country and community first, and work hard for the good of the state and its members. Now this is no longer sufficient, it is a person's access to hard currency that determines what they can consume" (Porter 2008, 145).

In the 1990s, when the state first opened the *diplotiendas* (also known as dollar stores), they were limited to foreign diplomats and visitors, or Cubans who had passports from other countries. One might have unlimited economic capital, but you could not enter the store and, therefore, you could not use that economic capital to buy the products available in the stores. Social capital, on the other hand, might connect you to foreigners or Cubans with foreign passports who could enter the store and buy you what you wanted.

By 1992, the value of state wages had fallen so precipitously that the average Cuban family needed twice its income to satisfy its basic needs (Togores 2000 in Burchardt 2002, 61). Economic capital, especially access to dollars or hard currency, became necessary to even partially meet household consumption needs previously satisfied through subsidized state distribution mechanisms. Many families turned to the informal sector to supplement their incomes; by 1997, almost 40 percent of the economically active population was working in the informal sector (Padilla Dieste 1997 in Burchardt 2002, 61).

After trying to ameliorate the effects of the crisis through deficit spending and courting foreign direct investment in tourism, the Cuban government implemented a series of economic reforms which changed the structure of labor, exchange, and consumption. A growing proportion of the population had access to dollars through work in the tourism sector or family remittances, but, because it was illegal to hold dollars, they were spent only in the black market, out of the reach of the state, which desperately needed hard currency to continue social spending and imports. The state legalized the dollar in August 1993 in hope of replenishing the country's critically low foreign exchange reserves. About $3 million of remittances entered Cuba between 1989–1996 (CEPAL 1997:124 cited in Barberia 2004:369). The state opened a chain of stores in which otherwise scarce goods were sold in dollars at high markups (an average of 240 percent on imported goods and 170 percent on domestically produced goods), the government was able to capture the dollars circulating in the economy and channel them towards national economic priorities (Barberia 2004, 376). Soon, a dual economy formed in which the majority of residents earned Cuban pesos, but a growing number of basic goods and services were available only in hard currency. Cuba came to be divided into new classes of "haves" and "have-nots": those with dollars (through remittances, informal or licensed employment, formal employment with foreign firms, salaries of professionals working abroad, and dollar incentives to workers in key industries) and those without (Ritter and Rowe 2002).

Suddenly, as the structure of the field changed, revolutionary cultural capital became increasingly irrelevant. As Burchardt explains, "the revaluing of wages in terms of the US dollar... eliminated the correlation between professional qualifications and standards of living," leading to a "shift of highly skilled labor to low skill jobs that dramatically devalues qualifications and specializations" (2002, 62). In Cuba, this situation is commonly referred to as the "inverted pyramid" because the most highly educated and trained professionals who are at the top of the occupational hierarchy are at the bottom of the income hierarchy, while those in low level service jobs in the tourist sector are at the top of the income hierarchy and the bottom of the occupational hierarchy (Uriarte 2008). The expected correlation between higher education and increased earnings is no longer the rule in Cuba.

Between 1990–2000, the percentage of the population working in the state sector fell from 90 percent to 73 percent (Galbraith, Spagnolo, and Munevar 2006, 3). Highly credentialed professionals, especially doctors and teachers, left formal sector jobs for informal, unlicensed and illegal work as taxi drivers and tour guides, where they could earn significantly higher salaries (Pérez 2006, 310). In the Special Period, economic capital became increasingly important, but it was still ideologically and morally questionable because its sources were likely connected to illegal or self-interested acts, which were considered immoral.

Those most visibly committed to the Revolution were among the most disadvantaged in the new economy, because they continued to work in the state sector, earning only pesos, and did not engage in black market activity to earn much-needed economic capital or take advantage of their position to gain benefits through mobilizing their social capital (Burchardt 2002, 62). The staunch revolutionary who refuses to engage in the shadow market or whose moral commitments to the Revolution prohibit them from using social connections to resolve personal problems is a stock character ridiculed in contemporary Cuban films such as *Cuerno de la abundancia* [Cornucopia] (2008) by Director Juan Carlos Tabío where the super communist father doesn't believe anything unless he reads it in the Communist Party's national newspaper, *Granma*, or sees it on the nightly news (Tabío 2008). The ceiling of the family's home is in extremely poor condition and his wife narrowly escapes injury when a chunk of cement from the kitchen ceiling falls, but he refuses to fix it because his state salary is not enough, and it would require buying materials in the black market, which are stolen from the state. *Guantanamera* (1995), by Director Tomás Gutiérrez Alea, offers another example of a film that mocks such stalwarts (Gutiérrez Alea 1995).

Francisco, "I didn't need to know what the laws were... I just needed friendships."

In addition to giving one access to goods and services not easily available through regular channels in the formal economy, social capital also provide entrepreneurs who do not have moral qualms about using their connections a clear advantage in access to opportunities. After renting rooms to foreigners was legalized in the 1990s, many of the first licenses were given to people who were former military officials or people with extremely high levels of revolutionary cultural capital. Hosting foreigners was seen as a very sensitive job that required a well- developed revolutionary consciousness. Any of these "tourists" could be a mercenary in disguise, and the hosts must be prepared to deal with such challenges to the Revolution and be trusted to inform on them. Today, among the long-term renters I know are a wife of a deceased Cuban general, one of the founders of *Radio Rebelde,* a military man who set up the first radio communications in the Sierra Maestra Mountains, various Communist Party members, and former directors of national projects.

One of the renters, Francisco, lives in Vedado in a large two story house now divided into three sizable pieces between Francisco and his two siblings. Francisco's father is from a wealthy landowning family in Trinidad who stayed in Cuba after the Revolution. The family lost its important properties to nationalization, but threw themselves into working for the Revolution. Francisco's father and uncles worked with Che in a government ministry. In the late 1990s, after working for the military for several decades, Francisco left his state sector job at the university to set up a private travel agency. The agency brought French students to Cuba on short-term trips. They were hosted in private homes around his neighborhood, and every morning about thirty kids and their teachers would have breakfast in his living room, converted to a cafeteria. He rented a bus from the Cuban state agency, *Transtur,* and would go to the airport to pick up his groups with a sign just like all the other foreign agencies.

For about two years Francisco took his groups all over the island and never had a problem, until one day he was called into the office of the Minister of Tourism, Osmany Cienfuegos. The Vice Minister of Tourism and the District Attorney, who were both Francisco's personal friends, were also present at the meeting. Francisco explains,

> I'm a person who has always lived in this neighborhood and I've worked a lot, and I have a lot of relationships through that. We [the agency] never broke the rules. There is nothing written that could have taken us to court or have fined us. Everything we were doing was simply not contemplated in the law.

I asked Francisco, "How did you know what the laws were? How could you make sure you weren't doing anything illegal?" He answered,

> I didn't need to know what the laws were… [*changes tack*] I just needed friendships. In Cuba we have a saying that is "If you have a friend, you have a *central,*"

which young people don't really know what it means anymore, because a central doesn't mean anything anymore.[2] Young people don't even know what it means, but in my time that really meant something. I am still the same person I've always been. I'm very loyal to people. Sometimes people don't reward that, but a lot of people still remember that loyalty.

So they called me into Osmany's office. Now if my answers had not been the right ones, maybe I would've gone to jail straight from there. Those kinds of things happen in Cuba and nothing surprises me, but the people I was doing this with weren't stupid either. The other Cuban in the agency was a journalist and we always talked about, "Let's figure out the legal way to do this," and we had people we could ask. Here it is not just what the law says, but if they want to let you do it. It might not be against the law, but if they want to get you they will invent a law to do so. So we knew that, and we knew that if we went too far, or if they didn't like it, we would have to stop.

So I went, and I knew how to handle the questions they asked me. They asked me if I knew that what I was doing was against the law, and I responded that "No, I know that what we were doing is not against the law, but I also know that it had not been contemplated in the law. I also know that perhaps you guys don't like what we are doing, but I know that we are not breaking the law." And they said, "But this is dangerous for the Revolution" and I stopped that train quickly by assuring them that, "There's nothing here that is dangerous for the Revolution." Many of the people who came were leftists and supported Cuba, and so I tried to manage it so that there was no way that they could attack us.

When I left, I got in my Fiat and drove away, and my friends (the Vice Minister and the District Attorney) were right behind me in their cars. In the meeting, they had acted like they didn't know me, but, when we were out of the area, they honked the horn and motioned for me to pull over. When I did, they told me "You know what you have to do, right? Tear it down, as fast as you can!" and of course we closed the business right away, because it didn't make any sense to keep going.

Thanks to his political connections, Francisco had access to high-level advice and protection, and the business was able to last as long as it did without getting in trouble. Francisco explained that the fact that he and his business partners were "known quantities" was an extremely important protective factor: "I am a person that there's no way that they can say that I'm not with the process or that I'm not revolutionary or that I am against the government or anything. That's something that I always have on my side. I'm not a person who doesn't *not* help things to work. I'm someone who thinks that things have to work, and the better they work the better it is for me and my people."

Without his unquestionable background of revolutionary cultural capital earned by coming from an *integrated* family and working in the Cuban military and as a *dirigente* for more than two decades himself, Francisco explains that things would have been different.

I think that it was just that they wanted to know what was going on and what we were about. I don't think that the intention of the meeting was to arrest me, because they could have done it, but they didn't. If they really wanted to catch me in something, if they had put listening devices or followed me, they could have found something that wasn't exactly "correct." They could have invented, or even proven, I guess, that I had bought beer from somebody that I shouldn't have bought it from. You know, not directly stolen, but they could've done it, because there's no one who can supply any sort of business unless you go to the black market, and I am sure that they knew that I had done thousands of things like that. So when I thought about it, I realized that they would have only have had to watch me for a little bit, and they would've found something on me, and that would have been it.

From the beginning, Francisco and his business partners were prepared for the possibility that at any moment they might have to dismantle the agency.

It was something that we knew could happen. From the very beginning, we had been warned that this was a possibility. I come from the military, so I know how these things work as well. Even though it wasn't my area, you relate to people who are in different areas, and you know how things work, the *Plan Maceta* actions, for example. This idea that there is now about self-employment did not exist back then. Things were really different back then and it was seen as bad by the majority of people.

From the experience, Francisco learned that it was important to him to always have both types of work: having state sector work makes your private work less threatening. You are a known quantity and less threatening to the state. Also, having a state job gives you something to fall back on when the riskier forms of business (inevitably) fall apart.

Even though Francisco had to fold up the tourist agency, he was still seen as trustworthy enough to get a rental license. He moved himself, his wife, and his two kids into his father's spare bedroom downstairs in order to rent out their apartment on the top floor. Living crowded into one bedroom was stressful for the family, and they decided to move back upstairs. They prepared a spare bedroom downstairs and another upstairs to rent out to foreigners. With separate streams of income for Francisco's family upstairs and his parents and sisters downstairs, they avoided conflicts around dividing the earnings. This business provided the two households with a steady income, charging $15 a day per room, a large sum at the end of the Special Period. In 2015, both households continue to rent to foreigners.

Both the story of Lourdes and Frank, and the story of Francisco, show a tendency towards the reproduction of economic and social privilege through generations. Generally, today, those who came from families with a certain level of economic and social capital and status before the Revolution were likely to maintain that status, holding important positions after the Revolution. With so many professionals leaving the country, those who stayed and were willing to put their skills and knowledge to work for the new social project were often put in place as directors of important projects, high up in political and professional hierarchies.

Both Lourdes' and Francisco's fathers came from important land-owning families in Guantanamo and Trinidad. They lost their properties, but became directors of important revolutionary programs and continued to receive relatively high salaries. In the next generation, the children of these leaders, like Lourdes and Francisco, tend to be professionals and live in large houses in desirable neighborhoods of Havana (sometimes as a part of inherited pre-Revolutionary wealth, sometimes given to their parents by the state for revolutionary service). In the 1990s, the next generation had the advantage of being able to use these properties to rent or start small businesses, combined with the advantages of social capital, connections to current government officials who can help find loopholes in state policies. Coming from families with social and economic capital before the Revolution contributed to their success after the Revolution but did not determine it. If they had not cultivated their revolutionary cultural capital they would not have been trusted to be directors of important revolutionary programs. As members of important and politically trustworthy families *integrated* into the revolutionary project, the concentration of wealth by these individuals in the current period is not a source of concern for the state, which does not see them as a risk to political stability.

CUBAN SOCIAL STRUCTURE
AFTER THE SPECIAL PERIOD

Perhaps the simplest way to describe the great social divide in Cuba after the Special Period would be a division between those who have dollars and those who do not, with gradations according to how much and how often (Brenner 2015, 21). But this definition looks only at economic capital and doesn't take into account the weight of social capital.

Anthropologist, Amelia Weinreb (2009), uses class as an analytical concept to explain the relationships between individuals and the state in Cuba based on fieldwork in Havana in 2003, during the liminal period between the first wave of economic reforms in the mid-90s and the second wave, which began after Raúl Castro took over the presidency. Weinreb's ethnography focuses on the formation of the class she calls "Unsatisfied Citizen-Consumers," which she sees as an important class, given its potential to lead the transition to capitalism. She sees monetary dualism and growing economic inequalities as desirable due to their potential to erode the power of the state.

According to Weinreb's political position, limiting the role of the state in people's lives is a positive step as "government discipline is intensive for those reliant on the state; access to dollars (through certain sources) may precipitate freedom from the state, due to decreased economic dependence on—and, therefore, interaction with—it" (Weinreb 2009, 105). She defines "civil liberties" as "immunity from the arbitrary exercise of government authority/ interference," and for this reason she is interested in the potential of social classes less dependent on the state for stimulating changes in Cuban society, leading to changes in its socio-economic system (Weinreb 2009, 105). She is more interested in the dual currency system and how it structures opportunities for gaining personal freedoms, the so-called "positive" effects of social stratification, rather than the ways in which it limits opportunities for food/ housing/survival in the context of declining state welfare.[3]

Despite Weinreb's specific political agenda, which reinforces transition narratives, it is still worthwhile to discuss her proposal for understanding stratification in Cuba. Weinreb presents a hierarchy of "five culturally and nationally specific late-socialist "classes." Weinreb's categories, the Red Bourgeoisie, Performers/Athletes, Dollar Dogs, Unsatisfied Citizen-Consumers and the Peso Poor are terms of Weinreb's own creation, not local folk categories (2009: 104). Particularly interesting is the fact that the word "citizen" is definitely not a local category and has a very negative connotation in Cuba. In the next chapter, I present my own model to understand social stratification and the diversity of practices of cultural consumption found in Havana based on local models for understanding social stratification and inequality.

As Bourdieu explains, "within any given field, different specific entities can be said to engage in the struggles ongoing within that field as bearers of different amounts and combinations of capitals, some yielding greater advantages within that particular field than others" (2005:691). In the following discussion of Weinreb's late socialist class structure (2009, 104), I will discuss the different combinations of capitals yielded by each of these groups.

Through connections with party members high in the hierarchy, Weinreb's *Red Bourgeoisie* have important social capital, through which they're able to access consumer goods and services not widely available for the general public. Most often, these benefits are achieved through in-kind access to products, rather than actual money, so although these individuals may derive many privileges from their relationships with important people, they are generally cash poor.

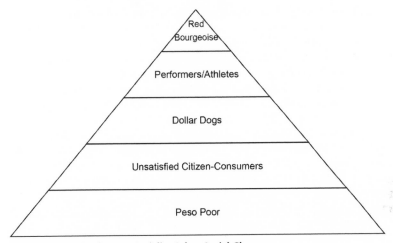

Figure 2.1. Weinreb's Late-Socialist Cuban Social Classes

The Revolution's commitment to the development of sports and arts mean that *Performers/Athletes* are generally well-respected for their talents and possess revolutionary cultural capital, which they are able to convert into economic capital. Because they are able to legally earn large sums of hard currency for their performances abroad, the state has allowed them to freely import and purchase commodities, like cars, that during the time of Weinreb's research could not be legally consumed (Weinreb 2009, 103). Since most Cubans living in the country would have no way of legally earning the tens of thousands of dollars necessary to buy and import a car, they do not have this option. This privilege is given to performers and athletes who can prove the legality of their earnings.

The *Dollar Dogs* earn economic capital through their legal small businesses, which allow them to consume goods and products unavailable to lower classes. Although their economic capital gives them certain privileges, unlike Performers/Athletes, they are likely to be disrespected by society at large and have low status due to the source of their capital, earned through capitalist practices which might be dependent on the use of cultural capital despised in the revolutionary habitus.

To meet their economic needs, members of Weinreb's lower economic classes depend heavily on their social capital, which Portes (1998) defines simply as the "ability of actors to secure benefits by virtue of membership in social networks or other social structures" (6). Weinreb claims that the largest group is the *Unsatisfied Citizen-Consumer*, who possesses varying amounts of economic capital from unreliable sources and, therefore, must also depend on social capital and revolutionary cultural capital to maintain their household economies (2009).

The *Peso Poor*, without economic capital of their own, must depend heavily on social and cultural capital and strategically engage with revolutionary habitus to access needed resources. As Portes explains, social capital is a double-edged sword: "just as it opens opportunities for some, serving as a source of family support and benefits thorough extrafamilial networks, it can also exclude outsiders, make burdensome claims on group members, restrict individual freedom, and enforce downward leveling norms"(1998, 15).

A joke told to me in Havana illustrates the negative side of the current importance of social capital: "What we have in Cuba isn't *socialismo* (socialism), but *sociolismo,*" a play on words in which an egalitarian *socialist* system is eclipsed by one based on connections between *socios*, or buddies. While social capital is used in Cuba to facilitate "access to resources, such as work opportunities for the well-networked, on the other hand, it distributes these resources very unevenly" (Powell 2008, 185). *Sociolismo* "works against the reproduction of broader social solidarity" (Powell 2008, 185). Members of the Peso Poor, whose social networks are more closed and limited to other peso-earning state workers, may be disadvantaged due to their lack of bridging social capital to connect them with individuals who have access to new knowledge and resources (Burt 2005).

In the current period, revolutionary cultural capital alone is largely irrelevant unless accompanied by social capital, which connects the subject to centers of power. Economic capital increasingly allows individuals to pay their own way, or pay their way around obstacles. Although its importance is growing, we are not yet to the point where economic capital alone guarantees access to opportunities and power. Social capital combined with economic capital is the configuration which in contemporary Cuba permits individuals to successfully pursue goals that may not yet be allowed under current regulations.

EDUCATION AND MOBILITY IN CONTEMPORARY HAVANA

By taking into account source, quantity, and regularity of dollar income, as well as consumption practices, Weinreb's claims that her model of Cuban social structure adds nuance to traditional employment-driven class models which she says:

> do not capture economically significant details, such as the mode of acquisition of taste for goods, the social pathways and underground routes to certain types of goods or services, the local irrelevance of educational status when education is nationalized or superfluous in the current economy, the social role of financial obligations to local family, dependence on dollar remittances and durable goods from abroad, and changing employment circumstances (2009, 104).

However, I strongly disagree with Weinreb's assertion that educational status is irrelevant in Cuban society. Logics of social differentiation are constantly being contested in the Cuban field, and educational status is connected with cultural and social capital in a way that is extremely important in contemporary Cuban society.

Even within a system which guarantees access to public schools and a standardized national curriculum, there are differences between Cuban public schools that help create segregated social networks which give students in certain schools the opportunity to create social networks which connect them with centers of power. During the era in which Havana high school students were boarded at institutions in the countryside (1970–2009), the schools were divided geographically based on the neighborhood of residence in Havana, reproducing structural dimensions of territorial inequalities. In the 1990s and early 2000s, when conditions in boarding schools were extremely difficult, many families used their social capital to avoid sending their children to the schools, securing phony medical exceptions to allow them to complete high school in the city or enrolling them in special schools for arts training or athletic training that would allow them to live at home and not board in the countryside.

In Havana, high schools like the *Vocacional "La Lenin," Humbolt 7, Saúl Delgado (Pre-Vedado)* MININT middle school (*Hermanos Tamayo*) and MININT high school (*Camilo Cienfuegos "Camilitos"*), sports training schools, and music and arts schools are sought out by parents with high levels of revolutionary cultural capital and social capital to guarantee high quality public education for their children. Many of these schools guarantee students conditions not present in regular schools, such as complete uniforms, transportation, experienced teachers (while other public schools may have shortages of teachers), good lunches, and preparation for entrance exams for the next level of schooling. While these schools are part of the public school system, the conditions (building, teaching staff, and material resources) are superior to other public schools. Admissions are based on passing rigorous tests, and social connections help in a way that lead my informants to question their truly public nature. These highly selective, limited access public schools function in the way that private schools function in other schooling systems.

In higher education, similar dynamics which tend to reproduce patterns of social stratification are also present. During the slight economic recovery in Cuba in the early 2000s, the Revolution began a campaign of New Social Programs [*Nuevos Programs Sociales-NPS*] to address social problems which had emerged during the economic crisis of the 1990s (María Isabel Domínguez 2013). One of these programs aimed to provide young people— who had dropped out of formal education to work in the state sector during the Special Period—the opportunity to return to school. The program for young people between seventeen and twenty-nine years old designed to give a second chance to these young people who were unconnected from the state [*desvinculado*]. They were able to return to school and become professionals, something that would benefit both them as individuals and the country.

The students in these Youth Comprehensive Training Courses [*Cursos de superación integral para jóvenes*] received a stipend to study that was higher than many salaries in the state sector at the time. Upon completing the program, they were offered the opportunity to complete a university degree at the SUM [*Sedes Universitarias Municipiales*] local extension campuses which were created in every municipality of the country as part of a campaign known as the Universalization of Higher Education [*Universalización de la Educación Superior*] (María Isabel Domínguez 2013). With the advent of the SUM, program enrollment in higher education was 4.7 times higher in 2009–10 than in 2000–2001 (María Isabel Domínguez 2013, 26). In the city of Havana, courses at these local campuses were taught by both regular professors from the University of Havana as well as other individuals without previous college teaching experience.

Cuban Sociologist, Yulexis Almeida Junco, explains that in the 1960s access to higher education was completely open, stimulated by the need to form professionals to replace those who were emigrating. In the 1970s and 80s, when university admissions were based on student's high school academic average and their social conduct (integration with revolutionary activities), there was racial parity in college graduation rates (Almeida Junco 2015). In 1987, the Seventh Congress of the Federation of University Students [*Federación de Estudiantes Universitarios-* FEU] approved the introduction of university entrance exams as an additional criterion for admission. Students were required to take a math entrance exam as well as two other subject exams (based on the major they hoped to study). Under this new system, by the end of the 1980s, there was a tendency towards homogeneity of the university student body (Domínguez García 1997a). Most students were white and came from families with parents who were professional or held positions of leadership [*dirigentes*]. The unequal access to higher education resulted in limiting upward social mobility through education for the children of laborers, rural people, and blacks (Almeida Junco 2015).

In the 1990s, university enrollments were cut. Enrollments in 1998–99 were 43 percent lower than in 1989–99 (Ávila Vargas 2011, 124). With restricted enrollment the access of vulnerable social groups such as blacks and the children of workers in the state sector to higher education suffered. There are special enrollment schemes for working adults, but the regular daytime program that takes students directly after 12th grade has become an elite space with predominantly white students (Martín, 2006). In the 2004–2005 school year, 79 percent of students in the regular university system were children of professionals and 63 percent white (Gómez Cabezas, 2004).

The municipal campuses were successful in providing access to higher education for black and mestizo students who, since the late 1980s, have been underrepresented in Cuban universities. The enrollment of black and mestizo students was higher in the SUM system compared to the regular university system. In the SUM 77 percent of students were children of laborers and 51 percent were black and mestizo (Gómez Cabezas, 2004).

While the SUM, opened up new opportunities for disadvantaged youth, there was also criticism of the quality of the education in the local campuses compared to the main campus. Despite the fact that they used the same curricula and often the same professors as the main campus, the SUM had more flexibility for promotion, and graduates were held to lower standards than on the main campus (María Isabel Domínguez 2013, 54). These students' diplomas are issued by the main campus and do not specify that they are SUM graduates. However, in the labor market, they may suffer discrimination because many employers feel that a SUM degree is not as rigorous as the regular university program. Some of this may be associated with subtle racism or classism towards the SUM's graduates because of their race and social origin.

Citing the Compendium of the Ministry of Higher Education, Almeida Junco shows that, in 2010, the racial composition of regular daytime students on the main campus of the University of Havana was 57.5 percent white, 14.2 percent black, and 28.6 percent mestizo (Almeida Junco 2015). For the 2013–2014 school year, whites made up 72.3 percent of the student population with blacks representing only 9 percent and mestizos representing 17.7 percent (Almeida Junco 2015).

More recently, as the number of Cubans with dual citizenship grows, some Cuban families have begun to enroll their children in private international schools in Havana. In Havana, there is a Spanish school, a French school, the International School of Havana, and a Russian school that accept students with foreign passports. These schools were originally established for the children of foreign diplomats and business people living in Havana but, today, Cuban children with dual citizenships are also attending. The International School of Havana (ISH), founded in 1965, is accredited by the Council of International Schools and the New England Association of Schools and Colleges (ISH 2017). ISH has 430 students from 63 countries and announced plans to open a new larger campus in the 2017–18 school year to meet growing enrollment (ISH 2017). Minimum annual tuition depends on the grade the student is in and ranges from $12,000–$14,000 CUC a year (ISH 2017).The French school, *Lycée Français de La Havane* has 310 students from thirty nationalities (Havane 2017). The *Lycée Français* is slightly more affordable ($6,440–$9,565 CUC a year) and offers discounts for multiple children (Carpentier 2017). The Spanish school, *El Centro Educativo Español de La Habana* (CEEH), was founded with the assistance of the Spanish Embassy in 1986. Today, at CEEH there are more than two hundred students in four levels, from two years old to twelfth grade (CEEH 2017). An article published in 2016 tells the story of a Cuban family who lived abroad and had dual citizenship. They decided to take advantage of the loophole to enroll their child in a private school for foreigners (Escobar 2016). This may be expected when one of the parents is not Cuban, but I have met a couple of families, in which both parents are Cubans, who are using capital from work abroad and small businesses in Havana to send their preschool-age children to these schools.

CONTEMPORARY CONFIGURATIONS OF CAPITAL AND DOMINANT HABITUS IN HAVANA

In a social world being transformed by a second phase of economic reforms, revolutionary cultural capital is increasingly losing ground as the dominant symbolic capital in the Cuban field. As demonstrated in the cases in the previous section, social capital is important in accessing opportunities, but economic capital has grown in importance as new opportunities for consumption emerge in the growing private sector. Since the Special Period, many important resources are no longer distributed by the state, and new types of cultural capital have emerged, shaped by the values of those who have control over the distribution of resources. How do Cubans today strategically negotiate between different forms of habitus in daily practices? How is the dominant habitus in Cuban society changing?

It is to be expected that in the emerging private sector showing one's revolutionary cultural capital will not help resolve problems, but many Cubans have found that in the second phase of economic reforms, state discourses have also changed to put greater value on individual initiative. The state now criticizes what it labels as the "paternalistic role" of the state. In chapter four, I explore how public narratives constructed by individuals entering the private sector are being impacted by changes in authoritative discourses.

Weinreb argues that declining state power and involvement in social welfare in Cuba should be read as a sign of progress during transition towards neoliberal modernity. However, Lynne Haney's work on social welfare in post-socialist Hungary (1999) explores how Hungarian women perceived new policies, which separated them from spheres of state power, as a sort of betrayal. Their alienation from the no-longer socialist state was perceived as resulting in a loss of entitlement and access to institutional resources. Rather than seeing a close relationship with the state as an oppressive one, the women in Haney's ethnography feel that their new lack of access to government services and the state welfare is dangerous, threatening to narrow the space they have to maneuver in their everyday lives (Haney 1999, 177–6).

As the rules of the game changed, the social contract was renegotiated without their participation, leading to feelings of disempowerment. Haney shows how these women make linguistic claims to identities once rewarded by the state: "But we are still mothers!" By doing so, they demand the state provide services that they were promised. In the post-socialist moment, however, these claims to legitimate socialist personhood are no longer rewarded.

Similarly, in Cuba today, linguistic codes which once proved one's revolutionary cultural capital and provided access to favors, subsidies, and opportunities don't always work to gain advantage. Economic capital is increasingly the most relevant, followed by social capital. Many people in Havana are finding that revolutionary cultural capital has lost much of its power.

To illustrate this, I give the example of the song "*En la pincha me quieren jubilar*" ["At work they want to retire me"] a satirical song by the Cuban humor troupe *Pagola La Paga* sung to the tune of the traditional Cuban song "*María Cristina me quiere gobernar.*" The song draws on anxieties that were common during the process of massive layoffs and is an example of how Cuban humor in 2011 reflected the population's discomfort with the changing social contract. The song is sung by three middle-aged male vocalists (a chubby black man, a thin mestizo man, and a white man with a mustache) all dressed in traditional white linen Guayabera dress shirts and backed by a traditional small format orchestra. In the song, the main vocalist begins talking about how he was very fed up and he couldn't believe this was happening to him. "I'm fed up!" [*berrea'o*] he exclaims. His companions asked him what's going on and he explained that he thought he was going to be laid off because there was a list with his name on it. The song begins with the chorus:

ALL (CHORUS):
At work they want to retire me,
and now they say that I am "surplus."
I'm outstanding, Vanguard, and efficient,
and I'm ideal for my work center.
But my boss has it out for me
and I explain to him, and I explain to him, and he doesn't understand
that I can't be laid off
for the reasons that I'll explain to you:
(Spoken)
Angry Man: I was the last cane in the sugar harvest of 1970.
[*Yo fui la última caña de la zafra del '70*]
(White Man looks at him with a slightly disbelieving look, but still going to
    hear him out. The black man folds his arms over his round belly and laughs at
    Angry Man's misuse of revolutionary codes)
Angry Man: but I tell you more: I was the last knot of the string of Havana. [*Pero
    te digo más: Fui el último nudo del cordón de La Habana.*]
(The White Man continues listening disbelievingly while the black man chuckles)
Angry Man: I went to the mountains to plant coffee
[*Y me fui a la Sierra a sembrar Café Caturra.*]
White Man: Uh huh?
Angry Man: And I came back full of mosquitoes and a cold [*catarro*].[4]

In this first part of the song, the vocalist tries to make his case as to why he should not be laid off by attempting to use state discourse to make claims to legitimacy as a proper revolutionary *compañero*, a person with revolutionary cultural capital. However, his usage of this old discourse is lacking in fluency and his claims fail to convince his listeners. The song is humorous precisely because of how inept he is at employing the revolutionary symbols. It appears that he is trying to mobilize revolutionary cultural capital that he does not possess in order to save his hide. For example, he claims to have been "the last cane in the sugar harvest of 1970," "the last knot of the cord of Havana," and to have "gone to the mountains to plant coffee" referring to three important (failed) campaigns of the revolutionary government in which large portions of the population were mobilized to do voluntary labor. But his phrasing makes it clear that he did not actually participate in any of the campaigns and lacks a clear understanding of what they were.

More appropriate statements would include references to how much sugar cane he had cut, or how long he had worked in the fields. Had he been involved, he would know that the *Cordón de la Habana* was not a belt or a string with knots in it as the name suggests, but an agricultural corridor around the city formed in the spring of 1967 (Salas 1968). The state planned to plant five million trees for fruit and timber which would also provide shade and protection for the 150 million *caturra* coffee plants that would make Cuba a leading coffee exporter in the world market (Domingo Cuadriello 2008). However, most members of the audience listening to the performance (or their parents) actually participated in these campaigns, and despite this, found themselves with few tools to make demands on the state as the social contract had been renegotiated from above.

After repeating the chorus, the white man with the mustache asks the *berrea'o* to explain what his problem is and he begins to answer the reasons why he should not be laid off by explaining that whenever the Revolution asked him to contribute, he did so. This song is structured as a call and response, in which the white man acts as the voice of the Revolutionary State asking for the Cuban population to hold up their end of the social contract. Like many of his generation, each time the Revolution asked him to volunteer [*Dar el paso al frente*], he did so, and, therefore, he does not understand why the state is not holding up its side of the bargain by providing him with employment that he had been promised in Cuba's socialist constitution.

White Man (WM): and go harvest sugarcane!	EL BLANCO: Y vete pa' la zafra
Angry Man: And I go!	EL BERREA'O: Y pa' lla voy
(The black man mimics cutting sugarcane)	(EL NEGRO imita cortar caña)
WM: And go to the potato (fields)!	EL BLANCO: Y dale pa' la papa
Angry Man: And I harvest potatoes!	EL BERREA'O: Y la recojo
(The black man mimics harvesting potatoes)	(EL NEGRO imita recoger papa)
WM: And go to the pineapple (fields)!	EL BLANCO: Y vete pa' la piña[5]
Angry Man: And I don't get offended!	EL BERREA'O: Y no me ofenda

(The black man mimics surprise at hearing what sounds like the insult "Go Fuck yourself!")

(EL NEGRO imita sorprendido al escuchar lo que parece ser el insulto "Vete pa la pinga")

WM: And join the micro![6]
Angry Man: And I joined!
(The black man mimics shoveling cement)

EL BLANCO: Y métete en la Micro
EL BERREA'O: Y me metí
(EL NEGRO palea cemento)

WM: And go to Angola!
Angry Man: And I went!
(The black man mimics shooting "pow pow!" with a gun)

EL BLANCO: Y vete para Angola
EL BERREA'O: Y me fui
(EL NEGRO imita po! po! con un arma)

WM: And come back with malaria!
Angry Man: And I came back!
(The black man and the angry man stumble like zombies)

EL BLANCO: Y vira con malaria
EL BERREA'O: Y viré
(EL NEGRO y EL BERREA'O caminan como zombies)

WM: And go donate blood!
Angry Man: And I donate it!
(The black man and the angry man stick out their arms to have blood drawn)

EL BLANCO: Y dale a donar sangre
EL BERREA'O: Y la dono
(EL NEGRO y EL BERREA'O extienden sus brazos para dar una donación de sangre)

WM: And go to the march!
Angry Man: And I march!
(The black man marches with a false smile on his face)

EL BLANCO: Y dale pa'l desfile
EL BERREA'O: Y desfilo
(EL NEGRO marcha con una sonrisa vacía)

WM: And you're made available.
Angry Man: Availa- WHAT??

EL BLANCO: Y quedas disponible
EL NEGRO: ¿Dispo… ¡QUÉ!

All: NO, NO, NO, NO!
Angry Man: If I'm out, everybody's out, if I go, why?!

TODOS: NO, NO, NO, NO. SE VA TO' EL MUNDO SI ME VOY YO, SI ME VOY YO. ¿Por qué?

For Havana audience members, the humor also derives from seeing how ineffective such arguments have become in making claims to the state. The state has changed the terms of the social contract. Havana residents listening to the song realize that the old claims to legitimacy through demonstrating one's revolutionary cultural capital no longer work the magic they used to. A lifetime of loyal action and building one's revolutionary cultural capital no longer guarantees access to social welfare in Havana today.

Once again, the dominant configurations of capitals in Cuban society have changed. The economic and policy changes made as a result of the 2011

Guidelines have succeeded in changing the social field. In Havana today, a new logic of social stratification is in operation, determining access to social mobility, consumption opportunities, and power.

NOTES

1. State pensions were increased in 2005 and again in 2008, but when adjusted for inflation, the average pension in 2008 was 55 percent lower than in 1989 (Mesa-Lago 2010, 707). Today, most pensioners in Cuba earn around $240 Cuban pesos (about 10 USD), but Felipe's widow receives a pension of almost $1,000 Cuban pesos based on his "historic salary" (Leyva Martínez 2010).

2. The *central* is the sugar cane mill where cane is processed into sugar and other derivatives. In the 1820s, sugar came to dominate the Cuban economy and the owners of the *centrales* were the most powerful and influential people in pre-revolutionary Cuban society. Today, however, sugar is no longer king. In 2002, the state began to dismantle what remained of the decrepit sugar industry, half of the *centrales* in Cuba were closed. At the end of the year, just 71 plants continued to produce sugar on the island (Álvarez Rodríguez 2013, 54).

3. It is interesting to contrast Weinreb's assumptions about state power and social welfare with the argument made by Lynne Haney's work on social welfare in post-socialist Hungary (1999:175). I discuss Haney's work and similarities with linguistic practices as part of claims to respectable personhood later in this chapter.

4. A play on words between the two similar-sounding words, *caturro* (type of coffee) and *catarro* (a cold).

5. The word pineapple [*Piña*] and the slang word penis [*Pinga*] sound very similar in Cuban Spanish. When you tell someone to "*Vete pa' la pinga*" (literally: "Go to the penis!") you're telling them to go fuck themselves.

6. In the 1970s, the *micros* were apartment buildings built using prefabricated construction systems by teams of workers with little to no construction experience recruited to build apartment buildings to provide housing for themselves and other coworkers. Between 1971–1975, the microbrigades built 18,000–20,000 new housing units per year in Cuba (Schmidt-Colinet, Schmoeger, and Zeyfang 2016, 195). *Microbrigade* workers worked for a term of two years that were renewable. They learned construction skills on the job while building homes for themselves and other needy workers while their coworkers worked extra to make up for their absence. Sometimes, not everyone in the microbrigade would be assigned an apartment after completing a building and they would have to continue working in the brigade to get another opportunity to be assigned an apartment. The program was reduced in 1978 due to a lack of building materials.

Chapter Three

Stratification, Income, and Cultural Consumption in Contemporary Cuba

The 2011 Cuban film *Habana Station* tells the story of two young boys who attend the same Havana elementary school: Mayito, from the wealthy neighborhood of Nuevo Vedado, and Carlos, the rebel with the upturned collar and un-tucked shirt who the teacher scolds at the gate of the schoolyard. After attending the May First International Workers' Day Parade with his classmates, wealthy Mayito gets lost and ends up in a formalized squatter settlement in the shadow of the Plaza of the Revolution. After being taunted by the neighborhood bullies, he is rescued by Carlos, whom he recognizes from school. Carlos takes him back to his humble home and shows true hospitality, sharing a simple plate of food his grandmother has left for him. The contrast between the lifestyles of the two classmates and their levels of consumption is extreme.

Cuban cultural products like *Habana Station* reflect the growing inequalities in Cuban society which have become increasingly visible in the last decade. Even as the film points out the presence of inequalities in contemporary Cuba, the filmmakers were politically astute in the way that they delivered this message. The characteristics of the film's characters somewhat justified the inequalities within the social norms of the current socialist system. The "wealthy family" came by their income honestly: the father is a famous musician who records and tours internationally (Weinreb's "Performers/Athletes" Class). The mother fits into traditional gender roles, managing her husband's career and the household (staff). The "poor family" on the other hand suffers because of its own ideologically incorrect behavior and misfortunes without structural causes. The father is in jail and, therefore, unable to provide for the family. The mother died, leaving the grandmother to raise the child alone.

The film does not attempt to provide a structural analysis of economic inequalities in urban Havana. The wealthy are well off because of their

53

artistic talents, and the poor are poor because of their bad decisions and illegal actions. Perhaps if the film had contrasted a privileged family of the political elite (Weinreb's "Red Bourgeoisie") with a household dependent on their completely legal peso salaries (Weinreb's "Peso Poor"), it would have gone too far. The film shows the inequalities present in Cuban society without pointing fingers at members of Cuba's economic and social elite whose sources of income are less ideologically or morally acceptable, such as nascent capitalists, small business people or middle men who may profit at the expense of workers and consumers, or officials trading on the privileges of their positions.

When I first started my research in 2011, I found my research participants were generally willing to talk about economic inequalities and social stratification. In fact, only one of my interviewees, Yessica, challenged my use of the word "class" to describe the relative privilege, access to economic resources, and consumption practices that distinguish the different groups present in contemporary Cuban society. Yessica was a college student and an active member of the Federation of University Students [*Federación de Estudiantes Universitarios*- FEU]. At the beginning of the interview, she corrected me, explaining that there were no class differences in Cuba. When I questioned her more she even denied the existence in Cuba of social groups with different levels and patterns of consumption. Her response surprised me greatly. I had not yet dealt with a person who denied the existence of social groups with different cultural practices or levels of consumption and income in Cuba.

As I reconsidered how to proceed with the interview, I was "saved by the bell." Yessica's cell phone rang. It was someone calling from a cell phone and she did what is customary in Cuba: she rejected the call without picking up. In 2012, calls cost $.35 CUC a minute, most people I knew didn't actually have conversations on their cell phones. At the time cell phones were more frequently used as beepers or to send messages than they were used for conversations. In Cuba, when someone calls from a cell phone the caller pays. Rejecting a call is a sign that one is aware that the person has called and will return the call from a landline as soon as possible. It is usually only if the caller repeats that one should answer.

When the caller repeated Yessica took the call. She quickly told the caller she was not at home and asked the caller if they wanted to call her on a landline or call her back that evening. The person on the other end of the line, however, appeared not to be concerned about the cost, and told her that it was fine to continue talking via cell phone at her expense. The caller was a student in the Law School who was trying to organize other students to participate in an intramural sports competition. Yessica promised to participate and help recruit others. The conversation lasted several minutes.

When Yessica hung up I asked her, "So what about the person you just talked to? From the way that she uses her cell phone it sounds like she might be a member of a social group that has more economic resources than most college students, right?" I asked.[1] This was the question that broke through the ice, and she explained to me that even though in the university they are taught that there are no "classes" in Cuba, she considers that there are some differences.

Understanding inequalities in Cuba is a complicated and controversial endeavor, as Cuban humorist Eduardo del Llano points out in an entry in his blog which uses irony and humor to challenge the dominant ideology which declares Cuba a classless society. The essay recognizes the existence of social and economic differences in Cuba and challenges readers to look for new ways to conceive of class beyond the archetypes taught in high school Marxist-Leninist theory class.

> In the period of the transition to socialism, the working class exercises its power over the remnants of the bourgeoisie until they achieve a more just society, in which we are all equal and each one receives what they need. This is what they told us; this, more or less, is what I copied in tons of notebooks during my years as a student. The dominant class is the owner of the means of production, and the relations of production are what determine the superstructure of a society. That's what historic materialism was about.
>
> Does this seem to describe contemporary Cuban society to anyone? Is the working class the owner of the means of production? That there's no bourgeoisie, and that if there are, that they languish under the power of the proletariat?
>
> It's been a while since I have mixed with Marxist theorists—or with theorists in general—but I suppose that it must not be easy for them to define social stratification in Cuba today. To begin, the national proletariat is not overwhelmed with class consciousness, nor feels part of the group destined to change anything; the only consciousness that it has of itself and its family is how to survive, and it's not rare for them to see their coworker or neighbor as a rival. Or worse, someone to screw over. They don't feel reflected in the parliament, and they do feel crushed by the state...
>
> The well off, the local middle class, are they really a true bourgeoisie? Or at least a true middle class? The guy that sells bootleg DVDs is the owner, perhaps, of a couple of computers which he uses to manufacture his merchandise. Does that mean he classifies as a bourgeoisie, even if it's a very petty bourgeoisie? The *botero* that converts his old car into a taxi, or the guy who has started a small restaurant or a cafeteria in his house and lives closed in by taxes. Did they transform into an exploiting class during a full moon, or are they merely

entrepreneurial proletariats? The manager of a corporation is not the owner of the hotel or the company, but his daughter dresses and acts like a bourgeoisie, is he not? Or someone with another nationality, or who is married to a foreigner, and talks like he is from Madrid or Mexico. The *nouveau riche* does not own large companies—because he is not allowed to—but has a ton of money in the bank. Is he part of a special class, or just a plain old bourgeoisie? *If it is green and has spines, guanábana...*[2]

Or is it about aristocracy? Many leaders and functionaries think that they are indestructible, and their children enjoy a lifestyle that is as far removed from that of an everyday worker as the 18th century king from the rank-and-file bourgeoisie. They are not completely dedicated to leisure, like aristocrats, but they do plan marriages to polish bloodlines and consolidate alliances and fortunes... Does Marxism still work to define this society? Or any other? ... Without Soviet tutelage, the local Marxists stopped thinking, and the government stopped listening to them.

What about the present? What classes are these? Where does an intellectual who doesn't have the least intention of standing up in the vanguard of the working class belong? Or the labor leader who doesn't represent anyone and who can't do anything, or the student who only wants to finish their degree and leave? What about a farmer who has never had any intention of aligning himself with the proletariat and is not the owner of his own cattle?

Will they tell us that what does not fit the theory doesn't exist? What are we? Bourgeoisie? Aristocrats? Proletariats? Slaves?

What language do people in Havana use to describe social structure in Cuba today? In the previous chapter, I described anthropologist Amelia Weinreb's model for describing social structure in late-socialist Havana. In this chapter, I ask a group of professionals working in the state sector in Havana to describe social stratification in the complicated and changing social field they inhabit.

FOLK TAXONOMIES AND SOCIAL REPRESENTATIONS OF SOCIAL STRATIFICATION, 2012–13

From October 2012–June 2013, I did fourteen in-depth interviews with professionals working in the state sector in the capital to collect information about their perceptions of economic inequalities and social stratification in contemporary Cuba. Given the difficulties in doing social science research in Cuba, and the impossibility of accessing the information necessary to build representative samples, many Cuban social scientists chose to stratify samples by quota to reflect the demographic characteristics of Cuban society to the extent possible (Pañellas Álvarez 2015, 165). Like many researchers in

Cuba, I depended on snowball sampling (or chain referral method) through the different social networks to recruit participants according to specific demographic criteria. I found that when dealing with sensitive or taboo research subjects, this method of finding participants through recommendations by people known to the interviewee can help create greater rapport between the interviewee and the researcher, and create a safe space to speak openly about difficult subjects.

My sample was stratified to include a representation of gender and race characteristic of the larger population. My fourteen respondents included seven women and seven men. All of the participants worked in the state sector, or were university students preparing for work as professionals in the state sector. The average interviewee age was 30.64 years old (average age of female respondents, 31 years old, and average age of male respondents, 30.28 years old). The racial breakdown, according to respondents' self-identification, was seven whites, five mestizos, and two blacks. While whites are overrepresented in the sample in comparison to the population of Havana at large, the racial breakdown of the sample is similar to the racial breakdown of university graduates in the 2000s. In 2004, whites were overrepresented in Cuban universities, accounting for 68 percent of traditional-aged university students who entered through entrance exams, compared with 9 percent black, and 23 percent mestizo first year students (González 2006; Domínguez García 1997b).

Because of the importance of territorial inequality as an axis of inequality in the city of Havana, I was careful to make sure that my sample of young professionals connected to the state sector included individuals from different municipalities of Havana. Mario Coyula, a Cuban architect and urbanist, divides the city of Havana into two zones: the "northern coastal strip, traditionally wealthier—where visitors now move around, and with them hard currency—and southern Havana, where the common folk live"(Coyula 2008, 6).

The CIPS Social Structure Research Group classifies the municipalities of Havana into three groups based on access to opportunities and well-being of the inhabitants: *privileged, semi-privileged,* or *disadvantaged.* These categories take into account the "high population density in the central areas of the city, the polarization of employment and unemployment by municipality, differences in municipal health situations, the impact of the zone of residence in length of school attendance, educational outcomes, and professional training, as well as the concentration in the coastal area of sources of employment, especially those that are a part of revitalized sectors of the economy" (Prieto et al. 2004, 10).

The inability of the state to keep up with the demand for new housing since the 1960s has created a dynamic in which most Havana residents continue to occupy the same dwellings and neighborhoods that they inherited from their parents and grandparents as I will discuss in chapter five. Although access to education led to occupational mobility after the Revolution, the state's failure to resolve the lack of housing in the city of Havana means that in the early 2000s many highly educated professionals continued to live in the same substandard housing that their grandparents inhabited generations before. Housing in Havana largely reflects the class status of one's parents and grandparents rather than one's own place in the social and occupational hierarchies.

As a result, today professionals working in the state sector live all over the city of Havana, even in disadvantaged municipalities. Although their status as professionals confers prestige, their place of residence confers disadvantages for them despite their high level of education and training. Although all of my interviewees were professionals or university students, their residence in different parts of the city created situations of relative privilege and disadvantage based on the quality of housing and services available in the area, access to networks of mobility (buses, collective taxis, private cars), and different opportunities for basic consumption, cultural consumption, and insertion into emerging sectors of the economy.

My interviewees resided in seven different municipalities, from the *privileged* Playa (Kohly, Miramar, La Sierra) and Plaza (Vedado: two interviews, Nuevo Vedado); to *semi-privileged* Habana del Este (Casablanca and Alamar), 10 de Octubre (Sevillano); to the *disadvantaged* Centro Habana (Cayo Hueso and La Victoria), and Marianao (100 y 51: two interviews). I chose to include residents of different areas of the city to broaden my scope in understanding social dynamics in Havana. In Havana, as in Cuba at large, social classes are geographically segregated (Martín Posada and Núñez Moreno 2013, 342). As residents of different neighborhoods of the capital, my interviewees have observed different social realities and subcultures in different areas of the city.

Table 3.1.   Municipalities of Research Participants

Privileged Municipalities		Semi-Privileged Municipalities		Disadvantaged Municipalities
Playa	**Plaza**	Cerro	Habana Vieja	**Marianao**
		10 de Octubre	La Lisa	**Centro Habana**
		Cotorro	**Habana del Este**	Arroyo Naranjo
		Boyeros	Regla	San Miguel del Padrón
		Guanabacoa		
My fourteen research participants came from the municipalities in **BOLD**.				

UNDP Human Development Index Classification of Cuban Municipalities from Espina Prieto, Mayra, et al. 2004. Heterogenización y desigualdades en la ciudad: Diagnóstico y perspectivas. Equipo de Estructura Social y Desigualdades, CIPS.

The interviews were a part of a three-part process. The first section of the interview began with mapping personal social networks and included questions focused on the role of social networks in resolving different problems of everyday life. The second part of the interview focused on the interviewee's practices of everyday consumption and cultural consumption. In the third section of the interview, I asked them to talk about how they saw social structure in contemporary Cuban society, and to draw a representation of how they see Cuban society organized and where they, and the people in their personal social network, fit into this scheme.[3] This chapter focuses on analyzing the results of the third section of the interviews.

MAPPING SOCIAL GROUPS:
SOURCE OF INCOME AND OCCUPATION

The major economic cleavage that developed in Cuban society during the Special Period was between households dependent on salaries in Cuban pesos as the main source of income and households that had been successful in accessing additional sources of income in hard currency (USD or CUC) outside of formal work in the state sector or thorough remittances (Mesa-Lago 2010) (Morris 2014:22). In 1989, salaries represented 78 percent of Cuban household income, but by 2002 salaries accounted for only 49.1 percent of household income (Togores González 2003, 5). In the 1990s, access to sources of hard currency, unrelated to formal work in the state sector, became one of the most significant motors of economic stratification in Cuba (Morris 2014:22). Unequal access to these sources of income has also had repercussions for racial equality (Blue 2007). The most common sources of hard currency during this period were through remittances, tips in tourism, self-employment (renting rooms and running home-based restaurants), temporary labor migration (national or international), and black-market dealings (resale of products, hustling, and prostitution, etc.).

Given this background, it was not surprising to find that the most common schema used by my interviewees to explain the social structure in contemporary Cuba was based on source of income and occupation. Most respondents described social stratification as related to occupational groups (intellectuals, taxi drivers, professionals, laborers, leaders, directors or state functionaries, agricultural producers, landlords, military, owners of private restaurants) or the sector of the economy in which one works (health care, education, self-employment, tourism, the state sector [recovered and non-recovered], manufacturing industry, services [state], joint venture or mixed companies [foreign capital], military, part-time non-state workers, individuals who neither work nor study, the retired, and the unemployed].

The graphic on the next page is a depiction of social structure in Cuba in 2012 based on the maps drawn by the interview participants that locate different occupational groups in a hierarchy based on amount of income and source of income. The Cuban state sector is portrayed on the left side of the graph. Three reddish squares depict three privileged occupational groups in Cuban society within the state sector: members of the military, government officials, and workers at mixed companies (joint ventures between the Cuban state and foreign capital). Each of these sources of income and sectors of employment are under direct state control, as expressed by the red lines that connect them to the state as children are connected to parents in a family tree. Blue arrows interconnect the three groups, representing both the social networks which connect people within the three groups and the circulation of personnel between the three groups.

The military, subordinate to the Cuban state, today holds many companies which are significant players in the Cuban economy. During the Special Period, the Cuban military was asked to take on new roles in the economy. It was tasked with putting its logistics experience and capacity at the service of the tourism industry which was a national priority. It also began to assist with the re-organization of state companies that required "the benefits of military discipline, hierarchy, structures, and the like in order to function efficiently" (Klepak 2004, 267). In these reorganizations, military officers were put in charge of state and mixed companies and military-style management was put in place. It was expected that militarization would provide them with easier access to transport, fuel, personnel and other necessities (Klepak 2004, 267). The State Administration Group [*Grupo de Administración del Estado*— GAE], is a holding company that belongs to the Cuban military. Today, the GAE is reported to control 20–40 percent of the Cuban economy and is run by General Luis Alberto Rodríguez, Raúl Castro's son-in-law (Cave 2014).

Members of the military also benefit from opportunities for subsidized consumption that are not available to the public at large. In-kind benefits received by members of the military include access to newly built housing and access to a network of cultural consumption spaces that provide high quality services at low subsidized prices (Cave 2014). Members of the military also have access to a network of hospitals and specialized health clinics that are not available to the general public. Schools designed to train future military officers are available to the public at large through specialized entrance exams, or with preferential entry for children of individuals related to the military. The resources available for students at these military schools, from uniforms, transportation, and room and board are of a quality far beyond what is available at schools operated by the Ministry of Education.

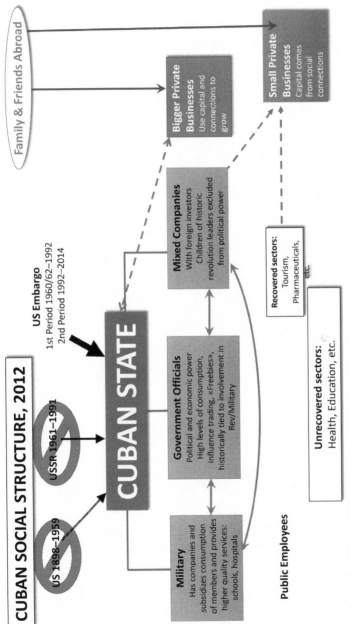

Figure 3.1. Cuban Social Structure, 2012

The second group, government officials [*dirigentes*], brings together an occupational group of individuals with political and economic power who are able to maintain high levels of consumption with income and in-kind products that come from their labor as officials at high levels of the state bureaucracy. Most people within this occupational group have historical family ties to the military, hold positions of leadership in government ministries, the Cuban Communist Party (PCC) at the national and provincial levels, or Cuban mass organizations which include the Cuban Labor Unions (CTC), Federation of Cuban Women (FMC), Committees for the Defense of the Revolution (CDR), and the Organization of Small Agricultural Producers (ANAP). Like people associated with the military, these individuals are able to maintain high levels of consumption due to the benefits of their position, which often include freebies such as access to a network of cultural consumption spaces that provide high quality services at low subsidized prices.

In their study of social identities in Cuban social structure, Cuban psychologists Daylén Rodríguez Alemañy and Jorge E. Torralbas, found two possible hypotheses to explain the privileged position of high government officials, military officials, and public servants [*altos cuadros del gobierno, los militares, o funcionarios*] (Rodríguez Alemañy and Torralbas 2011). According to their study, these groups receive economic benefits in the normal course of their exercise of power as well as, in some cases, wrongly appropriating the public resources under their control for personal benefit (Rodríguez Alemañy and Torralbas 2011). The privileges in income and consumption enjoyed by these groups is rarely explicitly recognized in the Cuban literature, but was often mentioned in interviews. Recent research on social structure in the Las Villas province also identifies these groups (Mederos Anido and Zabala Argüelles 2015, 192).

The third group, mixed companies, includes those individuals who work as local employees of Cuban-foreign joint ventures, or as local representatives of transnational companies. This group is located under the control of the Cuban state, but in a position that is close to the private sector on the extreme right of the image. All hiring for local Cuban staff in these foreign companies must be done officially through a Cuban state employment agency which has the final word on which Cuban citizens will be approved for employment in the foreign company. Decisions on local hires for these joint ventures and transnational companies are a negotiation between the interests of the Cuban state and those of the company. The state considers it important that those who work for these companies be individuals that are trustworthy and capable of defending the interests of the state and the Revolution in their position as executives for the foreign company.

Individuals get hired for these companies in two ways: more established foreign companies often identify individuals that they are interested in hiring through informal scouting through their personal networks on the island. Once the selection has been made, the "candidate" is asked to apply officially through the Cuban state hiring agency. If approved by the Cuban bureaucracy, they are officially hired. Sometimes foreign or joint ventures that are newer or less trusted by the Cuban state have no choice but to hire directly through the Cuban state hiring agency, choosing from an existing pool of applicants previously vetted by the agency.

Often these employees are the children and grandchildren of historic revolutionary leaders that have been excluded from positions of political power within the state bureaucracy because their parents' generation has not retired. Instead, they have found positions of power in these hybrid spaces that straddle state and private, Cuban and foreign. This group is described later in this chapter, in José's description of contemporary social structure.

The shapes at the extreme right of the social map represent the emerging private sector in Cuba. This emerging private sector is an economic space that is nurtured by investments from family and friends abroad, as represented by the arrows which originate in the oval labeled "Family and Friends Abroad." These arrows represent the support of the emerging private sector that originates outside of the Cuban social structure. This support from family and friends abroad comes in many forms: as investments of economic capital through remittances, as well as social remittances, and know-how, which they share with their friends and relatives on the island based on their experiences living in the capitalist world outside of Cuba.

On the right side of the map there are two blocks which represent two occupational groups within the emerging private sector: bigger private businesses and small private businesses. The first group, bigger private businesses, is located at the same level of society as the three privileged groups of the state sector because of the similarities in their levels of income and consumption, cultural consumption practices, and the common social network connections which link them informally. A dotted line with two arrows represents the connections between the Cuban state and these larger private businesses.

The second group, small private businesses, is located lower on the social structure hierarchy. The levels of income, basic consumption, and cultural consumption practices of this second group of private sector entrepreneurs are more similar to public employees working in recovered sectors of the Cuban economy such as tourism, pharmaceuticals, biotechnology, petroleum exploration, and mining, etc.

What distinguishes these two groups of private businesses is the scale of their enterprises and their connections with centers of state power. Cuban state policy aims to prevent economic and social inequalities in Cuban society by preventing the private accumulation of wealth. In a legal environment in which private businesses are very restricted in their access to raw materials and basic equipment, entrepreneurs are faced with two options for growth and economic success. Those with connections can seek to be granted exceptions to these policies, but those without connections must take the risk of breaking the laws or attempting to operate around them. Bigger private businesses are able to achieve this scale only with protection by someone within the Cuban state. In Cuba, there are a growing number of highly visible private enterprises that have managed to accumulate exceptional quantities of economic capital. The story of Francisco in chapter two illustrates how this exceptionality operates through social networks.

Small private businesses are those that do not have the capital and connections necessary to grow to the scale of bigger private businesses. In some cases, their growth is limited by the volume of capital that they have access to. In other cases, their success is limited by their knowledge of how to run a business, marketing, etc. For others, their lack of connections to centers of power and contacts who may offer spaces of exceptionality limit their success. This group is connected via dotted lines with arrows to mixed companies and recovered sectors of the state economy because, often, small business owners have migrated from work in these areas of the state sector to the emerging private sector, putting to use the skills and knowledge that they have learned in state businesses and the capital they have accumulated from working in areas of the state sector with higher salaries. It's quite common to see individuals who have worked in the state sector hospitality industry use this experience and the capital they have been able to save to begin their own private restaurants, bars, and bed and breakfasts.

The white rectangles in the middle left of the map represent different groups of public employees in the state sector. The smaller square, slightly higher in the hierarchy, represents a small minority of workers in the recovered areas of the state sector.[4] In comparison with other state workers, these employees receive higher salaries and benefits than those working in unrecovered sectors like health care and education. Workers in the unrecovered sectors of the economy are the largest group in Cuban society, have the lowest levels of income, and most limited consumption practices of all the groups represented in the map. Not included in this 2012 representation of social structure are individuals who are not economically active in formal employment. The unemployed, retired, students, and those who work in rural areas or labor only in the informal sector, are absent from this map of social structure in urban Havana.

CUBAN SOCIAL STRUCTURE AND THE INTERACTION BETWEEN ECONOMIC CAPITAL, SOCIAL CAPITAL AND REVOLUTIONARY CULTURAL CAPITAL

Most of my fourteen interviewees described the social structure in contemporary Cuba using the simple labels upper class [*clase alta, élite*], middle class [*clase media*], and lower class [*clase baja*]. Regardless of which social group the speaker belonged to, there was remarkable consensus about where different social groups in Cuban society were located within this hierarchy. Most interviewees were able to describe their own group and the groups immediately above and below them in detail, but claimed to not understand much about the social practices of groups "up there" or "down there." Many respondents identified as middle class when their basic food security needs were guaranteed and they felt that this made them better off than many others in society. These interviewees stated that they could not understand how people with fewer resources could make do since they themselves had such a difficult time with greater resources available.

To get an idea of what the class system looks like from the perspective of those near the top, I studied the transcripts of interviews with José and Rosa. Both come from families with low levels of economic capital, but high levels of social capital and revolutionary cultural capital. Rosa, 53, lives in Miramar and is married to the son of a martyr of the Revolution. José, 27, lives in Kohly and is the grandson of an important revolutionary political figure. Both focused on the importance of the combination of social capital, revolutionary cultural capital, and Economic Capital in determining access to consumption, opportunities for mobility, and access to power.

José

José was born in the Soviet Union when his father was studying in Moscow. When he was a toddler, the family returned to Cuba and settled in the neighborhood of Guanabo, on the other side of the bay from the rest of the city of Havana. His father was given a microbrigade apartment in a complex for members of the military who worked at bases in the area. José remembers the neighborhood as really picturesque, with a playground in the middle of the community. His father worked in a military base just meters away and José would go down the hill to school every day to the beachside town of Guanabo.

That was communism all right, there no one had anything! It was a military neighborhood. They teased me and called me "the little intellectual" because I liked to read. My father was a professional. My mother wasn't, but she really encouraged me to read and listen to music and those kinds of things. In the end, my family has always maintained a class consciousness: knowing how to use silverware, never raise your voice at the table, don't put your elbows on the table, you know those kinds of things that are hereditary. It doesn't matter how much money you earn, or where you live, that comes from your great-grandparents and your grandparents.

In 1991, the family moved to Havana when José's father was assigned to work for a company operated by the Cuban military. The family was given a spacious 3 bedroom apartment in a building in Kohly not far from his dad's new job. Right away, José began to be aware of the privileges that kids in his new neighborhood had. The family moved on a Saturday. On Monday at lunch-time at his new school, José pulled out his lunch: a bread roll with oil and salt. In Special Period Guanabo, this was the standard lunch, but in Kohly the little kid next to him pulled out a ham and cheese sandwich. José remembers think-ing, "Wait a minute, what's happening here?" He was 10 years old. "This was a shock that was really hard for me. I realized that I wasn't in Guanabo anymore. I was here and if I wanted to adapt to this new place that I was going to live in, I could. I could decide to be a different person from then on."

At the new school, there were other values, and the scales and measures were different. Over time, José began to adapt to his new surroundings, "But I didn't want to join in their game. I've always wanted to deny what I should be. This image was sold by other people, by those who have special access, or those who have CUCs and at the same time have connections, by the guys who are upper class. I've never wanted to accept this, even though I easily could have."

José spent his first two years of high school at the *Camilitos*, a boarding school run by the Cuban military in Havana to prepare future officers.[5] One of Raúl's grandsons was the officer in charge of his group. When the other guys found out who José's grandfather was, they invited him to be an officer too, but José refused. "No dude, no. I've spent the last two months marching, trying to march better than anyone else so that you would choose me to be an officer, and now you're coming to ask me?" He declined the offer. After two years at the *Camilitos*, José decided that he wanted to go to a regular high school. It was there, living with people from other neighborhoods, and later at the university, when he started to get to know people from other provinces that he was forced to come face to face with his privilege again.

When I was in the military service, one day I said that I had never learned how to play guitar, because in my house there wasn't money to buy a guitar, because the money we had was used for food. The guy sitting next to me

turned around and said, "You're a fucking idiot! [¡*Tú eres un comemierda!*]"
The word [*comemierda*] was full of so much venom, so much hatred for the
children of leaders [*dirigentes*]. This guy was from a family that had access to
CUC, but not to other benefits. There's always a competition between those
two groups and we are always going to win, at least for now. The guy said
it with such hatred that I turned around and punched him. I felt such hatred
inside against it all, against the way things worked. I knew it wasn't fair, but
it also wasn't fair because he was judging me for refusing to be what he hated.
He didn't know me, but he thought that I, because of the place that the stork
had left me, would be that way. This guy hated me for two reasons, one for
not being what I should be (which he hates) and then again because he doesn't
have that privilege.

What I have I have tried to earn on my own. One of my greatest professional
satisfactions was to be chosen to teach a photography course to a group of
foreign students, because I did it myself. It wasn't my dad, or my mom, or my
grandfather, or my aunt or anything. I was the one who convinced the professor
that I could do it. It was my work and my attitude. That's how I like to try to
live, trying to deny the idea that is out there of "the grandson" or "the son" or
whatever, but at the same time there's things that you cannot control. There's a
world that is in motion, functioning by an inertia that others invented. If I had
wanted the stork to leave me some place, I would've told him to leave me in
Paris, but he brought me here, to this family.

My father taught me what he learned from his father, that one has to earn what
they have, but it is not really true. We have the house in a good neighborhood
which I think someone gave to us, "You're going to work in a new military
company, so here is a house for you." That simple. Of course you work in the
company because, well, someone decided that among twenty people they would
choose you because you're "the son of"... so you are a trustworthy guy. Of
course you are intelligent, but there's a system that works behind the scenes that
is bigger than you, and in the end you come out winning. There may be times
when you might lose, but I recognize that, by coincidence, by act of Providence,
or intelligence or whatever, things are easier for me as a result. I can't change it,
but I've tried to at least deserve what they give me.

José has a couple of cousins, the grandchildren of his grandfather's wife,
who go to great lengths to make sure that everyone knows that they are related to his grandfather. Even though they don't have his last name, they use it
whenever they can, and they live a solid upper-class lifestyle as a result. Even
though José doesn't go around advertising that he is "*the grandson of*" there
are a lot of people who know. "Whether it is because they want something or
not, they choose you and pick you over someone else," José explained. "They
don't have to, but they do."

Although José's father has an important position in a state company, access to CUC in his house was limited at the time of our interview. His parents

earned enough CUCs to get to the end of the month, and he had sporadic gigs taking pictures of weddings and special events which allowed him to not be dependent on his parents. Most of the money he earned he invested in professional photography equipment.

When asked to describe social stratification in Cuba, José divided Cuban society into four groups: upper class, military oligarchy/revolutionary elite, the new rich, and those who only have social capital.

In his social circles he does not come into contact with people from social groups that are located below these four groups. The lowest group he mentioned are those with low income but high social capital.

José began his explanation of social structure in contemporary Havana with the social group he called the *Upper Class,* those who have access to CUC and benefits.

This would be like a famous person, or the son of a General, or the grandson of a General or whatever. Middle class is pretty much the same, but with fewer benefits. There is a difference between someone with benefits and contacts, someone who knows someone, and someone who has direct access to CUC. That's what makes the difference: the amount, the quantity, and combination of relations that you have. There are people who come from below and climb. They meet important people, and make connections and then they're part of it

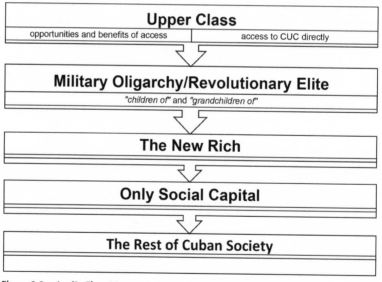

Figure 3.2.   José's Class Map

too, a part of the upper class. Middle class is the same thing at a smaller scale: less influence, less access to CUCs, the combination of the two. And lower class, that is the guy that has no other way and breaks in and robs your house.

According to José there are two ways of being upper class. The first subgroup is upper class because they have opportunities and benefits of access.

There are people that don't have a high income in CUC. They live off of their salary and maintain their household. But there are many things that they don't have to worry about. Even if they don't have an account in the bank, they have gas in their car, and they have a big house, nicely decorated, because they get gifts, and that is money that they don't need to spend. It's not physical money, it is not a bank account with millions, but it gives them a lifestyle that works.

I know people who work in foreign companies that work for $100 a month. But what happens is that they have a status: they have a car with gas, they have air conditioning, they have a lifestyle that makes you say, "Before working for $20 for the state, I'll work for foreigners for $100! Sure, I know they're exploiting me, but what the hell, it's okay because I'm taken care of!"

The subgroup of the upper class has access to CUC directly, often from private businesses or remittances.

There are other people who do have access to CUC, to good quantities of CUC! I don't know how they do it, I wish I knew, not to screw them over or anything, but so that I could do it too! There are people who are high-class even if they don't live in Siboney, Miramar or any of the good neighborhoods, but because of the income that they have from remittances or whatever.

Below the upper class José locates a group that he calls the *Military Oligarchy or Revolutionary Elite*, a group that is composed of social networks of carefully vetted families closely linked to the Cuban military and Ministry of Interior.

The children of important military people are considered trustworthy and often find themselves in positions where they have access to CUC, in a foreign company or a joint venture. These are the people who are part of what you would call the historical upper class here.

It's like the history of what happened here with the people who were part of the Ministry, of Interior's Special Forces [*Tropas Especiales del MININT*]. In the 1980s there was a sort of aristocracy made up of people from the Ministry of the Interior. Their cars were so full of antennas that they were called the sea urchins [*erizos*]. The more antennas your Lada had, more status you had. When the Special Forces were dissolved, all these people were left hanging around and when the foreign companies began in the 1990s these "children of" started to be located in the companies and began to have access to dollars, now CUC. In the end, the people that were born in Miramar are either living outside of Cuba, or they are the people who work for foreign companies in Cuba. There is a little group, not all of them, but many of them, are the same irresponsible "children of" from the sea urchin days who are now forty and fifty years old. They're the same folks, the ones that wore jeans when you couldn't wear jeans in Cuba. It's how social networks work, the guy in Miramar has his childhood friends, and, if he can, he helps them out. Or a buddy is working in the foreign company and brings him along so that he can work there as well.

These "children of" have the security of having been born in a good neighborhood. Your parents gave you that. They have the inheritance that their parents gave them which is not financial, but the security of living in a good neighborhood, and even legal security. Your job is to behave yourself, get to know your neighbors and the people who have the same origin as you and among that circle look for work.

The third social group José describes is *The New Rich*, an emerging upper-class of people who just have access to CUC. These are people who may invest their money in buying multiple properties in the city, getting around restrictions on multiple properties by buying in the name of their parents, children, and distant relatives. Many keep their money in bank accounts abroad. There are people in Cuba in this group who actually maintain their young adult children who are living or studying abroad in the United States and Spain. People in this group try to solve their everyday problems using money, since they do not have connections necessary to make things work through other channels.

These people just have money, no connections, but of course they start to buy the bureaucrats, and then things get more complicated. Right now I know of the case of a guy who has his own business. He built a house on top of his mother-in-law's house and when the house was finished he divorced his wife. So the woman said, "The house is mine, go to hell," and now they are in a legal battle. The guy has a lot of money and he's bought everyone: the housing department, the lawyer. He's bought a lot of people, and so there's a big mess.

I know another case just like this, the family of a friend of mine. At the beginning of the Revolution, they had a duplex and donated the house on the second floor so that another family could live there. They got along fine, but then about five years ago the family upstairs traded with another family, and now the new guy upstairs is trying to take over the common areas. He has bought the official at the housing office, he's bought the lawyer, he's bought everybody, and so now a guy comes from the housing department and tells the family that the passageway on the ground floor, that has always been theirs, from now on belongs to the neighbor upstairs. How does the first floor passageway belong to the neighbor upstairs? The next thing they know they're not allowed to go on the roof because it belongs to the neighbor upstairs. The guy is a damn octopus!

He began to take over everything. The guy works for a Chinese company or something like that and earns a good salary and bought everyone off!

But the guy only has access to CUC, and you can tell because he had the people at the bottom paid off, but he couldn't buy the ones at the top. Maybe he could have, but not with the amount of money he has. In the end, the family won the battle, but it made it to the Supreme Court! The municipal and provincial courts ruled in his favor, but in the end they won the case on appeal at the Supreme Court on a technicality. And they are people who are very "by the book." The guy was making their lives miserable every time he came through the door, but they didn't lose their cool or do anything shady. They took the long way around, but in the end they won.

On the other extreme of the spectrum are people with "Only" Social Capital, and limited economic capital. José told me about a friend whose father Miguel is a humanities professor. His salary in Cuban pesos from the university does not allow for many luxuries, but after more than thirty years working in the university he is very well connected. He holds an important position at the university that allows him to travel to international events a couple times per year to present his research and represent the university. On these trips he is able to import small appliances, and electronics for his household and the savings are significant when compared to having to buy these same products in state stores in Cuba.

In Cuba, as in much of Latin America, a daughter's 15th birthday [*Quince*] is an important event in which a girl is said to come of age and is presented to society as a young adult (Härkönen 2014; Pertierra 2015). In Cuba today, the event is often celebrated with a party, as lavish as possible, given the family's budget (Pérez Dueñas 2012).

> When Miguel's oldest daughter turned fifteen he had no money at all with which to throw the party, but he went to a restaurant in Old Havana and introduced himself to the manager of the restaurant. "Good afternoon. I'm a professor at the university and I'm with my daughter who's going to turn fifteen, and I wanted to see if we could negotiate something for a special dinner." Miguel is an academic and well-known in intellectual circles and right then Eusebio Leal walks in and says, "How are you doing Miguel? What are you doing here?"

Eusebio Leal Spengler has been the Historian of the City of Havana since 1967, and since 1981 he has been the Director of the Restoration of Old Havana (Lamrani 2014). He is perhaps the city's most important political figure. He is extremely powerful, as he controls the money for restoration in Old Havana, as well as the profits from the hotels, bars, and stores in the Old City, and decides how to use these funds. Profits are re-invested in the Old City for future restoration projects, but also for social uses such as building or rehabbing housing, schools, and health centers, etc. In the Old City, a simple letter from Eusebio can resolve all sort of problems, such as the distribution of housing, coveted spaces in a state daycare center [*círculo infantil*] or college and trades programs run by the Historian's office, and jobs. He is also a member of the Cuban National Assembly, the Cuban National Assembly's Permanent Commission on International Relations, the US-based National Geographic Society, and the Smithsonian Institute (Leal 2015).

> So Miguel begins to explain to Eusebio that his daughter is turning fifteen and that he wants to organize a lunch for her. The maître d' is listening and he's like, "Damn, this guy knows the chief!" All of a sudden, after Eusebio left, the negotiations got a lot easier. The maître d' told Miguel that the rice and beans are on the house, and don't worry about the champagne, it's all covered. In the end, the only thing that he had to pay for was the salad!

Although the professor doesn't have access to CUCs, he has connections which link him to people who are able to facilitate access to consumption that wouldn't have been possible for him otherwise. In this case, this social capital can be used to grant access to consumption. In this example, social capital connects the low-wage university professor with a center of power.

Rosa

Rosa, 53, has lived with her husband in Miramar, a neighborhood of large modern houses close to the western coast of Havana, for 35 years. Her husband Alberto's father and grandfather were martyrs of the Revolution. The seven bedroom modern split-level home where the couple lives was built in 1958 by a Mexican industrialist and was nationalized after he left Cuba a couple years later. Alberto's father and grandfather were from Eastern Cuba and fought with revolutionary forces in the Sierra Maestra mountains. After the revolution they came to the capital and were given the house in Havana where they lived briefly before being recruited to spread guerrilla movements throughout Latin America and Africa as a part of Ernesto "Che" Guevara's elite troop. After the deaths of his father and grandfather in the guerilla war in Bolivia, Alberto was raised by his grandmother in the house in Miramar and became a musician.

As the son and grandson of martyrs, Alberto's family had some privileges as he was growing up. His grandmother travelled to Canada as a passenger on a Cuban Merchant Marine ship in the 1980s and many of the appliances used in the household to this day were purchased on that trip. The family has a car today, a small barely running Fiat *Polski*. Alberto studied in Cuba's best military schools, but chose not to follow his father and grandfather's path. Instead, he dedicated himself to music and studied electronics. Today, he earns a living as a musician and enjoys fixing things, mostly for friends and family, but occasionally for pay.

Rosa grew up in Vedado, close to the corner of 23rd and 12th, an area that was expanding quickly in the 1950s. She considers that her fathers' family was rich. Her paternal grandfather was a Spanish immigrant. He married the daughter of a plantation owner from Guantanamo who had several bakeries and other businesses in Vedado and Santos Suarez. As the corner of 23 and 12th streets in Vedado were taking off, he made investments in the area that included a bakery, a bar-cafeteria, and a chain of small kiosks [*quincallas*]. When his male children came of age, he incorporated them into the family business, giving them each a small business to run as their own. Rosa's father managed a chain of small kiosks on 23rd street in Vedado.

Although her father came from an upper-class family, Rosa's mother was the daughter of a sugar cane worker who had work only a couple months a year during the sugar harvest, and suffered through the rest of the year, known in Cuba as "the dead season" [*el tiempo muerto*]. Since he was unable to provide for his ten children in rural Sancti Spiritus, Rosa's mother and her two older sisters immigrated to Havana as teenagers to find work as domestics before the Revolution. Rosa's parents met at a dance held at the Centro Gallego. At the time, these society dances were seen as respectable places for young people to meet and court. Despite the fact that the two young people came from families with very different economic and social positions the budding relationship was accepted by both families.

When asked to describe social stratification in Cuba, Rosa divided Cuban society into five groups: *The Elites/the Royal Family, the Favored and Protected, the Powerful, Middle Class, and Lower Class.*

At the top of the social structure, Rosa locates the group she calls the *Elites or the Royal Family.* This thin layer brings together a small group of ministers, vice ministers, and directors of national institutions.

These people live untouched by any social norms; they are an elite group far removed from any reality. Then there are the leaders [*dirigentes*]: the high up ministers, vice ministers, and directors of institutions at the top level like, for example, CIMEX and CUPET are a class.[6] Within this you can also include the Ministry of Interior, the FAR (Cuban Armed Forces). There is an idea that in order to protect this type of men, so that they don't fall into corruption, they should receive a special stipend and goods from the ministry. For example, the ministry doubles their salary, or gives them a special stipend every three months in CUC so they are taken care of and not tempted.

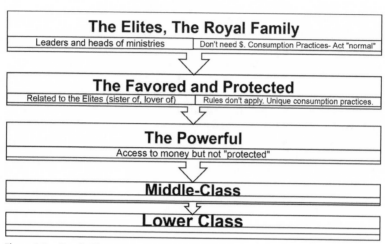

Figure 3.3.   Rosa's Class Map

As is logical, in all of this structure there are all kinds of people. There are the people that are good people, but because they're doing some sort of business or they are the manager, they are simply above the rest of the population. This doesn't mean that they are bad people, just that they are not regular people. These people want to be like you and me. Since they once were like you and me they remember what they were like. They can be relaxed, they're people who normally act just like you, but of course this only lasts until their cell phone rings, until they have to get going.

I don't really know anybody from this elite, but I know that they're there because you see them go by. For example, you see a bunch of balloons and cakes and you say, "Whose birthday is it?" And someone tells you, "Oh, it's the birthday of the granddaughter of the director of the Nacional" and then it makes sense why there were so many cakes and the whole circus spectacle, much more than a simple clown, like a whole circus! I don't know the director of the Hotel Nacional, but you know these people exist because we live together in society and they're not hiding under a rock. They're part of society and move around in their cars, they're out there. That's why I say that there are class differences. Without a doubt, even if they want to hide that, they're there. They are visible. It's not like they live in Cayo Coco and you only see them if you go there. No, they live here, they're your neighbors, but they don't live like you do. It's a group that is mostly composed of leaders [*dirigentes*] so that's why I call them the royal family.

Closely related to this top group of the social structure, Rosa places the groups which she calls the *Favored and Protected*.

They're very close to the elites and enjoy a measure of protection as long as they don't contradict them, but they're more relaxed. They're the ones that you see that they don't care as much that people realize that they are different. In fact, you can find people who are proud of it. They're showing off. They want people to see that they are different! They don't go to the same restaurants that you go to, and they are very close to the elite: it's the lover of, or the sister of, or simply people who have some sort of power, and the only way they can maintain this power is under the protection of the ones above them.

There are women who wake up in the morning with two kids, and from the second they wake up they are trying to figure out what they are going to cook, to put food on the table. And we have, in the same society, women who wake up in the morning who are only worried about getting to the gym early. At the gym, they pick up their cell phone to call the household help, "There's going to be three guests for lunch." I don't know these women, but they have picked up their phone next to me to make the call, [*imitating the tone of voice of the gym lady*] "Oh dear, no, no, no! You have to change the menu. Yes, so and so called me. At two o'clock... it's going to be three people. Yes, make it special!"

The third group that Rosa identified is what she calls *the Powerful* [*Los pudientes*]. This group is very similar to what José calls the *New Rich*. Just like José, she stresses the difference between the *Protected* and the *Powerful*.

The *Protected* have money and are above the norms. They don't even have to look out for themselves, because they are being watched out for. The Powerful have money and money is power to a degree, but they're not protected. Most of these people who have access to money, it is almost always from illegal sources, ill-gotten gains. There are maybe some people who, through TCP, can make it to this class, but even that isn't very legal, or at least it is not positively seen by society. If everything is prohibited, you always have to do something illegal, right? This is also where you'll see the managers of foreign-Cuban companies, who also have access to freebies. I also put here all the people who have money, whether it is from a completely illegal source, by doing dirty businesses, or the owner of a business, a restaurant, someone who rents their house, anyone who is above the mean. They make money, and then when things get hot they fold up shop for a while.

For Rosa, the middle class in Cuba is composed of people who receive a good salary from their work as professionals in the state sector, as well as others who are able to supplement their low state salaries through some other side job that allows them to bring home enough money to meet their household's basic needs and achieve a basic level of food security.

To reach the middle class, that comes from an extra personal effort, or the type of state job that you have. For example, the scientists who work in biotechnology, the state has tried to provide for them. If you don't have any absences, they double your salary and then you also have a bonus in CUC. So you might earn $1,400 Cuban pesos a month, plus $20 CUC. The company also tries to provide other incentives, like vacations, hotel reservations, things like that.

The people who are fighters [*luchadores*] are also in this group. They look for a way to get ahead, and they have initiative. The majority of people in the middle class are educated, but they have to do some extra little thing on the side to make money. For example, I have a job that might pay me $600 Cuban pesos, but I can't live on that, so I know how to make dolls, and I'm going to make dolls for the artisans, and in addition to that I will do something else. So, in addition to my salary, I have the doll making, and maybe I can bring in $2,000 Cuban pesos a month. That's around a hundred dollars [CUC], and with $100, more or less, you can live decorously. They can live. These are houses in which they have breakfast, lunch and dinner, and one day you can buy a bottle of rum and sit around with some friends to drink a little bottle of rum. This type of person lives. They're not down at the bottom.

Rosa considers herself to be a member of the middle class in Cuba. In addition to her professional work in the state sector as a manager for a musical group, she makes chocolates at home on her days off. She sells the chocolates by the hundred to a friend who sells them to coworkers from the reception desk where she works in a large state office.

I'm in the middle. I'm not at the very, very bottom. I know people who live much, much worse than I do. But I don't like to say that I'm in the middle class because I don't feel like it. I don't think I'm better than anyone else, but I have to recognize that the way that I live, my lifestyle and my level of consumption is above that of many people. So I can't say that I am lower class because what does that leave for everyone else? Where would that put them? So I've got to say that I'm in the middle.

I'm 53, and for the level of education that I have, and given the type of person that I am, I feel like I should have been able to achieve more. But I live in a society and have convictions that limit me, "You shouldn't do this. That's not done. That's not right." But I think that, given how I've been in my life, I should have a little bank account saved up to have some sort of security in my old age, or if simply tomorrow I get cancer and die, at least my kids got something from me, at least I was able to leave them something. I spent my whole life working. Do you understand? But despite the fact that I'm a professional, and despite the fact that I'm a good worker that wants to live from my work, I am forced to live day-to-day because it's not possible.

For Rosa, members of the middle class are those who have their immediate basic needs in the immediate short term taken care of by income that comes from a combination of work in the state and informal sectors.

The lower class in Cuba, according to Rosa, is composed of people who, for a variety of reasons, are not able to supplement their low state salaries with income from other sources. In Rosa's opinion, some people are held back because their beliefs do not permit them to get involved in any sort of illegal activity or business that feels capitalistic or individualistic.

The ones at the very bottom, sometimes we call them pejoratively *orilleros*, it's a term that we use for people who stay by the shore [*orilla*] (laughing). You know the ones who don't jump in, they don't get wet, they stay on the shore. There are various factors at play there. One is their convictions, their beliefs. There are a lot of people who, because of their beliefs, won't get involved in any sort of business or anything that's illegal. But every day these are less and less. They say, "No, count me out. I'm not getting involved in that," but they are living on the threshold of poverty and have really difficult lives.

There are others who are in this group because they simply can't do anything. They don't have any remittances, or a diploma, or an ability that they can use to get a better salary. They don't have initiative. Then there are the others: those already marked at birth by marginality because they grew up in dysfunctional homes with alcoholic parents, or because they have seen their whole lives that if there's food you eat and if there's no food then you go hungry. They're people with very, very few resources. They are practically on the threshold of poverty or below the threshold of poverty. There can be all sorts of people in the lower-class, and it is the largest class in society.

Rosa comments that, even for those with specialized training and talent, it can be extremely difficult to escape from a cycle of poverty without property or resources that can be turned into capital.

I know a playwright with a degree from the National Cuban Arts University [*Instituto Superior de Arte*] who sleeps on a cot that he folds up every morning and his breakfast is a glass of sugar water, because he comes from a very poor family where there are housing problems. There are small kids in the household, and there's not enough space. He only earns $400 Cuban pesos a month in salary. He usually gives $200 to his mom or to his sister, which isn't enough to do anything, and he is left with $200, which isn't enough to have a piece of bread with croquette in the street after rehearsal. He comes home at night and has to kick the TV to get it to work because it doesn't turn on. He is a graduate of Cuba's best arts university, but he doesn't have any other connections. He's good at his profession and everything, but he comes from a very poor family, and that keeps him down. They haven't gotten involved in any sort of business, because they don't have money to invest. They can't rent out their house, because they don't have an extra one, and they can't say, "I'm not going to rent the house, I'm just going to rent the pool," because they don't have one either. "I'll set up a fried food stand," isn't an option, because they don't even have space to live. So it's like a trap, and they keep falling backwards, because there's no way to escape.

One of the frustrations that Rosa expressed in her interview was the mismatch between discourses about poverty in the media and the reality that she observes in Havana. Many of the interviewees who considered themselves to be members of middle-class Havana expressed concern about the growth of urban poverty and the difficult economic situation that many of their friends, neighbors, and extended family members faced.

The discourse doesn't fit. We want to cover up the sun with a finger and forget that in Cuba today there are people who live in poverty. We are always criticizing Colombia or wherever, because we say that 50 percent of the population there lives in poverty. When I hear that headline, I'm laughing to myself bitterly because I'm reminded of Belkis' daughter who lives under a staircase with two kids. Her husband left her, and she works in something that has to do with quality control in a laboratory. She earns $265 Cuban pesos. That's not even $10 per capita. She lives under a staircase with one bed for the three of them, that they prop up in the daytime, and a board with a pot of water that they bring in from outside to wash. In the other corner, there is a shower curtain and behind it a toilet without a tank. That's where they take their baths, with a bucket that they fill up with water from the faucet outside. She tries to have her kids clean, and you see them with their clothes nicely mended. They're happy, but I can't handle that headline! The discourse is what bothers me. You can't mean to say that that's okay, because it's not okay. There are a lot of things that are bad, and mechanisms were created here so that this kind of thing doesn't happen, but it still happens.

You have to try to find some way to have a social security system like there is in developed countries. What distinguishes a developed country is not just its education system or its public health system, but a social security system that ensures that the individual is secure, that no one is unprotected. A social security system where a pensioner at the end of more than 35 years of service has a pension of just $225 pesos is not fair. That's not even $10 CUC, and you were the one that was saying that $10 CUC is an extremely low level of poverty! You are turning this person over to poverty. There's no protection: medication, for example, should be free, because you know that at that age a person is taking some sort of medication, whether it's for high blood pressure or arthritis, but they are taking medicine for something, and there's no protection. Maybe the medicine could be free, and transportation could be too, at least on state-run transport, but that doesn't exist here. You just get $225 pesos, and you're on your own. Hit up the bodega, which is not enough, and head to the market, and buy your medicines. That's what bothers me about what I see.

Members of two different generations, both José (27) and Rosa (53) stress the importance of economic and social capital in defining positions of privilege and power in the social structure of contemporary Cuba. Both stress the difference between those who have access to large quantities of CUC and those who have privileged positions due to their history of revolutionary cultural capital.

Changes in Cuban society, first in the 1990s and again at the end of the first decade of the 2000s, have led to the diversification of Cuba's upper classes and the emergence of new social groups, like the group that Rosa calls *The Powerful* [*Clase Pudiente*] and José calls *the New Rich*, or *CUC without connections*. Both members of what José calls the historical *Military Oligarchy/ Revolutionary Elites* and *the New Rich* have access to similarly high levels of consumption. While some of these "new rich" may differ in their practices of cultural consumption, especially those from rural areas, there are others who share social spaces frequented by members of the historical elite and, as a result, have opportunities for further social mobility.

CONSUMPTION IN CUBA

Given the methodological complexity, Cuban social scientists on the island frequently approach the issue of economic inequalities by studying differences in levels of consumption and consumption practices. In Cuba today, where the largest sources of income in most households come from non-salary sources (of varying shades of legality) it is difficult to approach the study of inequalities by tracking income. There is a refrain in Cuba that explains that "The streetsmart lives off the dummy/honest man, and the dummy/honest man lives from his work" [*El vivo vive del bobo y el bobo de su trabajo*]. When you ask people in Havana how much they earn in salary at their state sector jobs they are very willing to share what they earn, both in informal social conversations and formal research interviews. Sharing of how ridiculously low their salaries are seems to produce a cathartic effect. Talking about low salaries is like talking about the weather, it's something that is experienced by everyone. However, when I attempt to follow up by asking about non-salary benefits, or what the *búsqueda* is, the questions go unanswered, unless there is a high level of rapport.

Very few studies have been successful in quantifying the scale of income inequalities in Cuban society today. CIPS researchers provide a survey of research on economic inequalities and the different scales used to compare income groups in Cuba, and point out the strengths and weaknesses of various methodologies (Espina Prieto et al. 2003). Katrin Hansing and Manuel Orozco's 2012–2013 survey of 300 remittance recipients with small businesses includes a table with information on their reported monthly income from sales (Hansing 2014).

Cuban-American economist Carmelo Mesa-Lago published estimates of monthly incomes in several occupations in 1995 and again in 2002 (Mesa Lago 2002, 7). Mesa-Lago's data includes tables with estimated monthly incomes in several occupations in the state and private sectors, based on a dozen interviews with recent Cuban visitors and immigrants in Madrid and Miami in the spring of 2002. When comparing these numbers, he claims that there is a significant expansion in income inequality; however, he does not explain the units that he is comparing, making the data difficult to scrutinize (Mesa Lago 2002, 7). In a 2015 issue of *Temas*, Cuba's premier social sciences journal, actually not released until May 2017, Mesa-Lago attempts to establish a comparison between average wages and pensions in the state sector and what he claims are conservative estimates of income from remittances and private sector activities. According to his data, the yearly income of the average remittance recipient ($411 CUC) is 6.1 times more than the average pensioner ($67 CUC).

He claims that the yearly income of a person who rents a home to tourists ($77,500 CUC) is 1,156 times more than the average pensioner. In his calculations of the annual income of a person renting to tourists, he takes the example of a person renting a seven bedroom, seven bath mansion with a pool which he says goes for $5,000 CUC per week. This example is far from typical. In 2017, the average landlord in Vedado or Old Havana, the most sought after areas of the city, usually rented just one to two rooms in their home for $35-$45 CUC per room per night. Assuming, as Mesa-Lago does, 50 percent occupancy, earnings would fall in the range between $6,370 CUC (one room at $35 per night) to $13,650 CUC (two rooms at $35), to a high of $16,380 CUC (two rooms at $45). With these more realistic figures, the landlord's yearly gross income is similar to what Mesa-Lago had estimated as a landlord's weekly gross income. While Mesa-Lago estimated that the landlord is earning 1,156 times more than the annual income of the pensioner, my figures show the difference, depending on the number of rooms rented, to be closer to ninety-five times, 204 times, or 244.48 times more than the pensioner.

Rather than asking about income or salaries of household members, Cuba's 2012 Census of Population and Housing used levels of consumption as a proxy for income. The Census asked household heads what appliances are owned in the household, the origins of the appliances, and whether they are working or not. As a social practice, consumption "plays an important role in drawing class distinctions by providing symbolic venues for performing a changing sense of self and by conveying messages about one's position in a shifting social sphere" (Salmenniemi 2012, 13; Rivkin-Fish 2009). By looking at consumption practices of different social groups in Cuba, we can better understand the relative positions of these groups in Cuba's social structure.

BASIC CONSUMPTION: FOOD SECURITY
AND DECENT HOUSING

In my interviews about social stratification systems, several individuals categorized social groups based on consumption and differential access to material goods (housing and cars). One of the respondents constructed her map specifically around housing rather than income and occupation. She decanted individuals in her social network into members of what she called Cuba's upper class, middle class, or lower class, depending on their owner-ship of housing, its location, technical condition (in bad condition or in good condition), whether the dwelling was a detached single-family home or an apartment, and whether the apartment was in a microbrigade building, or a building built before the Revolution. In the 1990s, differences in hous-ing and the state of repair of one's home became an important element that distinguished social groups (Martín Posada and Núñez Moreno 2013, 338). CIPS researchers also consider that "the condition of housing can be used to measure relative social position and explain mobility" (Martín Posada and Núñez Moreno 2013, 327).

In my interviews, the individuals that interviewees identified as having "problems of housing" were labeled as members of a "more disadvantaged class" in relation to others. These findings coincide with the findings of CIPS researchers who explained that "for our interviewees housing is an important symbol of wellbeing and a generator of income, those who have homes in good condition—in many cases obtained through inheritance—often rent rooms as a source of income in hard currency" (Martín Posada and Núñez Moreno 2013, 334). They found that "once a family is able to obtain income in hard currency or increase their income in general they usually make im-provements to their property or move to "a better neighborhood" almost im-mediately" (Martín Posada and Núñez Moreno 2013, 334). Housing is key to social mobility. It is both a means to achieving further mobility, through renting rooms or spaces, or using spaces for household-based businesses, as well as being a concrete manifestation of upward mobility (Martín Posada and Núñez Moreno 2013, 342–3).

For most respondents, basic consumption and food security, the fact that a household was not concerned about where their next meal would come from and had steady access to three meals a day, separated Havana's middle class from its lower class. Lourdes, who appears with her son Frank in chapter two, makes a distinction between three groups: "the masses" [*El Pueblo*], middle class professionals who work for the state, and the upper middle-class, who may be professionals with high salaries, or new rich with non-salary sources of income. The distinctions between each group are made based on volume and source of income as well as patterns of consumption. As Lourdes explained to me,

> The *pueblo* is made up of the people who are the majority. The *pueblo* includes those who work for the state as well as those who are "inventing," and the retired people, the pensioners, students, and the people that are responsible for their families: the everyday people who are the most battered [*machucado*]. Those who, to eat, have to depend on the food from the bodega. The people that have to go running to the bodega when the "chicken for fish" comes in.[7] The people that have to go the very first day to get it because this is the food they are going to eat that day and the next day it's gone and they don't know what they're going to eat. That's the majority.
>
> Then there is a middle class, people that are professionals who work and "live from their salary." Well, in quotation marks, right? But it is a middle-class that has a standard of living that is a little higher. They have a house, almost always inherited from their family members, and maybe, just maybe, a car.
>
> So then there is what I would call upper middle class. They might also be professionals, but I think that I would also put the new rich here. They have cars and they also have money. In this group, the houses they have might have been bought. The new rich can buy them. These professionals also have the possibility of traveling abroad on a work contract, working for five years, and then coming back to buy it or something like that.

Lourdes considers her family to be upper middle class because her mother has a pension of $1,000 Cuban pesos, and her son Frank earns another $500 pesos. Lourdes considers that the household's Cuban peso income is not sufficient since it is spent quickly by paying the electricity, telephone, and gas bills, and going to the market a couple times.

> I tell you that we are above the norm, I can't complain because with $500 CUC a month and more than $1,000 something pesos anybody would say, "How is that not enough for her?!" But it's not enough. It's not enough, because, of course, you also know Marxism, even if you don't apply it. Your necessities continue to grow. I can't go backwards. If life gives me the way to do so I have to move forward, because I can't keep living on the edge [*machucándome la vida*] to save money. I can't suffer and sacrifice in the present, because I'm thinking and worrying about the future. So it's not enough, no matter how much you earn, you spend it. Before I didn't have the opportunity to make repairs to my house, and now I do and so I fix it. This month I do one project and next month I have a different project, and Frank says to me "What will you think of next?!"

The amount and diversity of products offered through the ration system has greatly diminished. During the Special Period, the state was unable to sustain this level of subsidized consumption for the entire population, and most of these products were disconnected from the ration system. When they were available, they were made available "*por la libre*" (not rationed) in Cuban pesos or in state-run *Tiendas de Recaudación de Divisas* (TRD), known popularly as "dollar stores." Consumers with the economic means to do so were free to decide where and how they would acquire these products. The reduction of products available through the ration system continued, even as the Cuban economy showed recovery at the end of the first decade of the 21st century (Bastian Martinez 2009; Grogg 2008, 2009; ETC). In November 2009, potatoes and chícharo beans were removed (Grogg 2008:124). Today, only a few products continue being distributed by the bodega for all consumers (rice, oil, sugar—refined and unrefined—black beans, matches, salt, pasta, coffee) are generally always in stock and available at any time of the month.

During the time in which consumption of basic products was regimented by the logic of egalitarian socialist distribution, rations were guaranteed for all Cuban citizens and permanent residents. Each household was assigned a *bodega* [small warehouse] based on the geographical location of their "home of reference," in which they could buy subsidized products with the household's ration book. People receive rations at the address on their *carnet de identidad* [national identity card]. For many reasons, this is often not the address the person really lives at. For example, in order to legally change their address to Havana, internal migrants must have a sponsor willing to agree to petition for them through a complicated bureaucratic process. Once legally registered at an address it can be nearly impossible to remove someone. In case of the property owner's death, all registered residents retain rights to continue living at the address. Due to the extremely poor quality of housing stock and overcrowding, some municipalities require people moving from other parts of the city to request special permission. The process includes a visit from the Community Architect to prove that there is sufficient space in the home for another person to be added. Sometimes, even when willing sponsors are found, the request is denied. Address changes are more likely to be approved for family members. This is especially an issue for same-sex couples whose relationships are not legally recognized. Such a difficult process for updating one's official address means that often the ID card address is not where one actually lives.

Even when it is possible to change one's address, sometimes people prefer not to. Often a person may be listed at one address in order to maintain their claim to inheriting a property in case of death or emigration. Until recently, when a property owner left the country, they lost their property, but other people residing in the property had inheritance rights. Family members maintained the address so that the property would stay in the family and not be taken by the state. Often young adults in Havana, who may rent or live with in-laws, will still be listed at their parent's home.

Since the ration book was the fundamental method of distribution of basic foodstuffs, Cubans of all walks of life were always in line with their neighbors. In my research, I found that as the quantity and diversity of products available through the ration system have decreased, so too has the centrality of bodegas as spaces for the creation and maintenance of neighborhood-based social networks. Economic differences between neighbors and the increased availability of similar products in non-rationed parallel markets mean that these neighborhood consumption spaces are increasingly economically segregated, frequented by individuals of limited economic means dependent on rationed consumption for maintaining household food security.

The economic inequalities that increasingly present in society at large, sometimes referred to euphemistically as "social heterogeneity" in Cuban academia, are manifested at the neighborhood level in different household consumption practices associated with subsidized rationed consumption. Observing which households pick up their rations during which part of the month uncover economic differences between territories and within seemingly homogenous territories.

People who are dependent on their quotas as major sources of household nutrition often go on the first day of the month, while households less dependent on the rations, for whom the quota represents a less significant source of nutrition, may wait till the end of the month and pick up the rations just before they "lose them." They may not even go through the trouble of picking up their quotas, as the few products available through the ration book today are also available in parallel markets in CUC or MN. Often individuals and households not dependent on the quota to meet household food needs gift their ration to a friend, family member, or neighbor with greater need, giving them physical possession of the ration book and the responsibility to pick up their monthly ration for their own consumption or to be divided between the households. Families with greater economic means often pay a messenger to collect their monthly rations in the bodega for them and deliver them to their home, never actually stepping foot in the bodega.

The *carnicería* is still relatively more important than the bodega in bringing together neighbors, forcing them to stand in line and socialize (potentially building and maintaining neighborhood-based social networks in the process) because the products produced there are more time-limited. For example, consumers only have three days to claim their ration of chicken before they lose the right. In many Havana neighborhoods, it is only on the days in in which eggs, ground meat [*picadillo*], and chicken are sold that lines form. Lines are still common when products become available, but these lines are now segregated by economic status: today individuals limited to state sector salaries must be aware of when meat and eggs arrive at their *carnicería*, as their dinner depends on it, while people with access to hard currency may not be aware that products have arrived or consciously chose to skip the line. Bodegas have lost the importance they once had in Cubans' everyday lives because the volume of products distributed are now minimal for most consumers.[8]

CONSUMPTION AND CONNECTIONS: INTERNET, EMAIL, AND TRAVEL

Others focused on distinctive cultural consumption practices such as the usage of email and internet as well as access to international travel and vacations. Idalys, now 36, studied chemistry and worked in a sugar laboratory at a port in Eastern Cuba from 1998–1999 before becoming an internal migrant settling in Havana. She told me that before coming to Havana she had a good salary, because all employees at the port were paid a bonus in dollars for the sugar that was exported. Idalys had grown up in a religiously active Protestant family and, in 1999, she decided to leave her job and her hometown to study at the seminary in Matanzas to become a pastor.

"From then on, I began to have access to things that I never would've had access to through my work: information and to be able to travel," she explained. From trips abroad that she took through the seminary, and her work for a Cuban religiously affiliated NGO, she was able to buy a small one-bedroom apartment on a *pasillo* in a peripheral neighborhood of Havana.

For Idalys, there are three specific reasons that she considers herself a member of the middle class: "I have my own house, I travel, and I have means of communication, I have internet. But I don't have a dime," she explained with a chuckle. "But these three things give me a status that many people don't have: they don't have housing, they don't leave Cuba, they can't travel, and they don't have access to information. These three things put me in a middle class in Cuba."

> If you look at my contacts, my father-in-law has a house, although it belongs to his daughters, but he has a house. He has a position in the government. He has a car that is falling apart, but it's a car. He has access to communications, and he can travel. For me, that's middle class. It is middle class and not upper class because he is living day to day... all of the people in my circle are living one day at a time. No one can afford luxuries, but everyone has their own house. My aunt is a professional. She has her own house and has access to information. She's never traveled, but I don't know, I couldn't put her anywhere else. My cousin is the same. He's a professional. Now he has a car, which he just bought, and he

has his own house. My friend Pepe is the same. He's a professional, although he's retired, but he has his own house, and actually he rents it out [to foreigners]. He has traveled to tons of countries and has access to information. All of these people travel through work. No one pays for their own travel.

If she had stayed in Eastern Cuba working at the port, Idalys believes that she never would have been able to buy her own apartment. Her life really started to change when she began to work in an NGO in Havana, as a professional outside of the state sector. It was through this job that she gained access to housing, travel, and means of communication; the three things that she considers make her and her friends members of the middle class in Cuba.

The question of how individuals identify and where they place themselves in the social hierarchy is an interesting one. In a 2015 research project about identity formation in individuals with high economic capital (tied to mix companies, self-employment, or with successful artist and musicians) Pañellas Álvarez found that "there is a certain resistance to recognize oneself as "high income" perhaps because they consider that there is a stigma in our society or because they compare themselves with professionals in the world [outside of Cuba] whose level of buying power is much higher" (Pañellas Álvarez 2015, 178).

The question of mobility and the ability to travel internationally was mentioned by several respondents as being something that made individuals members of the middle class (in the consideration of a respondent who travels), or near the top of the stratification system, only below remittance receivers (in the consideration of a respondent who has not travelled). Many interviews focused on how differences in consumption distinguished groups in different parts of the social hierarchy.

CULTURAL CONSUMPTION AND
IMPLICATIONS FOR UPWARD MOBILITY

By approaching economic inequalities from a theory of cultural consumption, Cuban researchers from the disciplines of Sociology, Social Psychology, and Cultural Studies have been able to focus on documenting the existence of social groups in Cuban society with different practices of consumption while avoiding the thorny political questions of what the presence of economic inequalities means for the legitimacy of a socialist state and its commitment to guaranteeing equal social outcomes.

Cultural consumption [*consumo cultural*] is "the process of adoption and use of products in which the symbolic value prevails over the use and exchange values, or where the latter are subordinate to the symbolic dimensions" (Linares, Riveros, Moras, Mendoza 2012:12). Cuban researchers have documented how social groups distinguish themselves from others in the social field through novel forms of symbolic consumption, similar to the way *New Class Studies* researchers abroad look at how people "do class."

Cuban social scientists write about the importance of "Spaces of Equality" in Cuban society: universal distribution mechanisms that are state-run, free of cost, or easily accessible collective solutions available to all members of society, regardless of their income, as a matter of right (Espina Prieto et al. 2003, 4). One of the most important of these spaces for consumption in Cuban families was once the local *bodega*, the store where products from the ration card are dispatched. As a result of fundamental changes in the organization of basic consumption towards market-based distribution, bodegas have lost their primacy as a territorially organized space in which Cuba's increasingly heterogeneous population once frequently socialized. Since the Special Period, in many areas of Havana, formal structures of community organization and political participation based on geographic proximity (membership institutions organized by the state, such as the Federation of Cuban Women [FMC], and the Committees for the Defense of the Revolution [CDR], etc.) have lost relevance as spaces for everyday socialization. As new private spaces of socialization around diverse cultural consumption practices grow in importance, these spaces of equality are gradually left to Havana's lower classes, those without access to CUC or connections to gain entrance to more desirable privately managed spaces.

Cultural consumption practices are of increasing importance in organizing spaces of socialization in Havana. The reforms in 2010 have stimulated the establishment of new small businesses in Havana which are creating new social spaces in which access is stratified based on income. For members of the middle class and below, the existence of segregated social spaces with different cultural consumption practices limit opportunities for building social networks that span different social groups and could provide people in lower groups opportunities for social mobility. Given the importance of social networks for social mobility in Cuba, the increasing segregation of social spaces has an important impact on social mobility.

Rosa explains that someone from the middle class or lower class who has a nice watch or a good pair of shoes might be able to go as a guest to one of the parties of the *Favored* and meet a partner there. One of her son's friends has an ex-girlfriend, Yanet, who married one of Fidel's grandchildren. How did she get there? Rosa explains that Fidel's grandson didn't go to regular discos or the same places that her son's crowd hung out. Yanet met her husband at a private party. She had an important position in the Cuban Institute of Radio and Television (ICRT). The communications sector is very controlled, and in that world she would frequently get invited to the type of private parties where she met her future husband.

> She is not a "daughter of," but her family has money because they have rented their house in Nuevo Vedado for years. In her case it's a combination, but it wouldn't be that easy for someone from the middle class to make the jump. The *Powerful* [*La clase pudiente*] can make it to the *Favored* because they move around in the same spaces. They go to Varadero, they might say "Let's go to Cayo Coco for the weekend," and they're at a resort in one of the Keys they meet someone from the other group and they might get along because they have certain things in common.
>
> Someone from the middle class might, through their talent or their intellectual achievements, publish a book or something and get invited to a party thrown by one of these people from the upper classes and maybe meet people there, but those are really exceptional cases. Usually the middle class and the people above don't mix socially. I can go into Club Habana, but there wouldn't be much of a point. If I don't have a car, once I got there all I would do would be to walk around a lot and not be able to enjoy anything. I don't have the $15 or $20 CUC cover to get into the pool, or the $15 or $20 CUC to get into the gym, or to go to the mini-golf, because I don't have the money. But the clients, the *Favored* and the *New Rich* who have the money, they can meet there. People like me or people from the lower class can't meet anybody in a place like that because we simply can't go. We don't have the buying power to go to Club Habana. There must be other places that these people share, but I don't know about them because I can't go.

In describing the processes of social mobility that he has witnessed, José also points out how differences in income create exclusive social networks that are reinforced through cultural consumption in segregated spaces of socialization.

> There's people that come from above and climb. They meet people and become a part of the upper class. The upper classes often cross between them, they're like royal families. It's not exactly like that, but there are spaces that they share. And the spaces that they share are spaces that you have to have either money or power to enter…in the end it's the world that you are born into [*Es el mundo que te toca*]. Maybe you want to go out at night. Sure, you go to the place you like, but the place you like costs $20 CUC to get in and inside you have to spend another $20 more. You have to go out with $50 CUC, and not everyone can go out with $50 CUC! So that means that you're limited to hanging out with people who have $50 CUC to burn on a Saturday night.

CONCLUSION

My interviews and research by Cuban colleagues describe recent processes of social stratification in Havana in similar ways. The professionals tied to the state sector I interviewed described a stratification system in which differences in income, occupation, sector of employment, housing, access to basic consumption (food security), and cultural consumption practices (media consumption, internet, email, international travel) were most relevant in understanding differences. This research corroborates research by Cuban colleagues describing the existence of different social groups in Cuba with unequal opportunities for mobility, access to consumption, and power.

The interviews also described the relative importance of different types of capital in the Cuban field, especially the conflicts that take place between those with high levels of economic capital and those with high levels of revolutionary cultural capital and social capital for dominance. Distinctive consumption practices have the potential to contribute to inequalities when differences in taste linked to cultural consumption lead to the segregation of social life. When spaces of cultural consumption become difficult to access, either because access is limited by entry fees (economic capital) or take place in spaces accessible only via private invitation (social capital), they may contribute to reinforcing differences in Cuban society and limit social mobility to members of those groups who are already favored by large endowments of economic or social capital.

NOTES

1. At this time, the Double Recharge had not yet begun. Double recharges allow people to receive extra credit by charging their phones online with a foreign credit card. Many family or friends abroad charge phones on the island with these periodic offers. In 2016, the recharges often gave the user an amount of extra credit that expired after a limited time. Since the credit expired, users who received these offers began consuming their credit before it expired leading to different calling practices.

2. Cuban saying: "If it is green and has spines, it is a *guanábana* fruit." Similar to the US saying "If it walks like a duck and quacks like a duck, it's probably a duck," or "What you see is what you get."

3. All interviews took place in a location chosen by the respondent, usually their home or mine, in Centro Habana. With the exception of one interview, which was a joint interview in which the interviewee's mother also participated, all interviews were private conversations between me and the interviewee (Respondent fourteen—Frank/Lourdes was the joint interview).

4. For a full discussion of the emergence of new economic spaces in the Cuban economy after the crisis and reforms of the 1990s, see studies by the CIPS's Social Labor Studies Group (Martín Romero et al. 2000; Martín Romero and Nicolau Cruz N.D.).

5. As discussed in the previous chapter, the conditions in the school, uniforms, teaching staff, meals, transportation, and dorms are better than regular Cuban high schools run by the Ministry of Education; the sons and daughters of Havana elite often study there.

6. CIMEX (Cuban Export-Import Corporation) is Cuba's largest commercial corporation which includes eighty companies including, Havantur, Fincimex (processes all credit cards and remittance transfers in Cuba), Melfi Marine container shipping company, Abdala recording studios, Imagines (Cuba's only legal satellite TV service), Cubapack (International package service), as well as 2,747 retail outlets (including 1,188 Panamericana stores, 1,128 eateries from fast food to full service restaurants, forty-nine photo shops, and fourteen video stores (Frank 2010b). In 2006, the company reported that it was responsible for 46.1 percent of retail sales in hard currency in Cuba and employed 25,000 people (Frank 2010b). Despite its importance in the Cuban economy, in February 2016 when I was looking for information about the corporation I was not able to find an active web presence! In June 2017, I visited the URL of the official site cited in the 2010 Reuters story (http://www.cimexweb .com/) and received a message explaining that the site was "being updated". CUPET operates 363 gas stations and is part of the CIMEX Corporation.

7. The Cuban ration book gives each household member a quota of fish each month. In Havana, more often than not, the state announces that the fish is not available and instead provides a quota of chicken per person to replace the fish quota. This is known as "chicken for fish" [*pollo por pescado*]. Cubans frequently joke about the substitution, as it feels surreal to them that on an island fish is not available and must be replaced by chicken (usually imported from the United States and Canada).

8. One possible exception might be families with small children or elderly or sick members who receive special diets and milk rations which are distributed more frequently.

Chapter Four

"Adjusting to the Adjustment"

Household Reproduction Strategies and New Economic Spaces in Havana, 2010–2015

The Cuban Constitution in Article 9(b) states that the Cuban state "as the power of the people, in service of the people, guarantees that no man or woman able to work be denied the opportunity to obtain a job with which they may contribute to the goals of the society and satisfy their own needs; and that all persons who are unable to work should have the means for a decorous subsistence." However, since the Special Period, low salaries in the state sector, where the majority of workers labor, have pushed Cuban families to develop household survival strategies that combine the labor of multiple members of a household across multiple economic spaces. Since 2010, the shift from a state policy of full employment, still guaranteed in the Cuban constitution, to a new state discourse which increasingly stresses personal responsibility, has generated an atmosphere of labor insecurity in the city.

In this chapter, I explore the decisions that Havana households are making about work and the way they relate to new economic spaces. I join many other researchers in arguing that the household is the most relevant unit of analysis for understanding life in Havana. According to Taylor (2009), 73.6 percent of Havana residents live in multi-generational, communal households (2009, 124). Taylor describes the importance of using the household as a unit of analysis for research in Cuba (123–4). Swedish economic anthropologist, María Padrón Hernández (2012), also took the household as the unit of analysis in her research into the relationship between morality and economy in Havana in the time period immediately preceding the most recent reform process. This chapter explores the impact of recent changes in state policies on the labor market participation of individuals in Havana and the households they live in. I have found that rather than making decisions as atomized individuals, many people in Havana make these decisions as members of households that contain multiple wage earners who work in diverse economic spaces, stretching between formal and informal markets and private and state sectors.

Despite the obvious differences in era, and the political and economic system, I approach the study of Havana households and the decisions they make about their insertion in the labor market in a similar manner to how Elliott Liebow (1967) attempted to understand the decisions made by "Negro streetcorner men" in Washington, DC the early 1960s regarding the jobs they accepted and those they chose not to. Liebow was committed to interpreting the "lower-class life of ordinary people, on their grounds and on their terms" (Liebow 1967, 10). In his classic urban ethnography, "Tally's Corner," Liebow explains that "behind the man's refusal to take a job or his decision to quit one is not a simple impulse or value choice, but a complex combination of assessments of objective reality on one hand, and values, attitudes, and beliefs drawn from different levels of his experience on the other"(Liebow 1967, 34). The decisions made today by members of households in Havana about their labor force insertion are also deeply rooted in the social reality in which they live. The reasons are multiple, and like the decisions about work made by the men in D.C., some of the reasons "are objective and reside principally in the job," while other reasons "are subjective and reside principally in the man [sic]," or woman, or household (Liebow 1967, 35).

In Havana today, household members commonly move between different economic spaces to make ends meet. In some cases, these maneuvers allow households to increase their consumption to desired levels, resulting in a sense of wellbeing and upward mobility that would not have been available to them had they continued working exclusively in the state sector. For those who have made the change, what do they see as the advantages and disadvantages to each space? How do people who have always worked for the state feel about moving into previously stigmatized spaces, and how does generation influence the meaning people give to their insertion into the labor market?

Despite low salaries, in 2015 the majority of the population continued to work in the state sector. In this chapter, I also look at the multiple reasons that people decide to continue working in the unrecovered state sector. Who are these individuals, and why do they continue working in positions that do not pay salaries sufficient to reproduce their labor? If it doesn't make sense in an economic sense, how can it be explained? In the final section of the chapter, I look at the transformations in the Cuban labor market from the perspective of Havana residents still committed to their work in the state sector. Why do people continue working in these jobs and what advantages do these workers find in the state sector?

JUAN AND MARTA, ALAMAR PIONEERS

Juan and Marta, consider themselves among the "founders" of the East Havana suburb of Alamar. The Alamar settlement was built in the early 1970s, by and for its residents, members of socially integrated revolutionary working class families. Before the Revolution, speculators, capitalizing on the newly opened tunnel under the Havana Bay, had built the streets and connections to public services for a planned upper middle class shoreline suburb easily accessible to the city by car. The suburb was never built, and the Revolution took advantage of the development to undertake an ambitious project to find a new socialist city on the land. The area swarmed with brigades of workers in white hardhats, who left their regular jobs for renewable two year terms to form the famous microbrigades.[1] On the microbrigades, workers from very different fields learned construction skills, coming together to build homes for themselves and their coworkers, who continued laboring at the office. A new state of the art elementary school for 1,264 students, with an Olympic sized pool, had been built to educate the sons and daughters of those new residents. Juan was asked to help get the school started and served as the principal for the school's first two years.

Juan and Marta met in 1961 when Marta, only thirteen at the time, went to Juan's small town in the mountains of Santiago to teach illiterate farmers to read and write as part of the Revolution's Literacy Campaign. It was love at first sight, but Marta told Juan that she wasn't allowed to date until she was sixteen. When she turned sixteen, Juan went to live with an aunt in Havana so he could study to enter the university, and he found her and they started dating. As they were both studying to prepare for the university entrance exams, a call went out for teachers, and they decided to join a program that would allow them to work in the daytime teaching classes and complete a university degree at night. They were married and were living in two rooms with a bathroom on the roof of Marta's aunt's house in the El Cotorro neighborhood with their four children when Juan began working in Alamar in 1973.

All schools in Cuba are named after revolutionary martyrs, and the Alamar Elementary school was named after the Chilean President Salvador Allende. The school was an experimental one which combined work and study, and at the time, all the important state visits included a visit to the school. Fidel would visit the school frequently, to give tours to visiting heads of state and other important visitors. He also dropped in on the monthly meetings of the school leadership to check on progress and offer whatever aid or resources were needed. During his two years as principal, Juan commuted daily almost two hours by bus from the family's home in El Cotorro. At the end of the second school year, the school had been set up, things were running well, and Juan had trained the new principal who would take his place, allowing him to return back to his regular duties in the municipal education office in El Cotorro.

But at the end of one of these visits from foreign heads of state, as Fidel was walking down the steps of the school with the visitors, he called out to Juan to say goodbye. Juan took advantage of the opportunity to introduce him to the woman he had trained as the new principal, "*Comandante*, the next time you'll be here, she will be your host."

"What do you mean? Why won't you be here?" Fidel asked. Juan explained that he had been asked to spend two years as the principal of the school in order to get it established, and he was confident that he had successfully completed the mission, leaving a very qualified leadership team in place. "Well, I'd really wish that you would continue as principal. Why wouldn't you stay?" Fidel asked him. And Juan explained to Fidel that he lived very far away and the commute was difficult, but that he had trained a very capable team to continue the work. Fidel responded by turning to one of the men in his entourage, "We could get him a house here in Alamar, right?" The man confirmed this and Fidel turned back to Juan, "We'll take care of that. See you next year then?"

A couple days later, the school closed for the summer, and in the fall, still living in El Cotorro, Juan began his third school year as principal. At the end of one of their regular long meetings about the school's progress, Fidel turned to Juan and asked how he was settling in to life in Alamar. When Juan told him that he was still commuting from El Cotorro, Fidel turned to one of his entourage and arranged so that as soon as the meeting was over the community architect would take Juan to see several houses. At lunchtime, a truck from one of the white hard-hat microbrigade construction crews took Juan to his house in El Cotorro to pick up the rest of the family and their belongings. Marta was surprised to see Juan arrive in the middle of the day, and he explained that there was a truck downstairs. They had been given a house in Alamar! Marta was in the middle of cooking lunch, and, after collecting the few belongings they had, they grabbed the kids and the steaming hot pressure cooker of bean soup still cooking on the stove and jumped on the top of the truck to head to their new home.

Marta and Juan raised three sons and a daughter in a simple four bedroom concrete block house in the center of the new city on the main boulevard, just a couple blocks away from the elementary school. Juan continued working as the principal of the elementary school until 1980. He then worked for a couple of years for the local *Poder Popular* and, later, taught Marxist philosophy at the high school level and for adults at the *Escuela del Partido*. From 1990–1992, he suffered from serious health problems and had two operations.

When he returned to work, it was as the principal of another elementary school in Alamar. After a third operation in 1998, he retired from state work at sixty years old.

In 1994, in the midst of the economic crisis, the government legalized TCP for a limited set of occupations, including transportation, housing repairs, agriculture, family and personal services, and home services. Originally only retirees, housewives or laid-off workers were issued licenses. Later, professionals were allowed to apply, but only with permission from their workplace and only in limited categories. An architect could get a license to drive a cab, but not to draw up blueprints. A nurse used to rent a room in her house, but never to do nursing care. Throughout the Special Period, Marta and Juan, teachers by profession, ran a series of small businesses out of their garage. At different times, they sold homemade wine, ice cream, snacks, take away meals, and sweets.

As Marta explains:

> When we began in self-employment we did it because we felt the need, more for our children than for ourselves, so our children, who are all professionals, could continue studying or working without the need to give up their work or their values. There's a lot of people who have had to do it because the salary is not enough, and they have had to do other things, *"por la izquierda."*[2] But we realized that here the professional has so much work, so many hours of work every day that when they get home they don't have time to have another job on the side. We saw what some professionals were doing, illegal things, including redirecting state resources. There are people who sell cotton or sell syringes; they take the things from the state, from their work in state institutions. But we had taught our children a certain set of moral values and we didn't want those values to become corrupted. We wanted them to be able to, with a fresh mind, dedicate themselves to their work and we would be there in the rearguard, supporting them as long as we could.

On the weekends, their four grown children would help their parents with the hard physical labor associated with the family business. When they were making wine, the boys would help sterilize the large glass vats and haul sugar. When Marta and Juan started selling ice cream, the boys would help stir.

At the beginning, there was a lot of hostility toward people involved in self-employment. Marta and Juan's first experience in TCP was when he was still working for the *Poder Popular*. In Cuba there is a *Casa de Cultura* community center located in each municipality that provides writing workshops, music, dance, and other art classes for the community, and also hosts cultural events such as concerts with neighborhood groups. The local *Casa de Cultura* didn't have any alcohol to serve at its events, and, since Juan knew how to make fruit wines, they asked him to make wine for the center's activities. The government gave the family the materials to produce the wine, and they sold it directly to the institution. The events were very well attended, and the local government was very satisfied with the solution, but Juan explains that the social pressure was intense:

> We decided to stop doing it, because I felt social pressure. I saw that many people thought that what we were doing wasn't correct, and we had an image in the community to uphold. I had been the principal of the largest school in this community. The young people knew me, and what would they think about me making wine? What we were doing, a lot of people didn't consider correct, not just because it was wine. I had always been a very revolutionary person, always supporting the Revolution and everyone thought of me as a very revolutionary person, so for a lot of people, they didn't think it was appropriate that I would do something like that. Afterwards self-employment was legalized, but when that happened, we had already decided not to continue. I tell you the story to give you an idea about what many people thought about self-employment. Many people didn't think that it was appropriate, even though it was the government who gave me the materials to make the wine.

Juan explains that back then a leader of the Revolution at the highest level said that TCP was a "necessary evil," and this really conditioned people's opinions towards self-employment and attitudes towards TCPers. People identified TCPers from many different sectors as "bandits and delinquents," as something negative that, given the unexpected and extreme situation, had become necessary.

"It was like if you have a family member who has gangrene, and, therefore, you have to amputate. If you don't do it quickly, you'll end up having to amputate at the knee, and you keep cutting and cutting, because the most important thing is preserving life, and if you don't do it the person will end up dying," Juan told me.

Marta remembers that, at the beginning, people would call self-employed workers "self-employed bandits." "Bandits of Cold River" was the name of a soap opera that was being shown on Cuban television at the time. In her ethnography of everyday moral economies, Marisa Wilson reports that people in a rural town she calls Tuta also complained about the "*Bandidos del Río Frío*" (Wilson 2014:139). Marta explains,

> The state would sell root vegetables for $.20, but the self-employed workers would buy them for $.60 and sell them at $2.50. It was highway robbery! But as the taxes went up and the prices went up, the self-employed had to do illegal things in order to continue supplying their businesses. The state media published

exposés on self-employed people who were committing illegal acts, who had suppliers who would even send them materials from abroad or who stole the materials from the state, and there was a lot of reporting on this in the newspaper and on television. This helped contribute to the idea that people who were self-employed were delinquents. And there were delinquents, but there were also honest people who were meeting a need in society as well as meeting the needs of their own families.

Juan remembers that, as people started getting established in these new businesses in certain sectors, some people started to develop *envidia* as they saw that these people began to resolve their economic problems. Others were inspired to become private workers themselves, and some began to see them as a part of the rainbow of diversity in society. But, from this initial growth, the taxes began to raise higher and higher, the materials needed to continue working were even more difficult to obtain, and although self-employment did not disappear, it declined drastically. Juan believes that it was a conscious strategy, a political not an economic one. "It was a "necessary evil," and if we are able to save the sick person using other methods, it is preferable. They went back to Che's position, that it was "difficult to build socialism with the corrupted tools of capitalism," he concluded.

Self-employment reached its peak at 209,606 workers in 1996, but from that point on the government stopped issuing new licenses and started to strictly enforce taxes and regulations, which pushed many people out of business. New licenses were not offered in 1998 or 1999 (Phillips 2007, 323). As the Cuban economy recovered in the early 2000s, increased inspection, taxes, etc. led to attrition in the number of licensed legal *cuentapropistas* (self-employed workers) from 209,000 by 1995 to 154,000 at the end of 2001 (*The Economist* 2004). In 2003–2004, it was reported that new licenses were no longer being issued in forty of the 157 self-employment categories available at the time (Henken 2004).

When the new economic activities were authorized under Raúl, Marta and Juan had already retired and were having a hard time surviving on their low pensions. Despite the fact that during their working life they had held important professional jobs with good salaries, as a retiree, Marta's pension was around $20 CUC and Juan's was only about $10 CUC a month. Through mutual friends, they began working for another retiree in Vedado, a former University of Havana professor, who was tutoring students to prepare for university and high school entrance exams. It wasn't long before Marta and Juan decided to start their own little school in their home in Alamar.

With the help of their kids and grandkids, they converted two bedrooms into classrooms. Using wood from a neighbor's rotting home entertainment center and the packing crates from the elevators recently installed in the twelve story apartment building across the street, they built three rows of rustic tables and benches for each room to fit ten students. Using celluloid scraps, they made dry erase boards for the two classrooms and installed wall fans in each of the rooms.

Marta explains that they structured things based on how things had worked at the other private afterschool program in Vedado where they had worked. Their school offers review sessions for middle school and high school students from seventh to 12th grade. In Havana, middle school lets out around 4:00 PM and high school a little later. Since kids already have classes every weekday, their school has its longest sessions on Saturdays. The classes are each an hour long and the basic package includes an hour a week each of Spanish, history, and math.

In the evenings during the week, there are additional classes in other subjects which are the most challenging for students. In seventh grade, natural science is very difficult, and so, on Tuesdays, they offer a review class. On Wednesdays, eighth grade physics and chemistry courses are offered. Each student decides which classes they will sign up for, but a package which includes the three core courses comes out at a discount.

> We don't offer all of the courses. For example we have Spanish, history, math and physics which are the most difficult classes in pre-university." Marta explains, "The students have other courses at school: political culture, civics, but those kinds of things they have to study on their own. They have chemistry as well, but it's very easy in the pre-university. There might be somebody who needs chemistry, but we don't have that course here. The student signs up for what they want to take, and the courses we teach them ourselves, my sons and my daughter. Each one teaches their specialty and has their own license, as if they were going to the students' house but they come here.

The new license has given Juan and Marta a way to supplement their pensions, but it is part of a family strategy for wellbeing that assists multiple households. Juan explains,

> In our case, it has not only allowed my wife and I to work, but also helped our family. Our children have their other jobs, but they also have their licenses, and they come here on certain days to teach classes. And each member of the family who works takes home exactly what their students pay to be in the classroom. Of course, we are not interested in charging them like another school would for using this space, or for finding them clients. It's also satisfying for us on an emotional and spiritual level. Two of my sons are doctors, and after the raise in salaries in the medical sector they are a little less squeezed than they were before, but they have their families, and this has been an important help for them.

The tax regimen for tutors is not a rigorous one. Each family member pays $60 Cuban pesos per month for their license, and there's no requirement to pay sales or service taxes at the end of the year. There are also no inspectors to deal with like there were when the family had a cafeteria.

Juan believes that, because this time in the political discourse, self-employment is not being introduced as a "necessary evil," the new opening for small businesses has opened up other possibilities. "The idea has changed. I am dialectic and I know that the moments, the situations change, the circumstances are modified, and the discourse has to be adjusted to the circumstances," Juan explains. "I'm not comparing two stages, thinking this one is worse or the other was better. The way it was before responded to an idea, and the way it is today responds to another. I really think it's been beneficial that one, in an honorable way and without being considered a bandit, can work towards the money you need to live."

Current research on occupational identity in Havana suggests that the image of the TCPers in the social imaginary in Havana is changing. Researchers from the University of Havana working on identity in workers in different sectors of the economy from 2011–15 found that with the exception of managers [*dirigentes*] working in commerce and food service, who perceive self-employed workers as competition and speak negatively about them, members of other groups talk about TCPers in what researchers call "the [new] politically correct discourse" (Pañellas Álvarez 2015, 173). Comments about TCPers from members of other occupational groups were positive and respectful: "They are a group of people that offer a service to society. They help to resolve problems in society; they are people like any other. They like to have a stable economic situation and a normal life..."(Pañellas Álvarez 2015, 173). Although other subjects recognize the materially comfortable lifestyle and distinctive consumption practices of this group, they also consider that self-employed workers work hard for their income (Pañellas Álvarez 2015, 173).

Despite being satisfied with the new family business and the opportunities now available in the private sector, Juan admits that he would prefer to be teaching in a regular public school.

> Maybe if I had to point something out, if I'm honest with you, I'd tell you that deep inside I would prefer to be doing this in a school. I can't help thinking about this. I wish I could be doing this the way I did for many years. But the circumstances change and my vision of my responsibility also changes. I also feel a responsibility so that my grandchildren can eat better and so that we can have a dignified lifestyle and help those who are around me who might need me. It's not that I don't wish I could do this in a school, but the circumstances don't allow it. What we would earn doing this in the school is a fraction of what

we earn now. And we do it in an honest manner and we do it not only to earn money, but also to help educate young people from the point of view of values.

The truth is that the Special Period not only affected the economy, it also affected the educational system. Because many of us older, experienced teachers decided to retire or do something different and we are no longer in the classroom. Today, many of the teachers in the classroom, I'm not going to say that they're lacking preparation, because it's really experience that is the most important for teachers. The experience that comes from facing the same problems over and over again and learning how to handle them, finding not the perfect answer, but the best one. You only get that with years of practice, and the young people who are there in the schools today over time will build that experience. They will achieve it, but there's no doubt that many of the young people today have serious gaps in their education. The situations at home have been greatly affected by what is going on in society, and it all affects the classroom.

GLADYS, NEWLY SELF-EMPLOYED ACCOUNTANT

In 2013, after 32 years working for the state, Gladys decided to quit her job as an accountant and shift to the private sector, keeping books for new private businesses. I met Gladys through her husband who works with a state sector institution in the Ministry of Culture. When she told me that she was now helping self-employed workers file their taxes I asked her for an interview to help me understand how the tax system worked for self-employed workers, but most of the interview ended up being about her recent decision to leave the state sector.

My father spent his whole life waiting to retire. He retired in 1998 and he died in 2000. That's one of the things that made me decide to leave. There is a moment for everything. They came out with the license for bookkeepers and I have 32 years of experience as an accountant. I knew I could do it. I left my work with the state not because I didn't like what I did, but because I was under-utilized. I had a boss who was 84 years old, and I had to do everything for him, it was like working in an old-folks home. I felt very underutilized. I felt horrible! You can't imagine how I felt.

I saw so many things growing around me, so many opportunities, and there I was, wasting my time. I started working on my own not because I didn't have a job, but because I didn't see the fruit of my labor. Living with $375 Cuban pesos a month. That was my salary when I began to look into self-employment and researched the laws to see how to prepare the tax statements.

When I began, I didn't even know how much to charge people! When I started, a guy came to me and asked me to keep his books. He came to see me at work, because when I first got started I began by passing around business cards. One day a guy called me on the phone. He said, "Listen I need your services." I said, "Okay you can come to my house tomorrow afternoon," but he said, "No I need it right now." I said, "Well I'm at work." He asked me where I worked and he said that he would come by. He explained to me that he was going out of town the next day and he wanted to have everything taken care of before he left. So I told him to bring me all the papers and wait for me around the corner.

That day I was alone in the office. My boss wasn't there. When I finished with the guy's papers I met him on the corner and gave him all the stuff. But I had no idea how much to charge so I said, "Give me $30 pesos." I really had no idea! He said, "No, no, no are you crazy?" and he gave me $50 pesos. $50 pesos! I couldn't believe it! Do you know how much I had to work at my job to earn $50 pesos?! A whole week. I said to myself as I walked back to the office, "What the hell am I doing here? This can't be! $50 pesos!" Later I found out how much people are charging to prepare a tax form: $100 pesos! So I said, "This is not the place for me. I'm done here." I decided I was going to keep working until I had a good base of clients and then quit. December 2012 was my first client, and in 2013 I started getting more clients by word-of-mouth.

I don't like to fight, I like to fix my problems by talking things out. My workplace is small, and people visit and they say this is such an awesome place, but I say *"Pueblo chiquito, infierno grande."*[3] At the end of a hard day at work, I took the checks to my boss for signatures and told her, "I have to tell you something. We've always got along so well, and we have a similar way of seeing the world, so there is something that I want to tell you. The last two months, in addition to working here, I've been working as a private bookkeeper. I have my license and everything. I can even show you."

She asked me why, if there was something wrong. And I explained:

"I'm doing it because I'm going to earn a lot more than I am earning here, and again I have time to spend with my mother. Since I graduated as an accountant at sixteen I have been working. I haven't even taken a vacation. I haven't had time to spend with my mother. There's always something: work, or I have to rush home to make dinner. That's life here. I don't know about in other places, but here that is what it is, and I need this time. Besides, I love to do yoga! I love to go to cultural events, and often there is something interesting happening in Vedado, and I am stuck here on the edge of the planet wasting my time working. You understand what I mean."

I knew that my boss understood exactly what I meant because she had talked with me about how she was crazy to retire already because she was tired. I told her, "It's just like you. You want to retire. I'm crazy ready to retire too, but I have eleven years left before I can do that. Can you imagine eleven more years! And I'll have more free time. For example, when my husband travels to other provinces, I could go with him! Sometimes I can't go with him, but when I can, I have to ask for permission at work, etc."

I've been working for thirty-two years. It's not a day; I've put in my time. To retire, you need twenty-five years of service and to be of retirement age. I worked thirty-two years but I'm not old enough yet to retire, but I deserve it.

I said to her, "You know that everything I am saying is true." Then she told me, a little resigned, "I can't say anything to that. The only thing I can tell you is good luck." Then I tried to reassure her. I said, "But don't worry, this is not going to be right away."

The next morning, I had my resignation letter on her desk, and she called me and she said "This wasn't what you talked to me about yesterday!" And then I told her, "You have to understand the opportunity that I was just given! Don't worry I'll leave you everything in order, and I will train the other woman who works with me, and you know where to find me if you ever need anything or have any questions." But that was just empty talk. We both knew that it wasn't going to be the same. We both knew that I was leaving. She knew that she had already lost me. So she signed the papers to approve my resignation, and I turned everything in that I had been working on and I never looked back. That was March 25, 2013. I have never regretted it. It was the best thing that could ever happen to me in my life, and every day I say, "Dear Lord, why did I not do this before?"

Since going into business for herself, Gladys feels like her life has changed. It's everything that she had hoped it would be. Her life is still busy, but she likes that she sets her own hours. She has set up systems to automate a lot of the monthly reports that she turns in to the ONAT tax office on behalf of her clients. With even a few clients and a fraction of the time, she makes as much as she did in her state job. A few clients more and she can multiply her previous earnings.

Going into the private sector as a self-employed worker has provided the family with a level of financial solvency that they hadn't had since the beginning of the Special Period. When both Gladys and her husband were working in the state sector, the only income in addition to their salaries came from the occasional guest lecture for groups of foreign students or tourists that her husband was able to give at his state job. The family's diet has changed since she started working for herself, and she is able to attend cultural events that she used to miss out on. The fact that she works as a TCPer allows the family enough income for her husband to continue working for the state, as well as supporting her son as he continues his university studies.

COMMITMENT, FEAR, AND GENERATION

For decades, not working for the state was read as a lack of commitment to the collective project of building a new socialist society. The development strategy adopted after the Revolution required huge increases in employment and deployment of labor (Karl 1975, 27). The utopian project needed all hands on deck, and dropping out of the state sector was interpreted as a form of dissent that put the person who was *desvinculado*, neither working for the state nor studying, at odds with social norms. Terry Karl explains in a 1975 article about how work was conceptualized in Cuba during this period:

Lenin wrote that "Communist work in the strictest sense of the word is work without pay for the good of society . . . work done without any regard to any kind of remuneration, without demanding any kind of remuneration (Lenin, 1969:80). In Cuba, these attitudes of communist work are referred to as *conciencia*, a mixture of consciousness and commitment. The "New Person," the person of *conciencia*, puts the interests of society before personal interests" (Karl 1975, 24).

By 1971, the Cuban state employed 90 percent of the population and the debate over the best way to motivate workers in Cuba during the transition to communism, whether through moral incentives advocated by Ernesto "Che" Guevara or through material incentives promoted by Carlos Rafael Rodríguez, was already a decade old (Karl 1975, 36). The debate had two dimensions, the type of reward (moral versus material incentives) as well as who was rewarded (collective versus individual incentives).

With moral incentives, a worker receives an award of purely symbolic value. There is no direct remuneration for work accomplished. Instead, the worker may be given banners, medals, recognition in newspapers, etc. In Cuba, moral incentives are illustrated through voluntary labor, workers mobilizations, renounced overtime, and socialist emulation. Moral incentives rely on sacrifice to fulfill socially needed tasks. Material incentives, on the other hand, award workers in some rough proportion to the realized monetary value of their labor. The award is generally in the form of higher wages, work bonuses, vacations, commodity prizes, etc...A collective award is given to a work center or a group of people. The award may be banners, medals, or certificates. It can be a monetary bonus, free vacations, or the allocation of some commodity to distribute within the group. Collective incentives encourage individuals to see themselves as part of a group. They must recognize common interests and cooperate in order to meet their goal. An individual who holds back the group effort is usually disciplined within the group. Individual incentives involve one person, striving to reach a personal goal. The awards may be monetary, banners, prestige, or recognition. Using these two dimensions, there is the possibility of four types of incentives: moral-collective, moral-individual, material-collective, and material-individual" (Karl 1975, 23).

Describing the debate over how to incentivize workers in 1975 Karl reports that:

Under communism, as defined by Marx and Lenin, people do not work for material awards or for themselves. Incentives are moral and collective. In the socialist stage however, a mixture of all kinds of incentives are possible. The question is not the existence of one type of incentive or another, but whether the entire incentive structure moves a society in the direction of communism. To reach communism, a socialist country should eventually show a long-range bias towards moral and collective incentives" (Karl 1975, 24).

In addition to the positive incentives aimed at incorporating more men and women into the labor force and fighting absenteeism, the government established an anti-loafing law in 1971 [*La ley de vagancia*] which acted as a negative incentive, requiring all able-bodied men between the ages of seventeen to sixty to work (Karl 1975, 37; Lewis, Lewis, and Rigdon 1978, 309 note 56). The measure was successful in incorporating more than 100,000 workers into the labor force, more than half of whom had never worked before (Pérez 2006, 269). Workers who were absent for more than fifteen days without authorization were considered "pre-criminal"(Karl 1975, 37).

Cuban filmmaker Sara Gómez's feature length film "*De cierta manera*" (1974) shows how the anti-loafing law was applied in a Cuban workplace when Humberto, a laborer, is called to an open disciplinary meeting as the result of a long unexcused absence. Finally, one of Humberto's friends breaks down and confesses that Humberto's excuse about visiting his sick mother in the hospital in Santiago was a lie. Humberto is sanctioned, but the friend has a difficult time living with himself, in his own understanding of honor and morality he failed as a friend and as a man. His partner and other friends try to convince him he did the right thing as a revolutionary, that the *machista* codes of male honor are a thing of the past. The other workers at the plant consider his action to be correct because Humberto's irresponsibility affected all of them who were left picking up the slack.

Although women were excluded from these laws, they were encouraged to enter the workforce through other policies aimed at making the workplace more family friendly. More than 350,000 women entered the labor force in the 1970s as a result (Smith and Padula 1996, 101).

In the early years of the Revolution, people who refused to work were seen as antisocial and risked being sent to labor camps.[4] More than seventy UMAPs (Military Units to Support Production) [*Las Unidades Militares de Ayuda a la Producción*] camps operated in Camaguey from November 1965–September 1968 (Hernández 2015). The camps were run by the MINFAR in order to reform men who were accused of anti-revolutionary or antisocial activities and attitudes, and were intended to contribute to reforming these people through physical work (Lumsden 1996, 66).

According to Rafael Hernandez (2015), 25,000 Cubans passed through the UMAPs. Hernandez's article provides important context for understanding the UMAPs and tentative recognition from an important academic in Cuba of the abuses which took place. Hernandez explains that, in Cuba at the time, there was required military service of three years for young men. Young men who were not seen as "trustworthy" enough to be trained for military service were sent to the UMAP to perform alternative service. Among those not deemed fit for regular service were gay men, religious men (immediately following an important conspiracy of pastors against the Revolution) and those whose families were planning on leaving the country (the young men would then become draft bait in the US in the middle of the Vietnam war and be sent to fight on the other side).The first group sent to the UMAP completed their military service there. The second group, which entered in June 1966, was sent home when the camps were disbanded, before finishing the three-year service term. In 1967, rumors of abuse led the leadership to consult with the department of Psychology at the University of Havana to assist in improving communication, deal with conflict in the camps, and demobilize the recruits (Hernández 2015).

These events live in the collective historical memory as a warning against stepping out of line, even among younger generations. This man, in his 30s, felt that:

> Working for the state is what you do. If you don't do it, you are not a good person. If you don't do it, you could have problems in your neighborhood. You could cause problems for your family. You don't even know what could happen, but you are breaking one of the basic societal rules and you're off to a UMAP. I work for the state, because I was raised to think that I had to. If I didn't, something bad would happen. And since I never broke the rule, I don't even know what that would be, because I've lived my whole life living within those rules. I am motivated by fear, of what I don't even know.

Although the 1971 loafing law apparently fell into disuse, it was reactivated in 1990 during the Special Period economic crisis. Cuban men who could not show that they made a living in some formal way risked being scrutinized (Rosendahl 1997, 116, note 9). Women who were neither students nor employees were often seen as housewives, and, therefore, excused, but men who were idle were suspicious in various ways in the eyes of the police, the Party, and neighborhood organizations (Padrón Hernández 2012, 131–22).

This history is one of the factors that contribute to older workers' discomfort with leaving the state sector. The story of Mercedes, in the following section, demonstrates the ways in which generation influences the meaning people give to their insertion into the labor market.

MERCEDES, TRANSITIONING TO TCP AFTER RETIREMENT

Mercedes is a *mestiza* woman in her early 60s. She is a professional historian and works as a researcher. She lives in a large three-bedroom apartment in Centro Habana. She has two children. Mercedes' daughter, in her early 30s, lives in the 10 de Octubre municipality with a two-year-old son. Mercedes' son, an engineering student in his twenties, lives with her. Mercedes' mother lives in Old Havana. Her work as a researcher allows her to set her own hours and often work from home and help her daughter with childcare.

Mercedes has worked for the state since graduating from college as a historian in 1983. She worked for two school years as a history teacher, teaching eighth and ninth grade students in Eastern Havana. In this first job, she started out earning $198 Cuban pesos. Later her salary went up to $231 pesos when she finished her social service. Next, she worked from 1983–1989 as a researcher at a research institute earning up to $341 Cuban pesos. In 1989, she began her current job where she earns $440 Cuban pesos. She really enjoys her job and feels it is her vocation, but like all of the people I have interviewed, complained about her salary.

> The level of salaries doesn't correspond to the level of what you need for life. That's the biggest change that there's been, because before with your salary you could cover your needs and now there's no way. It's been that way since the 1990s. If you can't with your income cover your needs…You have to find a way to try to stick within legality. We've become accustomed to being subsidized by the state, or as well as by those family members who have emigrated, and now (with the changes in the country) we are being invited to cover our needs. Now they are inviting you to take that on. You have to look at that and try to figure out how you can do it. To wake up to that sense of individual responsibility.

HB: What would be a "just salary" that would allow you to cover your needs?
In Cuba or as a philosophical concept? In terms of a definition, I would say a "just salary" would be something that allows you, in a day's work, to cover your necessities. The minimum of what you're going to consume in a day. Calculated in money, you don't consume less than $2 CUC a day. Calculated in Cuban pesos, it wouldn't be less than $50, $25 and $25, lunch and dinner, without counting breakfast, for one person. And then maybe you pay $4 pesos in electricity or $2 in telephone. So other expenses would be maybe $15 pesos a day. $65 pesos a day. Translate that into CUC and it would be like $2.50 CUC. For a family budget I would say multiply that by the number of people living in the household, but it wouldn't be less than $5 CUC. That's just to cover the basics. Assuming that your television doesn't break, and without counting on the fact that you want to go on vacation. You would have to find some other way to deal with that, but the minimum, the "just" thing would be that.

HB: How do you do it?
Like all Cubans do. We don't. [*No llegamos.*] That's why the salary isn't enough. It doesn't cover it. It's just enough to pay the electricity, the basic services that are still subsidized. Like telephone, electricity, gas, water… I use the

money from my salary for those things. As soon as I get my paycheck I pay the electricity and telephone and it's gone. The other money I spend comes from the savings that I have. I take money out, and then when something appears I put it back. I have to spend a minimum one dollar a day. But then there might be a day when I spent five. I spend at least $30 CUC a month beyond my salary and I never spend less than $30 a month.

More than anything, I get by through family remittances. I won't tell you about other things, because they're not legal. But the most visible, the most official, would be that I sell the coffee that I get on the ration book, or the sugar which I don't eat. There are thousands of strategies. You can get remittances or you can contract your services, for example, tutoring. Something that helps you earn a daily income. Professionals can tutor or take care of an old person in the hospital at night, something that pays you for your services. I don't have time to tutor and luckily I've always had the opportunity to do some work for some other research center, or give a lecture, or teach a class, plus the remittances, from my uncle (my father's brother). He sends $300 CUC every three months, $100 CUC every month. The money is not for me, it's for my mother, but I manage it for her. Because of the blockade they can't send more than that, they can only send $1,200 per year. I play with that money as well.

For Mercedes, the fact that she is approaching retirement helps her feel more comfortable about moving into the private sector, working for herself. She tells me that her generation was raised to think first about contributing to society, to make decisions based on what would be best for the country and how to be socially useful, often even at great personal sacrifice. Above all, they were taught that income should come from work, and respectable work was in the state sector. The changing discourse about self-employment coming from the state has helped her understand that self-employment is now an officially sanctioned option and opened her up to the possibility.

HB: What advantages are there today to working for the state?
None.

HB: Why do you do it?
I do it because…First, because I have the education. It's idiosyncrasy. For us professionals, it is hard for us to take the leap into TCP because we know that the private sector is very uncertain. We know as well that we've also dedicated an important part of our lives to preparing ourselves, studying, and it's very hard at a certain age to let go of that. There are different reasons: one, because of our *formación* [training] another because of our age, and another because that is just logical, from life experience, from knowing that self-employment is very unstable, and at least this gives you a guarantee of security, *fija* [steady, fixed]. The other no. It changes a lot. And when you have a family, you need something that, even if it gives you very little, you know that you have it. I guess

it's that. Without denying that I'm looking for a way, now that I'm at the end of my work life and now I have to enter the next stage which is retirement, where I will be less, less rich. Well so I'm looking for a way to insert myself in self-employment, which is also a legal option to make up for my salary.

My father was a car mechanic, and my mother was a housewife. They taught me that your income should come from your work. My dad wanted me to be a musician. He signed me up for music school and he took me to ballet school. He wanted me to be some sort of artist, but always something related to studying, working for the state, something official.

I give my kids the same advice my parents gave me, despite the fact that I recognize that the times are different, and that now self-employment is also an official option. Because we grew up in a generation where outside of the state there was nothing. But now, you have to understand that the state is offering us this option as well for self-employment. Before it was a capitalist alternative, now it's also like a combination of the state/official. It's difficult to let go of one's concepts and values. I always think that the state is the most secure option. That's why I have my money in the bank and why I keep working for the state.

But I also start to see the other alternative, and so I also invite my kids to think about some other TCP opportunities. But for that it's important to study because if you don't you become a person who is totally *metalizado*[5] who only thinks about income and doesn't think about offering society your service. I don't want my young people to become people who are only thinking about their income. They have the opportunity to interact with society through the opportunities that the state offers them, studying and also the opportunity to participate in something that needs you. They have both worked for the state, for the security that the state offers you, but I think they're going towards the new options that are available...

Mercedes is now doing renovations to rent a part of her house, and she hopes to find students or other professionals that she can rent to, never tourists. Even if they pay less, she says that it doesn't matter.

I'd rent to students or professionals in my field but never tourists. Never tourists, because that is really complicated. You don't know what they're here for. With students you have the assurance that they're here to study. It's safer. They pay less than tourists, but I'm going to have my fixed salary from my retirement so it's just to complete that. I'm not so interested in earning a lot of money as I am in having a decent old age. It's not to make money [*lucrar*] it's to survive [*sobrevivir*], not even to live [*vivir*].

About a month after our interview, her son left the university to move to Europe, where his father, a Cuban émigré, has lived for more than a decade, and she thinks it's quite possible that her son will stay to make his life there. A couple months later, her daughter and grandson left Cuba for Italy, where they had been invited to visit by an Italian friend. It is likely that visit will become permanent as well.

"SOMETIMES I DON'T KNOW WHY
I WORK FOR THE STATE…"

Despite the low salaries, the majority of the population continues to work in the state sector. Who are these individuals, and why do they continue working in positions that do not pay salaries sufficient to reproduce their labor in the most basic Marxist definition? If it doesn't make economic sense, what is going on beyond the surface? Why do people continue working in these jobs? What advantages do workers find in the state sector?

In our conversations about their employment in the state sector, research participants repeatedly refer to the stability that working for the state provides them with. Although salaries are low, far from sufficient to cover their basic needs, they are a stable contribution to a household budget. Whether your state salary is $350 or $500 Cuban pesos, it's $14 to $20 CUC that you don't have to *luchar* [struggle] to earn.[6] Padrón Hernandez describes the stories of economic stress and hardship of daily life and difficulties of meeting basic needs which permeated her fieldwork, as well as mine (Padrón Hernández 2012, 67–68). Among her research participants, even those who were the most vulnerable did not consider themselves "poor" because they saw "poor" people as those who were incapable of meeting their basic needs, whereas they felt confident that they would be able to find a way to put food on the table. The stress that they experienced was not of *whether* they would but over not knowing *how* they would be able to do it (67). The solutions they found in this daily struggle varied on a monthly or even daily basis, combining work in multiple economic sectors. One couple in her study, Celia and Juan, both held state jobs (earning $360 and $328 Cuban pesos, respectively) but their informal businesses selling air fresheners ($325 Cuban pesos) and roach poison ($770 Cuban pesos) accounted for more than half of the household income (Padrón Hernández 2012, 107).

This struggle was extremely common. State salaries, far from solving these problems, gave households a minimum that they could count on since all the other strategies were so dependent on opportunities that may or may not appear. These informal opportunities for income generating are so "touch and go" that they are often talked about as *me cayó algo*. Literally, an opportunity, *something* fell (from the sky?). But since these income-generating opportunities in the informal sector are often temporary, not fully legal, if things get too hot then the opportunity disappears ["*se cae*" *it falls down, losing its foundation*]. These informal jobs, usually based on oral agreements, are very vulnerable to falling apart. Padrón Hernández found that in 2006 many of her research subjects "had no stable and reliable solution to their livelihood that survived from one year to the other. This required much of a person's creativity, flexibility and wit" (140).

State jobs are very secure, but informal jobs are much more profitable. As the state discourses toward self-employment change, individuals are constantly debating where to put their energies. One of Padrón Hernández's interviewees was struggling to maintain a full time job in the state sector as well as a much higher paying informal night job. He found himself trying to decide between the benefits of each, and eventually chose the stability of the state sector over the profitability of the informal work (2012:134). When Padrón Hernández did her fieldwork in 2006, opportunities like this one were part of the submerged economy because licenses were not available or were not being issued. During my fieldwork, after the reforms, many of these informal jobs can be done with licenses.

Many who work in the state sector use their CUP salaries to pay their utility bills (gas, water, telephone, and electricity) and to pay for their rations. Gas and water bills are low. In her study in 2006, Padrón Hernández (2012) found that "the cost for electricity, gas, and water, was between $40 and $50 MN per month per household. Households with a telephone paid approximately $45 MN per month in telephone bills and the monthly expenditure on rationed goods was about $20 MN per person" (58).

Ten years later, my neighbor who lived alone in Vedado paid between $19–25 Cuban pesos a month (water: $2.60, gas: $4–5, local telephone: $8–10, electricity (no air-conditioners): $4–7). In 2016, a family of four in Alamar paid between $218–232 Cuban pesos. The family used natural gas "*de balita*" (canister) and received two canisters a month for $7 Cuban pesos each, but often ran out before the end of the month and purchased more on the black market. In telephone, they paid $15 pesos. Their electricity bill (with one air conditioning unit), came to between $203 and $189 Cuban pesos.

If there is anything left after basic services are paid for in Cuban pesos, most households use their Cuban pesos to buy food at the agricultural markets. The remainder of the household's basic necessities are sold in CUCs, and that money generally comes from the family's other sources of income, which are more likely to be in CUCs. This way they also avoid losing money on the exchange between the two currencies.

There has long been a social stigma attached to being "*desvinculado*," unattached to the state through either work or study. People who do not participate in the labor force are seen as antisocial and suspect. One research participant who continued to work in the state sector despite the low pay explained that, "If people see that you are living without working then immediately they know that you're not living on air. You must have income coming to you from somewhere, and unless there are relatives from abroad sending you money, then you are probably doing something illegal." To avoid being subject to this scrutiny, many people find it advantageous to continue working for the state.

In Cuba, the minimum wage for state workers is $225 Cuban pesos (ONEI 2014a). Within the state sector, workers in the Ministry of Tourism and food service have the lowest state salaries. In 2014, the average monthly salary in hotels and restaurants was $377 Cuban pesos, below the national average of $584 Cuban pesos (Tamayo 2015). While salaries are low, their incomes are quite high. These jobs are highly valued despite the low salaries because of the opportunities they provide to *resolver*.

Many in Havana also talk about these jobs as desirable because of the money that can be earned in tips. But Heidi, who migrated to Havana with her family from Eastern Cuba as a teenager, explained to me, "People will tell you that working in tourism is attractive because of the tips, but anyone who tells you that who actually works in tourism is lying to you. Working in tourism, you make much more money from what you can steal than you ever make on the tips." After moving to Havana, her father, a high school Spanish teacher, was recruited to teach in the newly formed Ministry of Tourism doing training courses for workers. From there, he was able to move into a position at an important Havana hotel and was able to find jobs for his brother-in-law and both of his children in the sector.

After graduating from 12th grade, Heidi worked at the front desk at a hotel in Old Havana. At the front desk, whenever a guest wanted to make an international call, she would connect the call, tell them how long they talked, and how much they owed. On every call, she would overcharge the client by fractions of a minute. Since the cheapest destinations were around $2.50 CUC a minute, overcharging by just a couple seconds made a difference. Each time she overcharged by ten seconds, she earned $.40 CUC. Sometimes she would be more daring, rounding to the minute, even though the hotel's system was much more precise. She always did it with a smile and sometimes the client would even round up to the next dollar and leave a tip. It was rare for a client to question her because she was so friendly. In the rare case where charm didn't work, she would act as if she had made a mistake and apologize, diffusing the situation before things went too far.

Workers in tourism and in food service at all levels have access to food and goods that are not available in the public market, or are available in limited quantities and in prices that are not accessible to the average family. Family members of people working in food service never have to worry about food, as they can bring food home for their households. However, many who work in food service go beyond this and resell products that they take from their workplaces. Indeed, someone working in the sector who does not participate in this common practice will likely not last long. They will be seen as a threat by their coworkers and quickly dismissed.

Redirecting social property for private good is generally accepted in Havana as a necessary practice. Jobs which *"tiene búsqueda"* give you access to goods that can be repurposed for personal gain are considered "good jobs" (see also Padrón Hernández 2012:126).[7] Upon finding out that a friend has changed jobs, Cubans rarely asks about the salary, because the difference between one state job and another is negligible; the real difference is whether the new position *"Tiene búsqueda,"* or whether it provides the worker with opportunities to "look for" something for themselves. People who repair things at state workshops can say that a functional part is broken, and replace it with either a working or nonworking "new" part and then sell it. People working in a dollar restaurant that sells sodas in CUCs may buy cans of the same brand sodas in a store in Cuban pesos, or on the black market, to hide under the counter. They first sell their stash, without recording the sale, pocketing $.55- $1 CUC for a soda they bought for Cuban peso equivalent of $.42 CUC, before selling the restaurant's own stock.

Most Cubans would agree that working in a bakery is a good job. By making each loaf of bread slightly smaller, the bakery can produce and sell many more loaves of bread than expected. The off-the-books profit from the sale of the "extra" loaves goes straight to the pockets of the workers. Employees also sell ingredients, such as flour and oil, through the back door to entrepreneurs with their own home-based bakeries, as well as to families looking to find staples at reduced prices. The side businesses that bakery employees engage in are so lucrative that they often hire others to do the actual work of baking!

People who work in the bodegas also steal a little bit from each consumer and sell the "surplus" at rates slightly lower than the government CUC stores. When I lived in Cuba in 2008, when our monthly ration of cooking oil would run out, we would first inquire discreetly at the bodega about the possibility of buying a little extra oil at the going rate of $30 CUP a liter ($1.20 CUC) before, as a last resort, going to the government dollar store down the block, where it would cost $2.15 CUC. At the bodega, we could often also buy meat, eggs, and fish beyond that which was available through the ration book, by applying what one housewife on my block humorously refers to as "CUC power."

This same profiting from state resources (and consumers) happens at the agricultural markets. Many women I interviewed, responsible for doing their household's food shopping, expressed the importance of owning your own portable scale to take with you to the market to verify that the pound of black beans, cheese, or pork chops that you buy is actually a full pound. By short-shifting each consumer, banking on their silence, the market vendor responsible for selling one hundred pounds of yucca can sell the same goods twice and pocket the profit. In each state-run agricultural market, there is a consumer protection area where people can bring their purchases to verify the weights. However, I don't know from personal experience whether shoppers take advantage of this safeguard or whether those scales are any more accurate than the ones used by vendors.

Even when buying high-priced goods in dollar stores, consumers must be wary. Even there, anything liquid is subject to adulteration: shampoos, vinegar, bleach, cleaning liquids, perfume, and even rum, by employees who sell the real product in nondescript containers on the black market, leaving stores full of pretty bottles with watered-down products and irate customers left complaining to the deaf ears of the very employees who adulterated the product.

Ironically, consumers are aware that this happens; at the bakery they will complain about the shrinking bread loaves to other consumers. They will try to defend themselves from being cheated by bringing their own scales to the market, but they also depend on this mechanism, which makes more affordable goods available on the black market. When the government takes actions to crack down on workplace theft and the black market, as they did after the 2008 hurricanes, everyone feels the pinch: Cuban consumers both benefit from, and are negatively affected by, the pilfering of goods from the state sector and their sale in the black market.

Many people told me that they don't see any problem with taking things from the state workplace. "There's nobody who defends the state," one respondent told me. "It's a victimless crime, and people only do it because they feel it is just. If the state doesn't pay me enough for me to provide for my family, I feel justified in taking what I need as long as it doesn't hurt anyone else. It just hurts the state and the state doesn't count, because it's the state that is exploiting me and not paying enough."

"The state" functions similar to "the man" or "the boss" in US capitalism. Despite the quite different contexts, employees who are being paid below subsistence wages believe that their employers "owe them" a living wage. If the boss (or the state) chooses not to provide fair pay for their labor it is the boss (or in the Cuban example, the state) who is being immoral, not the worker who attempts to rectify the injustice by adjusting accounts. Wilson (2014), in her ethnography of rural "Tuta," also reports that Tutaños "only take from the state when they feel that the latter is not providing enough for their family or community" (140). In Havana, I discovered that the same distinction was made;

taking things from the state was moral and taking things from other people was definitely immoral (2014, 142).

As has been commented on by many anthropologists, Cubans' linguistic practices reflect their acceptance of these practices. The word *robar* [steal] is only used to talk about stealing from a private individual. When the word *robar* is used, a value judgment is made about the immorality of the action and the person who performs it. Usually when talking about taking state property, people use the verbs *llevar* [to take] or *conseguir* [to obtain] (Padrón Hernández 2012: 125,139). In this case, the moral breach was made by the state, for paying salaries so low that people are not able to fulfill their basic needs. The action of taking things from work is seen as taking things that are due to you by the state who has failed to keep up its end of the social contract.

I return briefly to Elliott Liebow's classic urban ethnography "Tally's Corner" with which I opened the chapter to point out the striking similarities between marginalized workers in 1960s DC and the situation of state workers in post-Special Period Havana. In both places, low wages make it necessary for laborers to "steal part of their wage" (Liebow 1967, 37). In both contexts, one of the advantages of working in hotels, restaurants, and retail establishments is that "they frequently offer opportunities for stealing on the job" (Liebow 1967, 37). In Washington, DC, Liebow learned that "the wage level rests on the premise that the employee will steal the unpaid value of his labor, the man who did not steal on the job is penalized. And, furthermore, even if he does not steal, no one would believe him; the employer and the others believe he steals because the system presumes it" (Liebow 1967, 38). Liebow explains that in Washington, DC.

> the employer may occasionally close his eyes to the workers stealing, but not often and not for long. He is, after all, a businessman and cannot always find it within himself to let a man steal from him, even if the man is stealing his own wages. Moreover, it is only by keeping close watch on the worker that the employer can control how much is stolen and thereby protect himself against the employee's stealing more than he is worth" (Liebow 1967, 38).

In contemporary Cuba, a certain amount of stealing from low-paying jobs in state-sector workplaces is tolerated, probably because managers know that salaries are insufficient and that if the worker received no benefit from their labor than they would not continue working. At the end of the day, the manager needs someone to fill the position. Since they cannot offer higher salaries to keep workers they have to offer other benefits, such as flexible hours, and being willing to look the other way at certain times to allow their workers to "steal part of their wage." Managers are generally less worried about the workers stealing "more than they're worth" and more worried about ultimately being held responsible themselves for goods and income that may go missing. There is often collaboration between managers and employees where both benefit from stealing from the state and, if the worker doesn't share the wealth with coworkers and supervisors, they are unlikely to last long.

This system puts workers in a situation which all the elements of entrapment are present. As Liebow described, "The employer knowingly provides the conditions which entice (force) the employee to steal the unpaid value of his labor but at the same time he punishes him for theft if he catches him doing so"(Liebow 1967, 39). Many people who work in these sorts of jobs in Cuba often change jobs frequently and give little importance to trying to maintain them. As Liebow explains, to the person who:

> refuses such a job or quits it casually and without apparent reason, the objective fact is that menial jobs in retailing or in the service trades simply do not pay enough to support a man and his family, this is not to say that the worker is underpaid; this may or may not be true. Whether he is or not, the plain fact is that, in such a job, he cannot make a living. Nor can he take much comfort in the fact that these jobs tend to offer more regular, steadier work. He cannot live on the \$45 or \$50 he makes in one, the longer he works, the longer he cannot live on what he makes (Liebow 1967, 41).

In Cuba, the non-living wage offered in these positions, and the need to steal part of one's wage, often makes these sorts of positions temporary ones. As soon as something better comes up, or the work becomes too demeaning, people will drop these jobs. People often leave these positions when things get too hot. If one has "stole too much" they will leave the job before they get caught and move on to another position.

For professionals working in sectors of the economy that do not provide them with access to goods that can provide for their household's needs or be resold, the material motives for working for the state are less obvious. Some in the public health sector steal and resell syringes, cotton, and medicines, as mentioned by Marta, the teacher from Alamar. In the public health system it is also quite common for patients to give gifts to specialists who have provided high-quality care (Andaya 2009; Brotherton 2008). Before salaries in the health sector were raised in the summer of 2014, these gifts made up a significant part of doctors' incomes. More recently, I have heard an increasing number of cases in which the practice of appreciative gift giving after receiving good care described by Andaya has been replaced by outright bribes or payments in exchange to access to services that are limited, such as plastic surgery and fertility treatments.[8] Teachers have it much more difficult, they can only *resolver* notebooks and chalk, which do little to contribute to family meal planning and have very limited resale value. Depending on the school, relationships with the families of their students may provide social capital that can help the teacher *resolver*, but if the students' families have flat social networks which do not connect them with centers of power, the effectiveness of these connections for helping educators' household reproduction may be limited.

State workplaces also become sites for opportunities to exchange (Padrón Hernández 2012, 124). It is quite common to sell things to coworkers at the workplace. Rosa, a mother of two, who in in her 50s was helping raise her grandson, made chocolate Bonbons which she sold to a friend from college who added a peso each to the price and sold them out of her desk drawer to people at the office. One of her other clients was a US medical student in Cuba on scholarship who sold them to other students in her dorm. Their locations in state institutions with a steady flow of people gave them the customer base that Rosa, who did not work in an office, did not have access to.

Another person I interviewed who is in her late twenties, supplemented her salary of $515 Cuban pesos as a professor at a Havana medical school by selling clothes to coworkers. Before starting to work she had also sold clothes and other miscellaneous items to her classmates at the university. The clothes she sold at the medical school were sent to Cuba by the brother of the mother of a child that she tutored. The mother, who didn't work outside the home, gave her the clothes to sell. When they sold, she would pay the woman for the clothes and keep the margin that she added as her profit. Often, depending on her knowledge of the client, their circumstances and trustworthiness, she would accept partial payment from coworkers who would complete the payment on the next payday or over several weeks.

In her thesis, Padrón Hernández (2012) explains that in informal market transactions, trust is very important. Since the transactions are not legal, trust is important for both the sellers, who must trust the buyers to protect them from authorities, and the buyers, who must trust the sellers to sell them a good product and not cheat them. Between family members and close friends, this sort of trust exists, but social norms dictate that transactions between these close contacts should be disinterested ones and should take the form of a gift rather than a sale. In order to make money, sellers must look slightly further away, to friends of friends, neighbors, and coworkers. The social distances at state workplaces provide the "right balance of trust and social distance in order to conduct safe transactions that did not violate ideals of social obligations" (Padrón Hernández 2012, 124).

For many professionals, although their state-sector work does not provide salaries which cover even their most basic caloric needs, working for the state in their fields provides them with legitimacy and professional credentials which may help them obtain work on the side paid in CUCs. In the case of professionals in state sector professions that are high status but low paying (for example culture, research, education, and medicine), there are few opportunities for these workers to use their professional skills in the emerging sectors of the economy. At the same time, insertion in the state sector provides professional credibility and credentials, which sometimes can open opportunities for better remunerated work in their field in the non-state sector.

While directing a US study abroad program, I often contracted University of Havana professors or academics working at different research centers around the city to teach classes or give guest lectures for my students. I hired the professors based on their academic credentials and reputation in Cuban academia. While publishing widely in Cuban journals, participating in academic conferences and working for the Cuban University or research centers did not provide these individuals with salaries consistent with their experience, dedication, and expertise, it gave them the legitimacy and credentials needed to be hired by the US program, where they were paid in CUC for their work. Access to these opportunities depends on social networks as well. There is a relatively small nucleus of Cuban academics who, largely due to their language ability, have been able to take on these jobs. They are largely nearing retirement age, white, and come from families that were upper middle class before the Revolution. Many attended US schools in Havana before the Revolution, where they learned American English with near-native fluency. This group of academics are also frequently hired by large US "People to People" tour operators to give general talks on subjects like Cuban culture, women and gender in Cuba, LGBT issues in Cuba, Cuba's political system, US-Cuban relations, Afro-Cuban religion, and Cuban music, dance, and visual arts.

State-sector work may also open opportunities for economic growth through state-sponsored temporary labor migration. During the early years of the Special Period, health professionals were severely disadvantaged in their access to the dollar economy by the devaluation of professional salaries and policies to prevent brain drain, which prohibited them from legally working in the non-state sector or immigrating. Today, going on international missions allows health professionals to earn higher salaries working abroad without leaving their field (Andaya 2014, 2009; Blue 2010). As Andaya points out, the missions are "a form of lucrative and prestigious state-sanctioned remittance economy" (102). Through participation in international medical missions, health professionals have the opportunity to improve their family's economic situation, "while gaining experience and prestige in one's elected occupation" (Blue 2010, 45). From 1998–2008, around 185,000 Cubans participated in international medical missions, 37,000 in just 2008 alone (Erisman and Kirk 2009). In 2011, more than 41,000 Cuban health workers were working abroad in state-sponsored missions in sixty-eight nations (Kirk 2015, 251). Since Cuba's early international health missions in post-earthquake Chile (1960) and establishing a public health system in newly independent Algeria (1963), almost 130,000 Cuban health workers have served abroad (Kirk 2015, 252).

In 2003, a new cooperation agreement with the Venezuelan government traded Venezuelan oil for Cuban doctors. The deal provided primary health care to poor Venezuelans and new opportunities for Cuban doctors to use their hard earned cultural capital on international medical missions. The largest contingent of medical professionals working abroad at that time were in Venezuela (close to 30,000), 75 percent of all Cuban medical personnel working abroad (Romero 2010:110 cited in Kirk 2015:256). In Venezuela, Cuban professionals also trained 25,000 medical students from the region (Kirk 2015, 252–3). Nine medical schools to train doctors for underdeveloped or developing nations have been established in Venezuela, Cuba (Havana and Santiago), and as far away as the Southwest Pacific (Kirk 2015, 252–3).

As the country reorients towards policies increasingly made based on weighing economic factors rather than social or political goals, new formats for cooperation have emerged. Article 104 of the Guidelines signals the shift towards considering, "when possible, that at least the costs of the collaboration that Cuba offers be compensated" (Lineamientos 2010:16). In 2009, Cuba earned $11.171 billion through its exports of goods and professional services (Kirk 2015, 256). Reuters reported in 2010 that some $9.9 billion of this figure was from the export of medical services (Kirk 2015, 256).

Not all missions are created equally. Some missions offer workers higher salaries and more benefits than others. Andaya wrote in 2009 that doctors working abroad on government missions made $150–375 CUC per month and received a raise of $50 CUC per month upon returning to continue working in Cuba (Andaya 2009, 368). Sara Blue reported that at the time of her research, doctors working abroad on renewable two-year contracts received their regular salary plus a $50 CUC incentive (paid to their family in Cuba), plus $200 CUC a month placed in a savings account in Cuba that they receive when they return (Blue 2010, 35). Upon renewing the contract for a second two-year term, the incentive increases to $100 CUC a month (Blue 2010, 35). In the field, the health worker also receives a monthly stipend of $250-$375 a month to cover food and housing (Blue 2010, 35). Many international collaborators use this money in order to import consumer goods that are not available in Cuba.

In 2015, I spoke to a doctor who had just completed a two year mission in Venezuela. He earned a salary in Venezuela to cover his living expenses, his regular salary in Cuba plus $250 CUC a month. The $250 per month was divided into two bank accounts in Cuba. Half the money was paid to a "frozen" account that is only accessible after successfully completing the mission and returning to Cuba. The other half is paid to a Cuban debit card account that can be withdrawn while the collaborator is still on the mission. The collaborator can assign a portion of this money to be withdrawn by family in Cuba. He has decided to make $50 CUC of this money available each month to his mother in Cuba. She has the option of withdrawing $50 CUC in cash each month or making purchases with the debit card in state stores in Cuba where she receives a 30 percent discount. Many families of collaborators use the money on these cards to make purchases for others in the state stores. For example, with her $50 CUC of credit, the mother buys something for a neighbor in the store that costs $70 and the neighbor gives her cash. By using the purchase option, the credit the collaborator has earned stretches 30 percent further. Collaborators may also choose to save part of their living stipend, depositing it into the "frozen" account that is available to them when they return to Cuba after successfully completing the mission. If they are dismissed from the mission for a disciplinary issue, such as being identified as likely to defect, they lose all the money in this account.

Increasingly, these missions take Cuban doctors and health professionals to regions where Cuban doctors become the local public health infrastructure, and these positions are paid to the Cuban government at quite high rates. For example, there are 7,200 Cuban doctors currently working in Brazil through the program *Mais Médicos*. The program is funded by the Panamerican Health Organization (World Health Organization) and the Cuban state is paid $4,200 per month for each doctor. The doctor receives a monthly stipend of $400 CUC while working in Brazil, another $600 CUC is paid into a bank account in Cuba which they can access upon their return to Cuba.

Rather than hire local support staff abroad, the Cuban health missions often bring along their support staff. Sometimes, an opportune payment to the right person can result in cooks, warehouse administrators, lawyers, secretaries, and other support staff being offered one of these lucrative opportunities for state-sponsored temporary labor migration, which covers costs of travel, housing, and visas in addition to paying a salary much higher than similar positions earn on the island. Regardless of the differences between mission destinations, all missions abroad provide medical personnel and support staff the opportunity to earn relatively high salaries without having to abandon their field, but the social costs for Cuban families and Cuban patients can be high (Consuelo Martín Hernandez, Personal Communication December 16, 2015 (Cutiño 2015).

Andaya points out that often "gendered obligations on the homefront" limit female professionals' ability to take advantage of these opportunities

(Andaya 2014, 103). Many women find it challenging to arrange for care for their children and elderly parents in order to go abroad, while male health professionals can often count on multiple generations of female family members to provide care for family members left behind. Padrón Hernández also introduces us to a single mother who went on an international mission as a doctor and was able to go on the mission because her mother was able to take care of her daughter while she was abroad (2012:115).

Since the state removed restrictions on travel by health sector workers, it has become increasingly common for health workers to arrange their own temporary work contracts abroad rather than join state sponsored missions. In 2015, I met two young doctors, through completely different social networks, with five and ten years of experience respectively, who moved to different regions of China for work contracts that they arranged themselves. Both ended up working in private clinics that serve expatriate business people and their families in large Chinese industrial cities.

Despite their low Cuban peso salaries, the status associated with their work and their possession of high volumes of cultural capital is an advantage to Cuban doctors working on the island in the "favor economy" described by anthropologist, Sean Brotherton (2008). Although the low salaries of health professionals in Cuba put them at a disadvantage in the dual economy, patients often provide them with favors and in-kind gifts to show their gratefulness in recognition of the structure of the dual economy which undervalues doctors' socially important professional work (Andaya 2009). When I lived in Cuba in 2008–2009, I often saw patients discreetly offer doctors small gifts, products sold in CUC, such as shampoo, deodorant, razor blades, sandwiches, and sodas. These gifts were not demanded by the doctors, or seen as payment for services rendered but, as one friend explained to me, they were important gestures of solidarity and appreciation for the professional who continues to serve the community despite the economic difficulties that such dedication is known to occasion the individual and his or her family. Despite their low wages, doctors working in Cuba have access to significant social capital through their wide networks of patients and can call on these ties to *resolver*.

After graduation, university graduates in Cuba are required to perform three years of post-graduate training [*adiestramiento*] or social service in their field. If they do not complete this requirement, their diploma is invalidated.[9] Since college graduates are required to work for the state during this time and cannot quit without risking losing their degree, they often take advantage of this time to make plans to move to a better job at the end of the term. This may mean applying for scholarships for master's and PhD programs abroad, or moving into similar positions in foreign companies located in Cuba. Others decide to leave their fields completely after completing their social service and move into private employment as soon as completing their obligations with the state. De-professionalization [*desprofesionalización*] is extremely common in urban Cuba since the 1990s (Martín Fernández 1996, 96). Since the process of restructuring personnel began, many young people who wish to continue working for the state after completing their social service have found it difficult to find permanent positions once their period as trainees [*adiestrados*] expires.

For young Cuban professionals working in the state sector, connections with Cuban institutions help facilitate access to scholarships to study masters' and PhD programs abroad. Some young people use these scholarships as an opportunity to immigrate, with the advantage of being able to integrate themselves into the new host society as professionals rather than as working class immigrants. Others take advantage of their time abroad to save money and return to Cuba with capital that will allow them to improve their living conditions in Havana by remodeling the family's home, buying an independent apartment, or using the money to invest in the small business.

Although salaries are extremely low, some state workplaces provide other nonmonetary benefits which many employees consider important. Access to the internet or email allows individuals to research opportunities for professional development in Cuba and abroad. It also helps them maintain contact with family and friends abroad. I know several computer programmers who continue at state jobs to guarantee free access to the internet. With contacts made online, or through friends living in other countries, they are able to telecommute and take on programming jobs, such as developing smart phone applications.

I also know college graduates from diverse fields who take on translation or copy editing projects with clients abroad via email. Internet connectivity provided by their state workplace makes these side jobs possible. So, in the balance, they explained, although their day job doesn't pay well, the position does provide them with internet access as well as time and flexibility, which allows them to take on side jobs that are well-paying. One copy editor explained to me that, if she had to pay for the internet access that she used, her margins would be much lower. At the time, internet access was only available through pre-paid cards sold by the Cuban telephone company, which costs $4.50 CUC an hour, or through Wi-Fi in hotel lobbies, which ranged from $6 and $12 CUC an hour.

CONCLUSION

For families in Havana, work in multiple economic spaces is an important part of households' strategies to guarantee the resources necessary for social reproduction during the second wave of de-statization of Cuban society in the revolutionary period. This second stage of re-privatization of social re-production has come accompanied by a change in state discourse about the role of the individual and discourses of personal responsibility that, as Wilson (2014) observes, eerily mimics discourses that accompanied Welfare Reform in the US and other nations in the 1990s (112). As state discourses toward the emerging private sector have shifted, individuals and their households are beginning to feel more comfortable with experimenting with previously stigmatized economic spaces.

In this chapter I have shown how households in Havana weigh the advantages and disadvantages of their participation in the state sector and previously stigmatized non-state spaces to make decisions about their insertion in the labor force. My interviews with workers of various generations showed that the historical stigmas associated with not working in the state sector continue to be strong, and many workers prefer to maintain jobs in both sectors, at least until retirement helps them give themselves permission to "drop out."

NOTES

1. At the time they were active, the microbrigades were mentioned in Cuban films by Julio García Espinosa "*La vivienda*" (1959), Nicolás Guillén Landrián "*Para construir una casa*" (1972), Sara Gómez "*De cierta manera*" (1974). More recently, in 2013, the microbrigades were the subject of a 31 minute experimental film "Microbrigades—Variations of a Story" which also was presented as an installation in ALTERNATIVA in Gdansk and at the 11th Havana Biennal as an installation called *MicroE111b* (Schmidt-Colinet, Schmoeger, and Zeyfang 2016, 195).

2. *Por la izquierda* literally means "On the left" and means under the table, or informally.

3. Cuban refrain: "Small town, large hell". In a small town there are no secrets, everyone knows everyone else's business and this can create gossip, ill will, and conflicts that make a small town hellish.

4. Carrie Hamilton (2012) describes the impact of the UMAPs on gay men (forty to forty-two). Juliette Fernández Estrada (2012) explains the impact of the camps on Protestant pastors and laypeople. Hernandez's article was published in *Catalejo, el blog de Temas* in December 2015. As Miller (2003) notes, "Anniversaries—which can be commemorated with official blessing—provide the most usual pretext for a discreet reassessment of the past" (2003, 157). The timing of the article, perhaps the first from within Cuba's academic establishment to write publicly about the UMAP suggests that the article was written around the anniversary of the opening of the UMAPs 40 years ago (November 1965).

5. A person who is *metalizado* is a person who is thinking about and motivated by money all the time, who gives more weight to economic considerations than emotional or spiritual ties or motivations.

6. Other verbs commonly used by Cubans to talk about provisioning practices and frequently commented on by anthropologists are *resolver, buscar, inventar, luchar, tener chispa, estar a la viva and ser avispado, jinetear* (Solberg 1996, 50; Pertierra 2011; Padrón Hernández 2012, 142; Weinreb 2009, 65; Rosendahl 1997, 43; Gordy 2006; Powell 2008, 182-7).) In the Soviet Union, the Russian word *dostal* had a similar meaning to the Cuban *conseguir* (Ledeneva 1998, 13).

7. In their study of labor and everyday life during the first wave of economic reforms in the 1990s, Cuban researchers define *"La búsqueda"* as "an umbrella term which includes a range of illicit activities from doing private jobs with the means and resources of your workplace to redirecting resources or products" (Martín Romero and Nicolau Cruz N.D., 42, note 19).

8. I have been told by multiple sources that couples who pay $1,000 CUC can get put on the waiting list to receive fertility treatments like in-vitro fertilization (IVF). While the couples who told me this believe that it may be possible to receive the services without such payments, they were frustrated that they could not afford to do so and assumed that those who pay will experience a different level of care, and be served much faster. Brotherton (2008) also reports that Cubans with CUC often gain access to medical services through "privatized informal sector, including backdoor access to a well-equipped *clínicas internacionales*, or get access to x-ray equipment from a *socio* at another hospital for a fee and return to the original state hospital with the x-rays that the specialist needs to diagnose the case" (Brotherton 2008, 267). Brotherton's research participants also preferred to pay physicians on the side for plastic surgery and experimental therapies (Brotherton 2008, 267). In chapter six of her dissertation, Padrón Hernández looks at the relationship between interest and affect in relationships between health professionals and patients and how intimacy and economy are negotiated in terms of intentions (Padrón Hernández 2012).

9. Both male and female university graduates must provide three years of service to the state as post-graduate trainees [*adiestrados*]. This service is paid, but at a rate lower than the regular salary. For males, the post-graduate trainee period is two years long because they perform a year of military service before beginning university. Females begin university directly after graduating from pre-university and perform three years social service in a post assigned to them as post-graduate trainees. For example, in 2011, a psychology graduate was paid $455 Cuban pesos during her three years of social service as a post-graduate trainee. After finishing her social service, she continued in the same workplace as a psychologist with a salary of $515 Cuban pesos.

Chapter Five

The Rebirth of Real Estate

Reproducing Class Inequalities in Havana

In this chapter, I explain how the re-creation of a real estate market in November 2011, in response to Guideline 297, has allowed the descendants of pre-revolutionary and revolutionary elites to use the capital in their homes to reestablish themselves at the top of an emerging socioeconomic hierarchy in Cuba. Since the first wave of economic restructuring in the mid-1990s, people with valuable properties had the option of turning their homes into sources of economic capital by renting out rooms in their homes to foreigners. Today, they can also sell extra properties outright.

These influxes of capital are changing the social landscape in Havana, serving as a motor for development, but also a motor for growing inequalities. In 2012, the average monthly wage was $466 Cuban pesos ($18.64 CUC), but families with valuable properties who have the option of downsizing can gain access to tens of thousands of dollars of capital to supplement low salaries and increase consumption to socially desired levels unattainable through state sector employment (ONEI 2013). Other families are selling to gain startup capital for new businesses, recently allowed under new regulations, or to fund migratory projects.

Those who can take advantage of these new opportunities, the inhabitants of Havana's most valuable properties, are largely members of Cuba's two historical ruling classes: the children and grandchildren of pre-revolutionary elites who remained in Cuba after the Revolution, and the descendants of revolutionary leaders. Many revolutionary leaders were originally from Eastern Cuba, and when they moved to Havana they were given the abandoned properties of the pre-revolutionary elites. Today, both groups are using the capital in their newly re-commodified homes to successfully reestablish themselves at the top of an emerging social-economic hierarchy in Cuba. The re-commodification of housing has contributed to reproducing pre-revolutionary class structures that

125

were temporarily disrupted from the 1960s to 1980s when widespread access to opportunities for education and technical training and stable employment made social mobility possible for the majority of Cubans. The changes which took place in Cuba during the economic crisis of the 1990s put an end to this period of social mobility through education, once again reconfiguring Cuban social structure and laying the groundwork for a new system of social stratification in Cuba.

In addition to reproducing pre-revolutionary class privilege and pre-revolutionary racial inequalities, the way in which the housing market has been reestablished may demonstrate an ideological shift as the state begins to limit its role in the economy. The General Housing Laws of 1984 and 1988 permitted sales between private individuals on the condition that the state would retain the right of first refusal. However, in practice, resolutions at a lower level nullified this provision. A 2003 law decree eliminated this option completely (Herrera Linares, 2012:30). After decades of complicated regulations and oversight in the area of housing law (the *Permuta* system) to avoid the concentration of wealth and prevent profiteering from illegal sales, the November 2011 Law Decree 288 established new procedures for direct sales between private individuals. This new policy direction signals a fundamental ideological change from the idea of housing as a right to housing as a commodity to be exchanged at market-determined prices.

In May 2017, the state, worried about widespread tax evasion in real estate transactions, made changes in the tax code. With this measure, the state has further recognized the nature of housing as a valuable commodity in contemporary Cuba by defending its ability to profit from these transactions through taxation. It is too early to know how buyers and sellers will react to the new regulations, or what impact the 2017 tax code revisions will have on the housing market and the economic inequalities that have accompanied its re-creation.

THE REBIRTH OF "REAL ESTATE": IDEOLOGICAL SHIFTS IN 2011 HOUSING REFORM

In November 2011, Cuba's General Housing Law was modified to legalize the buying and selling of private property between individuals, reestablishing a real estate market in Cuba. Law Decree 288 responded to Guidelines 273–8 (Partido Comunista de Cuba, 2011:31). In January 2014, the state took a step further by announcing that Cubans could hire state real estate companies to manage their properties, paying the company a 5 percent tax. The measure further legitimized the ability for Cubans to retain properties that they do not need for housing, but to use as sources of income.

Legalizing these sales was a wildly popular move in Havana. Buying and selling is perceived by most homeowners as much less complicated than the previous procedure, the *permuta*, housing swap, which often formed extremely long and complicated chains as described in the early 1980s Cuban comedy, *"Se Permuta"* (Tabío, 1984). Transforming housing from a social good to a commodity legally exchanged on the free market, resulted in transforming *some* Cuban homes into legitimate sources of wealth and capital for the first time in half a century. To understand how recent reforms have reproduced pre-revolutionary privilege, it is necessary to understand the recent history of housing policy in Cuba.

EDUCATION AND SOCIAL
MOBILITY FROM THE 1960s–1990s

The early years of the revolution, from 1959–1975, were characterized by radical upheavals in Cuban society. In the name of eliminating inequalities, new laws expanded state control over the means of production and limited private property. Havana's "urban capitalist class" was targeted, as a series of laws slashed the profits of landlords, lenders, and developers, effectively dismantling the real estate market. In January, Law 26 immediately halted eviction processes (Herrera Linares, 2013:8). In February, Law 86 created the National Housing Institute (INAV) to organize the construction of affordable housing and to offer low-interest mortgage loans as an alternative to commercial lenders (Herrera Linares, 2013:8). In March, Law 135 reduced urban rents by 50–30 percent (Ley N°. 135, March 10, 1959). Rents of less than 100 pesos were reduced by 50 percent, rents between 100–200 pesos were reduced by 40 percent and rents of more than 200 pesos were reduced by 30 percent (Herrera Linares, 2013:8). On October 14, 1960, Cuba's Urban Reform Law nationalized all existing rental housing. The state allowed families with multiple properties to keep one in the city and one in a vacation area, and everything else was nationalized. The state indemnified landlords and a newly-formed Urban Reform agency began to collect rents, applying them towards the purchase of the dwelling after five to twenty years (Vega Vega, 2000:44). As a result of these new policies, the state quickly controlled 70 percent of vacant land in Havana (Núñez, 2012: 72).

From 1959–1962, 354,963 Cubans emigrated, many members of Cuba's urban upper and middle class (Domínguez, 1992:34). Law 989 of 1961 established that all émigrés properties would be nationalized (Herrera Linares, 2013:27–8). Large properties became health clinics, schools, embassies, offices, or homes for high ranking officials (Lewis 1978). More modest homes were redistributed to families in need of housing. Often when word got out about the empty dwelling, squatters would establish residency and most squatters were eventually granted legal rights.

New opportunities for education and training in the 1960s–1970s made widespread upward mobility possible. As elites left the country, the subsequent brain drain was filled by professionals of diverse backgrounds newly trained by the Revolution. Cubans of humble origins climbed occupational hierarchies, but housing construction in Havana did not keep up with Cuba's post-1959 baby boom, nor with high rates of migration from the countryside (Hamberg, 2011:84). Havana's population grew rapidly, and between 1953–1970, the city reported an average annual population growth rate of 2.1 percent (Bobes, 2011:23, Montes Rodriguez, 2007). By the 1970s, the housing shortage was acute (Bobes, 2011).

To address the growing need for housing while providing full employment, the state formed the "microbrigades." In all sectors of the economy, workers were temporarily released from their regular responsibilities to join construction brigades to build housing for themselves and their coworkers. In the 1970s, the modernist revolutionary project sought technological solutions to this pressing social problem. Prefabricated solutions from Eastern Europe, originally designed to meet the urgent need for housing after the Second World War, were adopted (De las Cuevas Toraya, 2001: 319–21). Alamar is the epitome of this type of construction. Built between 1970–90, Alamar is the largest housing settlement in Cuban history, housing 100,000 inhabitants (5 percent of the population of the city of Havana) in five and twelve story prefabricated buildings built by microbrigades (Coyula, 2009:43). These construction projects benefited average Cubans who were neither Pre-Revolutionary elites, nor had important leadership positions in the Revolution's hierarchy.

Although the state never succeeded in building enough housing in Havana to meet demand, it was extremely successful in turning occupants into owners. By 1972, 75 percent of homes in Cuba were owned by their inhabitants and another 18 percent paid minimal rents for usufruct rights (Rodríguez y Carriazo, 1983:147 cited in Rodríguez Ruiz, 2011:76). Between 1970–1981, only 167,024 new housing units were built in Cuba, almost entirely by the state, but the majority of resources went to rural areas (De las Cuevas Toraya, 2001: 315–16).

Until recent years, individuals had few opportunities to improve their homes or engage in self-construction. Self-construction was difficult for many reasons. First of all, materials were not available for sale, as the state prioritized materials for building educational facilities, hospitals, sports stadiums, and social infrastructure to meet collective social needs, not individual domestic ones. Since materials couldn't be bought legally, many people did so illegally. Secondly, permitting processes did not exist, and in their absence it was "illegal" to undertake self-construction (Hamberg 2011:95).

Although access to education led to occupational mobility, the state's failure to resolve the lack of housing in the city of Havana, by constructing a sufficient supply of quality housing, or allowing people to build their own dwellings, means that today many highly educated professionals live in the same substandard housing that their grandparents inhabited generations before. Housing largely reflects the class status of one's parents and grandparents rather than one's own place in the social and occupational hierarchies.

"SE PERMUTA": HOUSING MOBILITY FROM 1980s–2010

Until 2011, the little mobility that happened took place through an administrative procedure called "*Permuta*," regulated by Municipal Housing Offices, in which property owners or individuals with usufruct rights could trade dwellings. Between 2005 and 2006, around 15,000 units changed hands through *permuta* housing swaps, representing about 3 percent of the total housing stock in Havana (Núñez, 2012:107).

According to Núñez (2012), in the early years of the Revolution, from 1960–1970, housing swaps were relatively simple, rarely included financial motives, and were used to move into housing which more closely met the households' needs (96). Between 1970–1989 it became more common to see trades between households in traditionally upper-class neighborhoods, with insufficient income to sustain their desired level of consumption, swap with households with disposable income and "less valuable" properties, such as apartments in newly constructed microbrigades on urban peripheries (Núñez, 2012: 96).

Cubans found out about opportunities for housing exchanges through announcements published in local print media and in a special section on the radio. In the early 1960s, *permuta* advertisements were published in *El Mundo* newspaper. In the 1980s, *Opina* magazine was a popular source for finding out about opportunities for housing swaps (Domínguez Hernández and Saínz Padrón, 2011). Analyzing *Opina* magazine advertisements in the 1980s, Núñez (2012) found a "significant number of inhabitants wishing to move from new development areas to the downtown and high income residential areas. Although there are no references to values or compensation, the last lines usually include a short, but very powerful sentence, saying "*propositions heard*" (102–104).

As early as the mid-1980s people in Havana were selling their homes, although it was not yet possible to do so legally. By 1986, it had become common for farmers who had amassed wealth through "free market" sales to buy homes in Havana (Castro Ruz, 1986). In the opening monologue of the 2012

Cuban film *"Se Vende"* [For Sale], Nácar, a Cuban woman in her early 40s, tells the story of how her family, solidly middle class before the Revolution, used their properties to maintain their lifestyle:

> My mother had been an expert in the art of survival. I was born in 1970. I had a pretty comfortable childhood because my mother sold the beach house that belonged to my grandparents who left the country, and with that money we got through the "Great Decade," or the *grey quinquennium*, depending on who's telling the story. Afterwards came the 80s and my mother convinced my father to exchange the jewels that we had inherited from the family for cash in the famous "House of Gold and Silver," and with that money we kept going, plus the salaries, which more or less were enough to live on back then, when we were happy and didn't know it. The 90s were hard for us. Everything was upside down and not because of Perestroika, but because my father, who is the most communist of all of us, couldn't take it anymore and he died of a heart attack...Going back to the 90s and the so-called "Special Period," which wasn't special at all. My mother swapped our house in Vedado for the apartment in Old Havana. With the money they gave us we were able to hold on until the end of the century...In 2001, with nothing left to sell, my mother checked out against her will. She always said that she wasn't going to die until she saw the end of the movie (Perugorría Rodríguez, 2013).

From 1990–1994, with the start of the Special Period economic crisis, swaps were increasingly motivated by economic needs (Núñez, 2012: 97). Until the legalization of the dollar in 1994, uneven swaps were most often compensated by "payment" in material goods unavailable for purchase at the height of the economic crisis (Núñez, 2012: 97). Many families liquidated whatever assets they had in order to buy food. Valuables, artwork, antiques and properties started to be concentrated in the hands of the new elite who got hard currency through remittances, illegal work or trade in the informal sector, working in tourism, and other priority sectors of the economy in which hard currency bonuses were given in addition to low state salaries.

After the legalization of the dollar in 1994, compensation for unequal trades was increasingly offered in cash (US dollars) under the table (Núñez, 2012). State policy aimed to keep people from profiting off of real estate transactions to prevent concentrations of wealth, in keeping with state ideology that housing was a right, not a commodity. As compensated swaps became more common in the 1990s, the state began to introduce increasingly complicated regulatory procedures to prevent these illegal sales. The state modified housing laws to increase regulation of housing donations and *permuta* transfers to prevent speculation and profiteering.

Real estate speculation became increasingly common in the 1990s, due to the combination of high liquidity in the hands of some parts of the Cuban population and high prices for scarce basic goods (Herrera Linares, 2013:13). Responding to this new reality, the state attempted in July of 2000 to control underground sales and stem the tide of illegal housing construction. Another measure, Law Decree 211, sought to prevent the conspicuous consumption of Cuba's nouveau riche by limiting the dimensions of construction licenses based on the size of the family that would occupy the house. The same month, Law Decree 218 established a tax on the transmission of properties through inheritance and *permuta*. In July of 2003, Law Decree 233–2 increased administrative control of *permutas* to prevent illegalities.

Despite the multiple bureaucratic barriers put in place to prevent unequal trades, they were extremely common. Rather than stemming the tide of illegalities and speculation, these regulations became onerous barriers for most Cuban families. Rich Cubans were able to make the system work by bribing their way through the increasingly complicated *permuta* process, while families simply interested in swapping to meet changing lifestyle needs (moving closer to work or to relatives needing care, less bedrooms after younger family members leave the country or leave the nest, or more bedrooms for a growing family, ground-floor apartments for those who can no longer handle stairs, etc.) were the least able to overcome the new barriers. It was common to hear Cubans complain, "How can it be that the house is mine? I have the title to it, but I can't do what I want with it? If I can't do what I want with it then it's not really mine!"

WHO BENEFITS?

For homeowners of valuable properties that formerly housed Havana's elite and upper middle classes, today it is easier than ever to get a rental license or sell an unoccupied or underutilized property to have access to capital. This economic capital can be used to make productive investments in new businesses, to increase consumption to a socially desired level unattainable through state sector employment, or to travel abroad or immigrate. The children and grandchildren of pre-revolutionary and revolutionary elites are using the capital in their homes to successfully reestablish themselves at the top of an emerging social-economic hierarchy in Cuba. As the exchange-value of housing becomes more important than its use value, owners of microbrigade apartments in Alamar are finding that, while the Revolution may have provided them with housing, they cannot turn their home into capital to take advantage of new opportunities in the emerging economy. Such opportunities are limited to those with valuable properties, usually tied to elite status before or after the Revolution. Microbrigade apartments, like those built in Alamar, are valued poorly in the new housing market. As a measure of quality, online advertisements often take care to specify that they are *not* microbrigade constructions.

Cuban families have shrunk over the last decades due to lower birth rates, and, in the midst of a housing shortage, some families find themselves with surplus properties. As older generations are aging, moving in with adult children or passing away, their properties are being handed down to their children, grandchildren or others in the extended family. For example, a couple born in the Cuban baby boom of the early 1960s, both from pre-revolutionary elite families, were likely to have one to two children, born in the 1980s. As they start to couple in the 2000s, there are four sets of aging grandparents within the family network whose properties they stand to inherit.

In the absence of sufficient state production of new housing stock for newly forming families, the grandchildren of elites have a great advantage over their peers. First of all, they can dream of having their own home, something impossible for young people with fewer properties in their family network. Secondly, they have the option of selling properties that they inherit and using this capital for other projects which require extremely large initial investments. Projects like starting a business in Cuba or studying or working abroad, that were previously impossible without money from outside of Cuba, can now be achieved through selling property. It is now even possible to inherit a property, sell it off legally, and inherit again from another family member. Before the current changes, when older members of the network left Cuba definitively to join adult children living abroad, their properties had to be turned over to the state. Now, an elderly Cuban leaving Cuba to be cared for by adult children abroad has the option of selling the property first and taking that money with them or donating the property to an extended family member. The property, or the capital from selling it, now stays in the family.

WHO IS BUYING? WHO IS SELLING?

Today's seemingly simple sales are long chains, which begin when transnational social networks bring foreign capital to Cuba or when Cubans living on the island invest in real estate to hide ill-gotten gains. Cuban banks offer no mortgages to finance sales between private individuals, so buyers must pay for the property in full at the time of the purchase. For anything to happen *somebody* has to have money, and, in Cuba, the opportunities for legally earning the 12,000 CUC to one million CUC to buy a new home in cash are close to non-existent. In 2012, the state-published average monthly wage in Cuba was $466 Cuban pesos ($18.64 CUC) (ONEI 2013) At this level of earnings, unless they have other sources of income, the average Cuban living on the island can only buy a house after receiving the money from having sold their own house.

From 2012–2013, I observed three segments of the Havana real estate market. The top segment is composed of foreigners or mixed-nationality couples buying into the market, who buy from Cubans on the island interested in "downsizing," in order to convert some of the value of their properties into cash. By 2015, this segment also began to include Cubans on the island with funds saved from work abroad or legal work with transnational companies. The second segment of the market is composed of Cubans on the island who have sold and use a portion of that money to buy a less valuable home. The third segment of the market is composed of "normal" Cubans without transnational income sources who do not have property and are looking to buy into the market. This group includes young couples hoping to move out of their parents' or in-laws' house and people from the provinces looking for a permanent legal address in the capital. The $2,000–5,000 CUC price range that these buyers can afford gives them extremely limited options in marginal spaces in the city's distant peripheries. They are the buyers most in need of housing for its use value rather than as a commodity, and the new real estate system does nothing to improve their chances of finding suitable housing. They are largely unconnected to the chain I will describe below.

Havana's new housing market is set in motion by money coming from abroad or illicit money from within Cuba. Cubans on the island reducing or selling extra properties for economic motives are well served by the form the market has taken, but Cubans on the island whose primary motives for moving are non-monetary, such as seeking an age-appropriate dwelling for aging family members (moving to lower floors or a building with an elevator or moving closer to other family members), or looking to move out of a home they are unable to maintain before it collapses on them, are disadvantaged in this new market if they do not have a place to move to in the time between when their house is sold and when they are able to buy a new one.

According to my research, most sales take place between mixed foreign-Cuban couples buying and Cubans on the island reducing. The chain begins as foreign-Cuban partnerships snatch up the big valuable properties, often in the desirable coastal areas of Vedado and Playa, setting off a chain reaction providing the Cuban sellers with the capital to move down to smaller dwellings, often in the same neighborhood. One Saturday in June on the Prado, the Central Havana promenade where buyers, sellers, and intermediaries (known as "*corredores*," a term which has negative connotations) gather in an open-air real estate market, I talked to a *corredor* who told me that it was already quite hard to find one bedroom apartments in Vedado, because lots of the people who have sold large houses in Vedado now want to buy one bedroom apartments in Vedado, in order to stay in the same neighborhood (2013, personal communication). As this happens, the people who sold their one bedroom apartments in Vedado and other central areas of the city are pushed further south and further inland to maintain a similar quality of construction, contributing to a territorial economic re-stratification in Havana.

NEW VALUES, NEW CAPITAL:
STRAIGHT TO PRIVATE HANDS

In addition to turning some homes into sources of economic capital, the way in which the housing market was reestablished demonstrates an ideological shift in Cuba towards a smaller role of the state in guaranteeing equal social and economic outcomes. After decades of complicated regulations and oversight to prevent homeowners from profiting from housing transactions and prevent the concentration of wealth, the state seemed to have given up its regulatory role. For the first five years of the new housing sales, the state seemed to prefer to benefit indirectly from the foreign capital entering the country through transnational social networks to buy property which releases capital to be invested in family businesses or everyday consumption.

In the 2011 law, taxes on property sales were set at 4 percent of the legal value and these modest taxes on real estate transactions were commonly avoided. From November 2011 to May 2017, the taxes on real estate transactions were based on the legal assessed value of the property stated on the deed. The prices on the deeds were calculated based on formulas established before the economic crisis of the 1990s which privileged the buying power of state salaries over real construction costs in order to make housing prices affordable (Núñez, 2012). In reality, market prices were negotiated between buyers and sellers. During the first five years of the housing market, buyers and sellers took advantage of the assessed values, which are ridiculously low in the current post-1990s economy, to avoid taxation. As a result, these new real estate transactions were barely being taxed by the state.

In a speech to the National Assembly in June of 2013, Marino Murillo Jorge, chairman of the Implementation Committee for the Guidelines of Economic and Social Policy, mentioned that the state was aware that sale prices are commonly sub-declared in legal documents to avoid taxes. However, it wasn't until almost four years later, on April 11, 2017, that the state published Law Decree 343, which had been approved by the Council of State in December 2016, and accompanying regulations (March 23, 2017) by the Ministry of Finances and Prices to change the system of taxation on real estate transactions.

Law Decree 343 modified articles 44 and 203 of the 2012 Tax Code Law (Law 113). It established that the value of the property upon which the tax is levied would be the declared sale price, or a referential value, whichever is higher. The law decree gave the Ministry of Finance and Prices the responsibility to establish, and update as necessary, referential values and the corresponding minimum taxes for different types of properties in five different tax zones across the county.

Tables were published in Cuba's legal Gazette by the Ministry of Finances and Prices on April 11, 2017 which established base referential values for properties located in five regions: 1) housing located in special economic development zones, 2) in the Havana municipalities of Playa, Plaza de la Revolución, La Habana Vieja, and in the towns of Trinidad and Cárdenas/ Varadero, which are located in a Zone of Importance for Tourism, 3) the Havana municipalities of Cerro, Centro Habana, Diez de Octubre and the coastal area of Guanabo in the municipality of La Habana del Este, 4) the remaining Havana municipalities of Guanabacoa, Regla, Marianao, La Habana del Este (except Guanabo), San Miguel del Padrón, Cotorro, La Lisa, Arroyo Naranjo and Boyeros, and all provincial capitals, 5) the remaining municipalities of the country.

The new base referential values for properties in Havana range from $471,000 CUP—$24,000 CUP ($18,840–$960 CUC). These values take into account factors like the type of construction (single family home or apartment), quality of construction (as referenced by roofing materials and wall materials), and number of bedrooms (1, 2, 3, and 4 or more). Supplements are added to each type of property if it has private garage or parking space in a collective garage, or a front or backyard mentioned in the deed. These measures went into effect in May 2017, thirty days after being published in the Gazette.

MARKET VALUE?

In December 2012 and January 2013, I had the opportunity to observe two real estate transactions in Havana from beginning to end. Data from interviews with other buyers and sellers and expert interviews confirm that what I observed is representative of how these transactions took place during the period after sales were legalized and before the 2017 modification of the tax code. The first property, a one-bedroom apartment in Centro Habana, close to the University of Havana, listed for $15,000 CUC on the online classifieds (Revolico.com) legally sold for its state-assessed value of $4,000 Cuban pesos. The second, a two-bedroom apartment in Vedado, sold for $38,000 CUC, but on paper went for its state-assessed value of $6,000 Cuban pesos.

The 2011 law stated that sale prices are to be set by agreement between the buyer and seller, and set the minimum sale price at the assessed value. The system of state-assessed property values is based on state-sector salaries in the 1980s, guaranteeing that even the most expensive dwellings would be affordable for the average Cuban worker (Núñez, 2012). It is easy to do a study of asking prices based on online listings on websites such as Revolico.com and Cubisima.com, but getting a handle on actual sale prices is much more complicated, as no official published sources exist. Given the widespread distrust of the state, it is extremely rare to declare the real sale prices on official documents. The actual prices being paid today are based on market factors, limited only by what the highly-transnational market will bear. The gap between assessed prices and the prices being paid for homes in the market is significant. New regimes of value are applied in these sales which make the process through which the state had previously determined housing values irrelevant in determining actual practice.

In both of the cases that I studied, the buyer/seller dyads chose to declare only the minimum state-assessed value of the property, rather than the actual amount of money that changed hands. They each made this decision based on advice from family and friends, and even lawyers and other employees of the notary offices which handle the sales. I have yet to meet a person involved in these transactions who claims to have declared the actual transaction price. So, in the case of the first sale, instead of paying 4 percent of the $15,000 CUC actually exchanged for the property, both parties paid 4 percent on the assessed value of $6,000 Cuban pesos or $240 Cuban pesos ($9.60 CUC) each. If the parties had declared the real value of the transaction, they would have each paid $600 CUC in taxes.

Although the state tries to convince buyers and sellers that it is in their best interest to declare the real value of the property, it appears that most people are not convinced. For the buyer, there does indeed seem to be a clear advantage to declaring the real transaction price. Even if they have to pay 4 percent tax, in this case $600 CUC, if something happened later down the line that reverted the sale, they would have a way to reclaim the money they paid. However, chapter II (articles 161–68) of the 2011 law establishes a property tax of 2 percent based on the purchase price listed in the title of the home (article 166). At the time of my research, there was speculation that, although the state had not implemented the property tax, it could be implemented at any time. Buyers who were considering declaring the true transaction value of the property for their own peace of mind feared that they might later come to regret doing so, as in the future their property tax would be assessed on the CUC transaction price rather than the Cuban peso assessed value of the house.

According to the government discourse, declaring the real value of the property is also advantageous for the seller, who is able to legally justify the licit source of their income. However, the most common uses for this income, downsizing to a smaller home, paying expenses for international travel or spending money abroad, buying construction materials, hiring contracted workers, increasing household consumption, or investing in new startup ventures, do not require showing the source of income.

Most dyads do, however, recognize a clear financial advantage for both parties in *not* declaring the real price. The negotiation of whether the real transaction price should be declared is a delicate one that depends on the trust of both parties and their interests. Generally, both parties recognize that declaring the real transaction price is a greater advantage to the buyer than it is to the seller. Usually the formal paperwork will reflect the official state assessed price unless the buyer prefers to declare the real transaction price and assumes payment of both parties' taxes. It is believed that the seller should not be expected to carry the tax burden of declaring the real price, a move which ostensibly only benefits the buyer. Some sellers prefer not to declare the actual price of sale as they would prefer there not be a record of the income they received for the sale: either because they plan on cheating the buyer, or because they simply don't trust the government. Beyond simply wishing to avoid paying taxes, they also fear that if there is proof that they have received such a large income, it will somehow be taken away from them, or they might be forced to later provide documentation of what they spent it on.

This of course means that buyers are faced with the choice of whether or not to declare the real sale price and the supposed advantages that it will afford them. In making this decision, the buyer must evaluate a situation fraught with uncertainty. They must weigh the multiple risks in the situation: If they pay the seller under the table, what risk is there that they might be cheated and left with no recourse for complaint? Without legal recourse, do they have access to informal means to fix the problem, and are they willing to use them? What risk is there that, if they declare the real price, they may be stuck with high property taxes in the future?

For the seller, what risk might it pose to declare the true income they are receiving for the sale? How are they planning on spending the money from the sale? Do they need to be able to legally justify its licit source or do they prefer to avoid a situation in which they might, in the future, be called upon to justify how each penny was spent? By deciding what value to declare for the sale, the buyer and seller must make a decision based on incomplete information about the potential risks and future implications of the decision. In the end, they have to decide who they trust more: the state or the person with whom they are undertaking the transaction.

In the case of the two sales I observed directly, and in others which I have learned about in my fieldwork and interviews, it appears to be common practice that the bulk of the payment is made in cash and only a small sum close to the official assessed value is declared. This practice follows the long standing practice of informality in real estate transactions, despite new laws which provide a legal structure for such exchanges. The fictitious property prices mean that, for the first five years of sales, these real estate transactions were barely being taxed by the state.

In 2017, the tax code was changed to bring the process into closer alignment with the real sale values of properties and strengthen the mechanisms to fight tax evasion. This change will likely not be popular with those who will now pay higher taxes on real estate transactions, but it is too early to know what the full impacts of the new policy will be. The new referential values are still lower than the real prices being paid for properties today. Will the state take further measures in the future to regulate these transactions or to prevent real estate speculation? Will the population resent having to pay these higher taxes, or appreciate the state taking action to tax and redistribute wealth with the goal of building a more just and equal society? The answer likely depends on who you ask, and how much they believe that the state is effective in not only taxing, but using this new income stream in transparent ways.

CONCLUSION

Despite 56 years of socialist revolution, recent reforms have highlighted the advantage that the children and grandchildren of pre-revolutionary elites maintain in access to economically valuable and socially-desirable housing. As a result, these groups have access to opportunities for economic mobility not available to the descendants of the pre-revolutionary working classes, who acquired their homes through revolutionary reforms or socialist construction projects which have little value in the new real estate market.

The problems with overcrowding and crumbling homes in Havana are unlikely to be ameliorated by the creation of a new housing market. Rather than contributing to solving the serious housing problems experienced by Cuban families, the re-creation of a housing market has attracted hard currency investments from outside the island. Cubans abroad bring in capital, buying properties either to live in themselves in the future or to improve living conditions of their relatives on the island. Increasingly, after the normalization process began in 2014, the boom in individual travelers from the US has intensified the Airbnbification of central areas of the city like Old Havana and Vedado. These injections of hard currency to buy properties are later recycled through private hands and serve as start-up funds for small businesses, to increase levels of consumption necessary to provide a customer base for new enterprises, or to fund temporary labor migrations.

In May 2017, the state changed the tax code after five years of losing tax revenue due to an unrealistic and outdated assessment structure. This action seems to show that the state is aware of the tax evasion and interested in establishing control to increase contributions to the state budget from these transactions. Will these new higher taxes be sufficient to counteract the way in which the new housing market is reproducing generational privilege? It remains to be seen what use the state will give to this growing stream of tax revenue and how the state's new intervention will be seen, both those paying the taxes and those excluded from the market due to historic disadvantage.

Epilogue

New Social Groups in Havana, 2015–2016

In many ways, the social structure in Havana in 2016 still looks a lot like the society described by interviewees in chapter three. However there are new social subjects in Havana that have emerged as a result of modifications in state policies in Cuba and abroad that were not visible in Cuban society in 2012 when I did the original interviews. In this chapter, I look at contemporary Havana and how the social structure of Cuba's "Post-Soviet normal" described in chapter three has been modified by the changes in state policy from 2011–today. Using participant observation and interview data from 2015–16, I will describe three new social groups that have gained importance in Havana as a result of recent policy changes: circular migrants, employers and employees, and (satisfied) consumer-citizens.

EMPLOYERS AND EMPLOYEES

When self-employment began in the 1990s, it was true self-employment, but in 2016, the term *trabajador por cuenta propia* or *self-employed worker* is becoming increasingly inaccurate to describe those employed in the non-state sector. There are large internal differences within the sector, between those self-employed workers engaged in survival (ambulatory peanut and newspaper vendors, manicurists, domestic workers, telecommunications agents), true self-employed workers, and small business owners and their salaried workers (Hernández 2013).

An important new divide is rapidly growing within the non-state sector into groups of individuals who employ others in their small private businesses, and those who are employed by other "self-employed workers": in other words, employers and employees. Comparing tax office (ONAT) statistics from 2011 and 2014, the CIPS Social Structure Research Group found that, in 2011, only 10 percent of licensed TCPers were salaried employees. By 2014 salaried employees represented 20 percent of the total "self-employed" population (Social Structure Research Group Results, PPT, slide fifteen, CIEE IFDS Course, June 2015).

The growing diversity of roles within the private sector was made possible by changes in domestic policy to stimulate small business development that allows for the hiring of employees, first in 87 license categories, and later in all of them. These policy changes brought people who were working informally in small businesses into the taxable economy and included them in Cuba's Social Security system. Self-employed workers, as well as workers employed by others in the non-state sector, are now covered by social security and are required to pay into the system. They can choose to contribute to the social security system at different levels. The highest contribution levels will result in higher pensions upon retirement, but many of the newly incorporated workers I have spoken to prefer to pay the lowest level of social security taxes. They are more concerned about the wages they could earn today than planning on actually receiving a social security pension payment someday. This new influx of contributions to the social security system will surely benefit the state that, with an aging workforce, faces an increasing number of Social Security payments in the near future. In 2010, 1.9 million Cubans were over age sixty, and by 2020, there will be 2.9 million Cubans over age sixty (ONEI 2010).[1]

From 2012 to 2015, Daybel Pañellas Álvarez, a social psychologist at the University of Havana, has studied the growing diversity of roles within the private sector, focusing on social perceptions within the sector of the three main groups: the employee, the employer, and the truly independent self-employed worker (Pañellas Álvarez 2015, 175). The study shows structural differences between each of these roles and in the structure of opportunities available to each. Employers tend to be male, white, professional, middle-aged individuals with large social networks, while independent workers tend to be black and mestizo men, young and middle-aged, with poor social networks and, in many cases, immigrants from Eastern Cuba. Entrance to the sector depends on one's access to capital: many employers receive remittances to help establish their businesses, while many of the independents are involved in businesses that require minimal initial investment. Across the three groups, interest in beginning in the private sector is related to the autonomy that it offers (Pañellas Álvarez 2015, 176). For those who are employers, their intentions are motivated by desire, for employees, the reasons for entering are more circumstantial, while the independent workers began in the field stimulated by economic stress and need.

The social representation of the three categories by subjects in the private sector reproduces a relationship of power, and often exploitation, between the employer and employee who is expected to be obedient and submissive (Pañellas Álvarez 2015, 176). When asked about their expectations for the future, employers speak of their desire to expand and become business people, independent workers hope to improve their conditions of labor, sometimes by changing activity, and employees hope to become employers. Independent workers and employees working in the private sector consider themselves to be in a disadvantaged position and perceive that their level of education, color of skin, and gender create obstacles for them in the private sector (Pañellas Álvarez 2015, 177).

Since the 1990s, international tourism has been one of the pillars of the state's economic growth strategy and tourists come to Cuba from all over the world. Canadian, Italian, and Spanish tourists are the most common. The reestablishment of US and Cuban relations announced on December 17, 2014, has led to an explosive growth in international tourism. Almost immediately after the announcement that diplomatic relations would be restored and the two countries would embark on a path towards the normalization of relations, international tourism to Cuba began to surge. The first wave of visitors were Europeans and Canadians who wanted to "get to Cuba before the Americans arrived" and "before things changed." In 2015, Cuba received a record 3.5 million visitors (Trotta 2016) and, not far behind the Europeans and Canadians, were US visitors.

In 2015, the number of US visitors grew by 77 percent for a total of 161,000 (not including Cuban-American visitors) (Trotta 2016).[2] In January 2016, 417,764 tourists visited Cuba, setting another record for the most visitors in a single month (Trotta 2016). January 2016 arrivals represented a 12.7 percent increase from the same period the previous year (Trotta 2016).[3] Increased tourism means that money is coming into Cuba to be spent in the service sector and this increased demand means that businesses have to grow and hire employees because mom-and-pop can't handle the work anymore on their own.

Most employees in the new private sector are earning much more than they could in the state sector, however, there are no real labor protections or regulations. There is no minimum wage in the private sector. In a televised meeting of the National Assembly in December 2015, delegates during a commission for the protection of youth talked about the common practice of young people being hired in small businesses without the legal paperwork for trial periods in which they received no salary. Often their employers tell them that they have not passed the trial, they are dismissed, or they decide to leave, and receive no pay for weeks and even months of work.

In her essay on the impacts of the changes in Cuban society since 2011 on social equity, Cuba's leading expert on social structure, Mayra Espina, points to a number of positive and negative impacts on social equity that can be expected in the medium term. She projects the consolidation of layers of poverty and vulnerability within the self-employed sector. While currently workers in the private sector earn incomes that are relatively high in comparison with similar work in the state sector, she predicts that the growing diversity in the sector, which includes everything from "petty bourgeois middle class, well set up with businesses renting rooms and homes, restaurants and the businesses of construction contractors, to low income employees and people who are self-employed in services in a survival economy"(Espina Prieto 2015, 215). She also predicts that in the future individuals working in the state sector who are laid off or those who enter the labor force without the necessary skills and resources necessary to set up their own small businesses will be concentrated at the lower extreme of income in the sector (Espina Prieto 2015, 216).

Access to the emerging non-state sector of the labor market is highly dependent on social networks, which connect potential employees to people with economic capital who are starting businesses. Today Havana's non-state sector service industry is high-paying in comparison to state sector work, and racist hiring practices based on Eurocentric standards of beauty appear to be common.

The new employer class is comprised of individuals with economic capital which they have invested to make money off of the labor of others, something that supposedly doesn't happen in a socialist country.[4] Article 14 of the Cuban Constitution promises that "in the Republic of Cuba, the economic system is based on socialist ownership by the people of the fundamental means of production and the suppression of the exploitation of man by man." The contrast between the socialist constitution, which promises a society free of exploitation, and new economic policies, which provide no such protections, may be resolved in a future constitutional reform or by enacting new labor regulations that provide protections for non-state-sector workers.

Further research should explore the relationship between employers and employees in the workplace and provide more information about these preliminary observations. How do employers seek out new employees? What role do social networks play in hiring? In the absence of laws and regulations to determine minimum wages, how do employers set wages and determine payment systems? What recourse do employees have if they feel like they are being exploited? What role may Cuban trade unions or other spontaneous formations of workers play mediating in these conflicts in the future?

CIRCULAR MIGRANTS

From the colonial era until 1930, Cuba was an immigrant-receiving nation (So-rolla Fernández 2011). With the economic crisis in 1930, this trend reversed, and Cuba began to send more emigrants abroad than it received (Sorolla Fernández 2011). After 1959, many people who had left Cuba during the eco-nomic stagnation and political violence and repression of the 1950s returned to the island, resulting in a temporary positive migration balance (Sorolla Fernández 2011). But, by 1960–62, the previous pattern of emigration was reestablished when the first wave of emigrants left Cuba. Significant waves of emigration occurred in 1965, 1980, and 1994 (Sorolla Fernández 2011). By the end of 2010, there were between 1.6–1.8 million Cubans living abroad as either temporary or permanent emigrants (Sorolla 2011; ONEI 2011).

Table E.1.   Cuban External Migration (Selected Years)

Year	Emigration Rate[1]	Year	Emigration Rate
1900–1904	55.300	1965	–18 003
1905–1909	96.100	1980	–141 742
1910–1914	79.300	1990–1993	–18 059
1915–1919	157.00	1994	–47 844
1920–1924	232.900	1995–1999	–125 340
1925–1929	32.600	2000	–29 322
1930–1934	–95.800	2001	–33 043
1935–1939	–48.300	2002	–30 985
1940–1944	–38.100	2003	–28 675
1945–1949	–17.100	2004	–35 429
1950–1954	–4.200	2005	–33 328
1958	–4 449	2006	–35 267
1959	12 345	2007	–32 811
1960	–62 379	2008	–36 903
1961	–67 468	2009	–36 564
1962	–66 264	2010	–38 165

1. *Emigration rate* is "the number of emigrants departing an area of origin per 1,000 population in that area of origin in a given year" (Population Reference Bureau). This is the English translation for the term *saldo migratorio externo*.

Today, the average Cuban immigrant is a young, white, female, urban resident (Sorolla Fernández 2011). Cuban immigrants are present in 146 countries (Sorolla Fernández 2011). Due to reforms in Cuba, and new laws in the United States and Spain which facilitate international travel for certain sectors of the population, the migration patterns that became common in the 1990s have been replaced gradually by new patterns that have become increasingly circular since 2013 (Sorolla Fernández 2011).

In January 2013, Cuban immigration reforms announced in late October 2012 went into effect, removing obstacles to international travel. From 2012–2015, almost half a million Cubans traveled abroad on personal trips (rather than state business), an 81 percent growth in relation to the 2010–2012 period (Cubadebate 2015). The majority of these trips are, to the United States, Mexico, Panama, Spain, and Ecuador and are considered temporary trips "to visit family members, work for a period, or undertake other activities"(Cubadebate 2015). Cuban immigration reforms in 2013, the Spanish Historical Memory Law of 2008–2011, a dramatic increase in the number of US visitor visas issued by the US Interests Section from 2013–14, and the continued application of the Cuban Adjustment Act in the US, have all contributed to Cubans' increased mobility. These factors may change the characteristics of Cuban migration from a one-way permanent emigration to a cyclical phenomenon, similar to other regional migrant flows. In the last fourteen years, 456,000 Cubans have emigrated, 80 percent of them to the United States (Antonio Aja, December 16, 2015 conference presentation). This is the second most important migrant flow since that of the 1960s (Antonio Aja, December 16, 2015 conference presentation).[5]

January 2013: Cuban Immigration Reforms

On October 16, 2012, the *Granma* newspaper announced that the Cuban exit permit [*permiso de salida*] would be eliminated (Juventud Rebelde 2012). This change was made possible by Law Decree 302 which modified Cuba's Migration Law 1312 of September 20, 1976. The Ministry of Foreign Relations also published Resolution 318 (October 13, 2012) which removed the requirement that, to travel abroad for personal reasons, Cubans on the island must present a letter of invitation by friends or family members in the country they planned to visit notarized by the Cuban consulate.[6] These two measures removed significant bureaucratic and cost barriers to international travel for Cubans on the island: the letter of invitation used to cost $140 CUC, and the exit permit, when approved, cost $150 CUC, valid for only thirty days. Longer trips required that the traveler extend the permit at rates which depended on the country that one visited (between €60 and US$140 per month). A traveler who did not pay to renew the exit permit or did not return to Cuba within eleven months lost their Cuban residency and any properties they owned on the island.[7]

With the new resolutions, Cubans traveling abroad for personal reasons are now allowed to remain outside the island for up to 24 months without losing their Cuban residency. In special circumstances, which prevent their return to the island within 24 months, individuals can even apply for an extension at their local Cuban consulate (Juventud Rebelde 2012).

The new measures also opened the possibility for professionals, doctors, and athletes who abandoned the country while abroad on official missions after 1990, and those who immigrated illegally after the 1994 migration accords, to receive visas from the Cuban government to visit the island as long as eight years had passed since their desertion (Juventud Rebelde 2012). This measure benefitted some 100,000 Cubans living in the US who were blacklisted from visiting Cuba as punishment for having left the country illegally while performing official duties abroad (Redacción [Café Fuerte] 2012a).

In the same package of reforms, a process is established for Cubans abroad who have lost their residency in Cuba to apply for repatriation. In order to apply to reestablish residency in Cuba, emigrants must present their up-to-date Cuban passport and an application with information about how they emigrated, the reasons why they desire to return to Cuba, and a person of reference in Cuba who commits to providing them with housing and maintenance until they can become self-sufficient, and pay a tax or consular fee for the application (Redacción [Café Fuerte] 2012b). The fee for the application is $100 CUC (Redacción [Café Fuerte] 2012a).

In a press conference at Havana's International Press Center, Col. Lamberto Fraga Hernández, deputy chief of immigration for the Ministry of Interior, announced that these requests are now routinely approved and that answers to these cases are given within ninety days of application (Redacción [Café Fuerte] 2012b). The official explained that about 1,000 Cuban emigrants return to establish residency in the island each year (Redacción [Café Fuerte] 2012b).

When the new measures were announced by Homero Acosta Alvarez, Secretary of the Council of State, on Cuban television on October 24, 2012, he explained that Cuban emigration has changed from being an eminently political flow in the early years of the revolutionary process to one motivated today by economic concerns. Acosta explained, that in recognition of this trend, it is important that Cuba's treatment of its emigrants change: "Today we are changing because our homeland is changing" (Redacción [Café Fuerte] 2012a).

The immigration reforms are also contributing to changes in the homeland. The extension of time that Cubans can spend abroad from eleven months to twenty-four months has made it possible for Cubans visiting the US to apply for and receive US residency through the Cuban Adjustment Act while still returning to Cuba in time to maintain their residency on the island. In the US, Cubans can claim adjustment of status under the Cuban Adjustment act after having spent one year and one day in the US. The process to be granted residency usually takes about six months, leaving time for a Cuban visitor to return to Cuba with US residency before the 24 months have expired. This measure has contributed to increasing the number of Cubans with residency on the island who are also US permanent residents. This dual status allows them to travel freely between the two countries. These new US permanent residents now have the option of working temporarily in the United States as part of a longer-term project of returning to invest in Cuba.

In 2013, a joint workshop—"Cuba: Updating the Model" co-sponsored by the Cuban *Temas Journal* and the David Rockefeller Center for Latin American Studies at Harvard University—brought together fifteen Cuban, US and European scholars to discuss the roots, characteristics, and impact of what the Cuban government calls the "updating" of its policies on the island. The group noted that increased circular migration has given rise to a new social actor in international relations and in Cuba's development. They call for the establishment of norms and policies to facilitate the incorporation of these new actors "in the development model triggered by the updating process"(Hernández 2013).

2008–2011: Ley de Memoria Histórica

In 2007, the Spanish government approved the Historical Memory Law (*La Ley de Memoria Histórica*) known as the "*Ley de nietos*" (Grandchildren's law). The law entered into effect on December 29, 2008, giving a period of three years for the children and grandchildren of Spaniards who were exiled during the Spanish Civil War and the Franco dictatorship to apply to recover their nationality (Cancio Isla 2011). Before the measure expired on December 27, 2011, more than 66,000 Cubans had already received their Spanish passports (Álvarez 2011). The consul general of Spain in Havana, Tomás Rodríguez-Pantoja, estimated that when all the cases had been adjudicated the number of new Spanish citizens in Cuba would be between 180,000 and 190,000, close to 1.7 percent of the population of the island (Álvarez 2011). These figures do not include the underage children of new Spanish citizens who would then become eligible to apply for citizenship as well (Álvarez 2011).[8]

Many of those who applied for Spanish citizenship did so in order to obtain a European Union passport to make it easier to travel to visit family abroad, or leave Cuba temporarily to work in Spain. With a Spanish passport, Cubans can travel to the United States without applying for a visa and can get US residency through the Cuban Adjustment Act upon arrival.

As a result of these changes in policy in Cuba and abroad, the mobility of the Cuban population has increased. With the removal of the exit permit process, the Cuban state no longer has the final say in deciding who can and cannot travel. If before revolutionary cultural capital was decisive in overcoming the obstacles to being able to leave the island, today mobility depends on being able to obtain a foreign visa. This depends on being able to convince a second country of one's financial solvency and prove that one is not a potential migrant. Economic capital becomes more important in opening opportunities for mobility because that is what foreign embassies look at when they decide whether to issue a visa.

Access to international mobility is also correlated with race, giving white Cubans an advantage. One of the largest categories for being able to travel is holding Spanish citizenship (usually white), or family abroad who can provide invitations, or apply for visitor visas or family reunification visas, in the case of the United States. Although during the 1990s Cuban emigrant flows began to include more mestizos and blacks, who can now invite family members, Cuban emigrants since 1959 have been majority white, as are their largely homogenous family networks.

Increased access to the internet, and relief from the high prices of international communication, make it easier for families to stay closely connected despite the distance. In Cuba, many families use Wi-Fi devices in public parks with Wi-Fi to video call family members abroad using a program called IMO for the cost of $2 CUC per a one-hour Internet access card. When commercial flights between the United States began, the price of the 45 minute roundtrip flight between Miami and Havana, fell from almost $500 USD, to about $200 USD, making travel more affordable and will likely increase the frequency of visits.

Increasing numbers of Cubans are beginning to live trans-national lives. Many new Spanish citizens have used their Spanish passports to travel to the US and get US residency through the Cuban Adjustment Act. Many Cubans with family in the United States who have been issued five-year visitor visas travel frequently to the United States for multiple reasons. While many use their visas for short visits, there are also cases of those who visit and work under the table in Miami with the support of family members. Others go to assist family in the US by providing home care for sick relatives or to assist with childbirth and child care, services that would be prohibitively expensive if their family members had to hire non-family members in the US to do the work.

An increasing number of Cubans are traveling abroad to work temporarily on labor contracts that they have organized themselves. Before the immigration reforms, work contracts abroad were state-sponsored. To be chosen for one of these state-sponsored labor contracts abroad, revolutionary cultural capital was key. Today, individuals with internet access (through state workplace or, increasingly, through paid access economic capital) and contacts abroad (social capital) can organize their own work contracts, often with higher pay and benefits and fewer restrictions than state-sponsored contracts. My own personal network includes two doctors who have organized their own temporary work contracts in China. Both work in international clinics serving ex-pat populations who prefer to be treated with allopathic medicine rather than by local Chinese doctors. Although both are part of my social network, the two doctors do not know each other.

Similarly, many young Cubans with internet access and contacts abroad are looking for scholarships to do masters' and PhD work abroad. This sort of temporary immigration allows them to continue furthering their professional qualifications while earning money abroad. Many have chosen this path with the hopes that they will be able to earn enough money to return to Cuba to purchase independent housing or set up a private business.

Since the 1990s, marriage-based migration in Cuba has been responsible for the slightly higher rate of female migration. Increasingly, Cubans married to foreigners are returning to settle in Cuba. In my research on the housing market in Havana, I have heard many stories of Cuban women who immigrated with their foreign spouses in the 1990s, who are now upon retirement, returning to Cuba to buy a house and bringing capital to start a business. It has also become common for women who live abroad with their foreign spouses to invest in a small family business to provide for a livelihood for extended family living on the island, rather than sending regular remittances.

CONSUMERS

The last five years in Cuba have brought about an expansion of opportunities for consumption on new levels, beyond basic needs. The new small businesses and cultural consumption spaces which have emerged after the 2010 reforms are extremely economically segregated. As new private spaces of socialization around diverse cultural consumption practices grow in importance, public spaces are gradually becoming stratified spaces, left to Havana's lower classes, those without access to CUC or connections needed to gain entrance to more desirable privately managed spaces. Cultural consumption practices are of increasing importance in organizing spaces of socialization. For people who are members of the middle class and below, the existence of segregated social spaces with different cultural consumption practices limit opportunities for building social networks that span different social groups and could provide people in lower groups opportunities for social mobility.

Cuba's new small and medium-sized entrepreneurs are among those who are consuming in these new economic spaces, and they are accompanied by circular migrants, people receiving remittances, and those who work in high income sectors of the economy. These economically privileged groups are not new in Cuban society. Since the 1990s, people linked to the recovered state sector, mixed sector, and emerging private sector, have earned higher incomes than the average state worker. However, often these people didn't have opportunities to invest or spend this economic capital. Weinreb focuses on the formation of a class of "Unsatisfied Citizen-Consumers," a social group characterized by its frustration with the lack of opportunities for consumption on the island in the early 2000s (Weinreb 2009). In this period, many domestic policies limited citizens' access to non-basic consumption: Cubans living on the island could not stay at hotels, rent cars from the state, have a cell phone line in their name, or buy many small household appliances in state stores, such as microwaves, computers, toasters, VCRs, and DVD players. Cuban immigration laws made traveling abroad for personal reasons an extremely difficult, expensive, and bureaucratic process.

The biggest change experienced in the last couple of years in Cuban society is not just the growth in economic inequalities but the growth in opportunities for this small group of Cubans to become "*Satisfied* Citizen-Consumers." Today this group has new options for investing and spending their relatively high incomes. New opportunities for conspicuous consumption have made the increasing inequalities in Cuban society since the 1990s much more visible. Post-Soviet and post-socialist societies around the globe have given birth to diverse social systems with some common characters: "New Russians," petty traders, entrepreneurs, state workers, and the unemployed (Ratilainen 2012; Round 2012; Caldwell 2004; Stenning 2005; Yurchak 2003; Burrell 2011). These ethnographies help us learn about the everyday lives of both the winners and losers of these transitions, of those who have been successful in adjusting to new values and norms and those that haven't been able to triumph under the new rules.

Before, when opportunities to legally earn large quantities of hard currency were limited, and equality was a dominant social value, those who had more attempted to hide that difference from others. Sharing is an important social value in Cuba. Cubans have learned to share, not their leftovers or what they don't need, but rather to share the little they have with others also in need. Many adults who grew up in socialist Cuba consider it unethical to have something that someone else needs and not share it with them.

In the 1990s and early 2000s, people who had more than the average often had earned it through "less than legal" means. They maintained consumption practices similar to their lower income neighbors in order to avoid calling attention to themselves that might lead to state scrutiny. Fewer places to spend or opportunities to invest combined with lower thresholds of perception of needs made it easier to share. Others hid what they had, because they either felt that they didn't have enough to share or didn't want to. In the last five years, changes in state policy have gradually shifted these norms. As spaces for conspicuous consumption multiply, people with higher incomes seem to feel much more comfortable with openly adopting consumption practices not possible for most of the population.

With the recent expansion of self-employment, many people who had started earning hard currency in the 1990s found an opportunity to invest that money by using the experience they gained in the state sector to go into business for themselves. Many new business owners of large bed and breakfasts, restaurants, and bars have been working in emerging sectors of the economy since the 1990s. This experience has helped them gain the know-how, as well as amass the capital needed to launch their business, and now they can get business licenses to do so. They are likely to be successful, because they already made their mistakes more than a dozen years ago, as managers for similar state businesses.

Every week, new places to spend money appear in Havana. Here, local consumer desires, constructed through consuming foreign media, stories from family abroad, and the firsthand experiences of returning migrants and medical professionals, are satisfied for those with money to burn. Changes in state discourses toward self-employment and small businesses have helped de-stigmatize consumption.

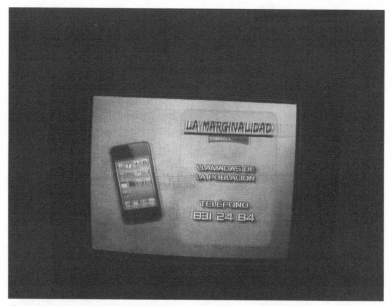

Figure E.1. Screenshot of *"Sobre la Mesa"* program on Marginality
"Sobre la Mesa" section of the Cubavisión Channel programa *Mesa Redonda*, Instituto Cubano de la Radio y la Televisión (ICRT)

There are many signs that the state is stimulating consumption. In the early 2010s, US anthropologist, Maya Berry, began to observe how the Cuban media had begun to adopt new technologies in their news broadcasts (personal communication). Instead of using the classic unobtrusive tele-prompter, or index cards, news hosts began to read their stories from lap-tops and tablets. This happened at about the same time that tablets appeared for the first time in state stores, and were still a rarity in Cuban society. For example, in December 2013, during the call-in section of the program, "*Sobre la Mesa*," during a discussion of economic inequalities and marginality, the program producers put the call-in phone number on the screen next to the image of an iPhone!

The number of cell phones in the country is growing quickly, but in 2013, there were only 17.71 cell phones per one hundred inhabitants (ITU 2015). Only a small portion of Cuban families had cell phones, and those who have them rarely use them to talk. Most people with cell phones use them primar-ily as beepers (Pertierra 2011, 216). Even in 2017, it is still uncommon to see people using cell phones to carry on long conversations. Certainly, those calling in to the show would have called from a landline, rather than paying $.35 CUC per minute, but the program producers chose the iPhone image for their call-in advertisement.

Many household electronics were previously prohibited in Cuba, with the justification that they created a demand for energy that the national power grid could not provide. Today, state stores are better stocked with deep fry-ers, rice cookers, electric pressure cookers, tea kettles, washing machines, sound systems, air conditioners, deep freezers, blenders, plasma televisions, fans, food processors, tablets, and USB memory sticks. The prices of these products have dropped and are increasingly competitive with prices abroad. There is an active black market in products bought abroad and resold in Cuba, through social networks in neighborhoods and workplaces, and online adver-tising sites like *Revolico.com* and *Porlalivre.com*.

The new private service sector is also creating new needs for people with money. Entrepreneurs are working to build their customer base and stimulate desires to consume in new spaces. These spaces use sophisticated interior de-signs to replicate the social spaces that Cubans are used to seeing in foreign television and movies. Now those who have more than others have many places to spend their money: gyms, spas, pet grooming parlors, juice bars, tattoo stu-dios, bakeries, spinning competitions, and gelato shops. They are also visiting all-inclusive beach resorts, vacationing abroad, and buying and rehabbing prop-erties. Social groups in Cuba are increasingly defined by changing values and consumption practices, and research on the newly rich and their conspicuous consumption practices is of interest to foreign market researchers looking to get a foot in the door and begin shaping new consumer loyalties.

CONCLUSION

Cuban society is changing quickly. The three groups introduced in this epilogue: circular migrants, employers and employees, and (Satisfied) Consumer-Citizens, were not mentioned by research participants in the interviews I did in 2012, but have become an important part of the social fabric in Havana that should be studied further. Also of interest for further research is to understand how social dynamics of life in urban Havana described here may be similar or different from dynamics in the provinces, and in rural areas. Understanding these dynamics in Havana and in other regions of the country is important work for all of us who are committed to social justice and equality in a rapidly changing Cuba.

NOTES

1. By 2030, Cuba will be the most aged country in Latin America and the Caribbean, and in 2050, it could be among the eleven most aged countries in the world with 38 percent of its population over sixty years of age (ONEI 2010). In December 2000, the Cuban Parliament agreed to extend the retirement age in Cuba to sixty-four years for men and fifty-nine for women (ONEI 2010).

2. Cuban officials estimated a 77 percent increase in US visitors in 2015 while US officials only reported an increase of 50 percent. The discrepancy can be explained: the US figures count legal travelers and the Cuban numbers include actual arrivals. Those who travel through third countries are included in the Cuban figures, but not in the US figures (Spetalnick 2016).

3. Before the announcement, tourism growth was slower. Between 2011–2013, the number of visitors increased from 2.7 million to 2.85 million (Economist 2012; ONEI 2014b). Both figures were recent records.

4. The preamble to the Cuban Constitution states that "regimes built on the exploitation of man by man cause the humiliation of the exploited and the degradation of the human condition of the exploiters and that only socialism and communism, where man has been liberated from all forms of exploitation: of slavery, servitude, and capitalism can the true dignity of the human being be achieved."

5. At the same conference, Consuelo Martín Fernández, a University of Havana psychologist whose research has focused on everyday life and how families are affected by emigration, pointed out that it is now common for family businesses to be supported by family members who migrate temporarily to send back money to help fund the project. She has also observed return migration of Cubans abroad who return to the island to inherit a property or to buy a property.

6. Cuban law accounts for different status for Cubans who were born on the island who have emigrated and those who continue to be in residence. Cubans born on the island, who have left Cuba permanently immigrating to another country, retain their

Cuban citizenship but lose many rights that are only available to Cubans resident on the island who have not left. For example, Cuban residents receive rations and can be treated by the national health care system. Cubans who have emigrated must apply at a Cuban consulate for permission to visit Cuba and are limited to how long their trip can last. If they need health care in Cuba, they must be treated through the international clinics for foreigners where they are charged for services in CUC.

7. Cubans who leave Cuba permanently now have the right to sell their homes before emigrating.

8. By April 2013, out of the more than 192,000 applications that were made under the Law of Historical Memory, 75,800 cases had been granted Spanish citizenship, 9,918 applications had been denied, and another 106,412 files were still pending awaiting further evidence (Barros 2013). According to the Spanish consulate in Cuba, the number of Spanish citizens residing in Cuba has more than doubled, from 44,000 Spanish citizens registered before the law to 100,600 registered Spanish citizens in February of 2013 (Barros 2013).

Appendix A

Frequent Research Contacts, Informal Interviews

Individuals in **bold** are people that I interacted with daily or multiple times a week during some part of my research period.

Pseudonym	# Kids	Race	Age	Housing/Household	Vocation/Occupation	Economic Spaces
Juan & Marta	5	white	70–80	Alamar. Independent detached home. Lives with wife. Daughter lives next door and two grandkids are always in the house.	Teacher and proprietor of private *repasos* school for 7–12 graders in afternoons and Saturdays.	Retired from education, now private freelance in education
Camila & Julian	0	white	20s	Vedado. Independent detached home. Rent out part of house to a small business.	Sociologists. Camila works for foreign company in Miramar Trade Center. Rent space to TCP.	Foreign company
Esperanza & Manuel	5	white	70–80	Vedado. One bedroom apartment in 1950s building.	Retired.	Retired
Lina	1	black	42	Centro Habana. Lives with husband and son.	Licenciada in Computer Science.	Foreign company
Marcelo & Sara	2	white	30–40	Marianao. Self-built property in marginal area far from work and family.	University professor and theatre actress.	Higher education and art in Old Havana
Humberto & Cary	2	white	40–50	Alamar. Microbrigade. Live with 2 sons and daughter-in-law and granddaughter in 3 bedroom apartment.	State taxi driver (public health) and housewife. Oldest son works in religious ceremonies.	State, Private [unlicensed]
Michela	0	mestiza	28	Vedado. Subdivided 1 bedroom apartment. Lives with father and his wife. Previously in Altahabana with boyfriend.	Psychologist, University professor, private English tutor, sells imported clothes.	State non-recuperated, Private freelance

Fidel & Maria	1	white	Playa. Bi-planta. 2 bedrooms. Daughter and son-in-law and two kids upstairs (2 bedrooms). Rent in MN part of house as separate apt (1 bedroom).	Fidel: Retired, mixed companies; Maria: Retired but working in tourism as administrator. Daughter: Lawyer working in tourism as sales person, Son-in-law: Diplomatic Corps. Rent room in MN. Teach cooking classes.	Mixed company, State
Alberto & Rosa	2	white	Miramar. Modern house 1958. 6 rooms: 3 bedrooms + service room in garage, 2 bedroom apt above garage (lives adult son, partner and 2 kids).	Alberto: Musician, Rosa: music agent.	State non-recuperated, Culture
Idalys	0	white	Marianao. 1 bedroom apartment on *pasillo*.	Pastor.	NGO, church
José	0	white	Kohly. 3 bedroom apartment in propiedad horizontal (3 floors, 3 apts) from 1950s. Lives with mom, dad, and sister.	Photographer, university professor.	State non-recuperated, education, culture
Elvira	0	white	Guantánamo. Not a homeowner: renting a 1 bedroom apartment. Immigrant from Las Tunas/Guantánamo. Lives alone in Havana.	Licenciada en History. Works as a domestic in Havana.	Private

(continued)

Pseudonym	# Kids	Race	Age	Housing/Household	Vocation/Occupation	Economic Spaces
Marielena & Carlos	2	white	55–65	Centro Habana. 5 bedroom house. Originally 4 bedrooms. Turned one bedroom into a bakery. One of the rooms is an addition (2nd floor apt built by daughter for her and her partner). Immigrants (35 years) from Granma.	Licenciado in Filología. Retired High school teacher and principal, also worked in hotels. Housewife, baker, business person.	Retired. Private
Ana Maria	0	white	40	Vedado. Sold 2 bedroom and bought a 1 bedroom. Invested difference in sister's business. Rents out apartment and lives at parent's house in marginal neighborhood.	Licenciada in Psychology, works in research institute.	State non-recuperated, education
Judith	0	black	38	Buenavista. Substandard home. Lives with mother, sister and grandma.	Licenciada in Foreign Language (English and French)	NGO, international collaboration
Ricardo & Carmen	1	white	25–30	Centro Habana. Both came to Havana to study and are trying to stay in the city after graduation. Not home owners: renting 1 bedroom.	University professors (UCI) and private software developers.	State recuperated, Private

Name		Race	Age	Housing	Occupation	Sector
Mercedes	2	mestizo	55	Centro Habana. Microbrigade 3 bedroom apartment. Son lives with her when not abroad living with father. Takes care of grandson while daughter works.	Historian, Researcher.	State non-recuperated
Marcos	0	mestizo	40	Sevillano. Lives with mother. Small detached home in backlot of another family's house. Self-built.	Licenciado in Art History. Works in international relations for a prestigious Cuban cultural institution.	State, culture
Rembert	0	white	25–30	Santiago de las Vegas. Substandard home. Lives with mother.	Studying MA in Political Science.	State, higher education
Tamara & Tanya	2	white	35–40	Vedado. Ground floor 2 bedroom apartment in 1940s building. Lives with two children.	Licenciadas in Engineering. Sell stuff on the black market.	Private [unlicensed]
Vanessa & Irina	0	white	25–35	Centro Habana. Live in brand-new luxury apartment they built on roof of parents' house	Business owners. Bakery in Vedado.	Private
Lucy	1	black	55	Vedado. Lives with husband, daughter, son-in-law, and grandson in 2 bedroom 1950s apartment.	Human Resources.	State non-recuperated, restaurants in MN

(continued)

Pseudonym	# Kids	Race	Age	Housing/Household	Vocation/Occupation	Economic Spaces
Sandra	0	white	25	Habana del Este. Lives with parents and brother in self-built home.	Studying night school Licenciatura in Historic Preservation Management. Day job state cultural institution.	State, culture
Adan	0	white	34	Playa. Lives with parents and grandfather in large 1940s house in poor condition.	Licenciada in Library Science. Has begun to teach private photography courses to tourists. Day job state cultural institution.	State, culture
Melissa	0	white	29	Vedado. Lives with parents.	Licenciada in Sociology. Works in State research institute.	State non-recuperated
Nyade	0	mestizo	25	Alamar. Lives with parents and sister in 3 bedroom microbrigade.	Licenciada in Computer Science.	Mixed
Yessica	0	mestizo	22	Centro Habana. Lives with parents.	Licenciada in Law.	State, university student
Ernesto	0	mestizo	23	Centro Habana. Lives with parents.	Licenciado in Law.	State, university student
Ariel	0	white	25	Vedado. From Eastern Cuba. Lives with aunt who rents out rooms to foreigners and assists with family's room rental business.	Studying medicine.	State, university student and private
Yanet	0	white	33	Nuevo Vedado. Lives with parents and sister.	Licenciada in Library Science.	State non-recuperated

Name		Race	Age	Housing	Occupation	Sector
Frank	0	mestizo	20	Vedado. Lives with mother. Rents to foreigners (long term).	Student.	State, social service trainee and private
Mariela	0	white	30	Centro Habana. Lives alone. Responsible for care of grandmother in Guanabo.	Licenciada Cultural studies and theatre. Actress and producer.	State non-recuperated
Fatima	1	mestizo	55	Vedado. Lives with son. Independent home.	Licenciada in Engineering. Takes care of elderly mother and rents apartment to foreigners.	Private, rental in CUC
Osmany	1	white	40	Cienfuegos.	Electrician. Car mechanic. Current taxi driver for tourists (between cities).	Private
Ramón	2	white	60	Víbora. Lives with wife.	Retired military. Cuban security. Current taxi driver for tourists (between cities).	Private
Gladys	1	white	52	La Lisa. Lives in apartment (biplanta) with husband and son.	Private tax accountant.	Private
Donna	1	white	60	Playa. 1950s 1 bedroom apartment.	Private [unlicensed] bakery.	Private freelance (unlicensed)
Miriam	1	white	45	Centro Habana/Plaza. 1 bedroom with boyfriend and his son.	MA, Literary critic. Organizes international courses for foreign students in Cuba.	State, culture

(continued)

Pseudonym	# Kids	Race	Age	Housing/Household	Vocation/Occupation	Economic Spaces
Pedrito	2	white	47	Vedado.	Driver for state cultural institution, possibility to use car for side work.	State, culture
Lourdes	1	mestizo	56	Vedado. Beach home in Guanabo.	Rents 10 plus rooms to international visitors.	Private
Leticia & Estebán	1	white	60–75	Vedado. First floor 3 bedroom apartment in 1950s building.	Rents room to foreigners.	Private
Annet & Francisco	1	white	55–65	Vedado. 3 bedroom apartment in 1950s building.	Rents room to foreigners, works in airport traffic control.	Private
Osmany & Laura	0	white	20s	Vedado. 2 bedroom luxury apartment in 1950s building.	Rents room/apartment to foreigners.	Private
Yoan	0	white	40	Centro Habana. Renting 1 bedroom from friend of a friend. 60 cuc/month.	Designer and Film editor.	Private
Manolito	0	mestizo	28	Centro Habana. Bought 1 bedroom apt in 1950s building. From Camaguey.	Masseuse. Licenciado in Fitness.	Private
Lisset	0	white	30	Cárdenas.	Musician. Repairs and resells guitars.	Private
Yuniesky	0	white	34	Cárdenas.	Baker.	Private

Name		Race	Age	Location	Occupation/Education	Sector
Amalia	0	mestizo	26	Santiago.	Licenciada in Journalism. Journalist.	State
Renier & Dianelys	0	white	20–25	Sancti Spíritus.	Licenciado in IT, Licenciada in Psychology. Psychologist.	State non-recuperated
Reina	0	white	37	Santiago.	Teacher.	State non-recuperated
Miriam	0	white	24	Jamanitas.	Works for Cuban NGO.	NGO
Maite & Elio	0	white	25–30	Lawton.	MA in Teaching Spanish as a Second Language, Professor of Spanish (tour guide), unemployed.	State non-recuperated
Elias	0	mestizo	26	Vedado.	Licenciado in Journalism. Journalist.	State non-recuperated
Lauren	0	white	26	Playa. Lives with parents.	Licenciada in Journalism. Journalist with state, also writes for new glossy magazines.	State non-recuperated, Private freelance
Delia	2	white	66	Marianao.	Physical Education teacher, retired.	Retired
Taty & Pedro	3	mestiza white	50-60	Vedado. Pedro's mother moved in with them when she sold her apt in Centro Habana (and they bought a car).	Rental in CUC.	Private, State recuperated
Diego	0	white	20	Santos Suárez. Lives with parents and brother.	Paquetero. Sells stuff on the black market.	Private (unlicensed)

References

Almeida Junco, Yulexis. 2015. Políticas de acceso a la Educación Superior: Un análisis a las desigualdades por color de la piel. In *Taller Internacional: Repensando la Antropología para las políticas públicas y la práctica antropológica. Sponsored by the Wenner Gren Foundation.* Havana, Cuba.

Álvarez Rodríguez, Maylan. 2013. *La callada molienda, Coloquios y testimonios.* Havana: Centro Cultural Pablo de la Torriente Brau.

Álvarez, Soledad. 2011. "El 'boom' de los 'cubañoles.'" *El Mundo*, December 22, 2011.

Andaya, Elise. 2009. "The Gift of Health." *Medical anthropology Quarterly* no. 23 (4):357–374. doi: 10.1111/j.1548–1387.2009.01068.x.

———. 2014. *Concieving Cuba:Reproduction, Women and the State in the Post-Soviet Era.* New Brunswick, NJ: Rutgers University Press.

Ávila Vargas, Niuva. 2011. "Características sociodemográficas de los jóvenes que ingresaron a la Educación Superior en los cursos de 2003–2009." *Novedades en población* no. 7 (14).

Baker, Peter and Randal C. Archibold. 2015. "Starting Friday, U.S. Will Ease Restrictions on Travel to Cuba." *New York Times*, January 15, 2015.

Barberia, Lorena 2004. "Remittances To Cuba: An Evaluation of Cuban and US Government Policy Measures." In *The Cuban Economy at the Start of the Twenty-First Century*, edited by Omar Everleny Pérez Villanueva and Lorena Barberia Jorge I. Domínguez. Cambridge, MA: David Rockefeller Center for Latin American Studies. Harvard University Press.

Barros, Manuel 2013. "En Cuba ya se aprobaron 75.800 expedientes de nacionalidad de las más de 192.000 solicitudes y todavía hay pendientes más de 106.000": Iago Losada Maseda, responsable del Registro Civil Consular de La Habana." *España Exterior*, 16 de Abril de 2013.

Berdahl, Daphne, Matti Bunzl, and Martha Lampland. 2000. *Altering states : ethnographies of transition in Eastern Europe and the Former Soviet Union.* Ann Arbor: University of Michigan Press.

Blue, Sarah A. 2007. "The Erosion of Racial Equality in the Context of Cuba's Dual Economy." *Latin American Politics & Society* no. 49 (3):35–68. doi: 10.1353/lap .2007.0028.

———. 2010. "Cuban Medical Internationalism: Domestic and International Impacts." *Journal of Latin American Geography* no. 9 (1):31–49.

Bourdieu, Pierre. 1986a. *The forms of capital*: Wiley Online Library.

———. 1986b. "The Forms of Capital." In *Handbook of Theory and Research for the Sociology of Education*, edited by JG Richardson, 241–258. New York: Greenwood.

Brenner, Philip, Marguerite Rose Jimenez, John M. Kirk, William M. LeoGrande. 2015. "History as Prologue: Cuba Before 2006." In *The Revolution under Raúl Castro: A Contemporary Cuba Reader*, edited by Marguerite Rose Jimenez Philip Brenner, John M. Kirk, William M. LeoGrande, 1–33. Lanham: Rowman & Littlefield Publishers.

Brotherton, Pierre Sean. 2005. "Macroeconomic change and the biopolitics of health in Cuba's special period." *Journal of Latin American Anthropology* no. 10 (2):339–369.

———. 2008. "We have to think like capitalists but continue being socialists": Medicalized subjectivities, emergent capital, and socialist entrepreneurs in post-Soviet Cuba." *American Ethnologist* no. 35 (2):259–274. doi: 10.1111/j.2008.1548–1425 .00033.x.

———. 2011. "Social Relations and the Cuban Health Miracle." *Contemporary Sociology: A Journal of Reviews* no. 40 (4):459–460.

Brundenius, Claes and Andrew Zimbalist. 1989. *The Cuban Economy: Measurement and Analysis of Socialist Performance*. Baltimore: Johns Hopkins University Press.

Burawoy, Michael, and Katherine Verdery. 1999. *Uncertain transition: ethnographies of change in the postsocialist world*. Lanham: Rowman & Littlefield.

Burchardt, Hans-Jurgen. 2002. "Contours of the Future: The New Social Dynamics in Cuba." *Latin American Perspectives* no. 29 (3):57–74. doi: 10.1177/0094 582x02029003004.

Burrell, Kathy. 2011. "Opportunity and uncertainty: young people's narratives of 'double transition' in post-socialist Poland." *Area* no. 43 (4):413–419. doi: 10.1111/j.1475–4762.2011.01024.x.

Burt, Ronald S. 2005. *Brokerage and Closure: An Introduction to Social Capital*. Oxford: Oxford University Press.

Buyandelgeriyn, Manduhai. 2008. "Post-Post-Transition Theories: Walking on Multiple Paths." *Annual Review of Anthropology* no. 37 (1):235–250. doi: 10.1146/ annurev.anthro.37.081407.085214.

Caballero, C. 2013. *Redes sociales de cuentapropistas habaneros* Facultad de Psicología, Universidad de la Habana, La Habana.

Café Fuerte. 2013. Cuba: 429,458 cuentapropistas registrados.

Caldwell, Melissa L. 2004. *Not by bread alone : social support in the new Russia*. Berkeley: University of California Press.

Cancio Isla, Wilfredo. 2011. "Más de 60 mil cubanos han obtenido ciudadanía española." August 11, 2011.

Carpentier, Lycée Français de La Havane Alejo. 2017. *Tarifas Escolares 2016/2017*. Lycée Français de La Havane Alejo Carpentier 2017 [cited May 31 2017]. Available from http://www.ecolehavane.org/es/tarifas-escolares-20162017.

Castro Ruz, Raúl. 2016. "El desarollo de la economía nacional, junto a la lucha por la paz y la firmeza ideológica, constituyen las principales misiones del Partido. Informe Central al 7mo Congreso del Partido Comunista de Cuba. 16 de abril del 2016." *Granma*, 14 de mayo.

Castro Ruz, Raúl. *Closing Ceremony Speech at Sixth Session of the Seventh Legislature of the National People's Power Assembly* 2010 [cited May 31, 2017. Available from http://cuba.cu/gobierno/rauldiscursos/2010/ing/r181210i.html.

Cave, Damien. 2014. "Cuba's Reward for the Dutiful: Gated Housing." *New York Times*, February 12, 2014.

CEEH. 2017. *Centro Educativo Español de La Habana* 2017 [cited May 31 2017]. Available from http://correo14.ceehabana.com/ceeh/index.php.

Coyula, Mario 2008. The Taking of the Great White City. In *Enfoques*. Havana, Cuba: IPS-Inter Press Service.

Cuba, Partido Comunista de. 2011. Información sobre el resultado del Debate de los Lineamientos de la Política Económica y Social del Partido y la Revolución.

Cubadebate. 2015. "Declaración del Gobierno Revolucionario: "Cuba reitera su compromiso con una emigración legal, ordenada y segura." *Cubadebate.cu*, December 1, 2015.

Curbelo, L. 2013. *Ser cuentapropista hoy: relación entre identidad y movilidad social*, Facultad de Psicología, Universidad de la Habana, La Habana.

Cutiño, Claudia 2015. *Abandono familiar en Cuba.* , Department of Psychology, University of Havana.

de la Fuente, Alejandro. 2001. *A nation for all: race, inequality, and politics in Twentieth Century Cuba*. Edited by Louis A. Pérez, *Envisioning Cuba*. Chapel Hill: University of North Carolina Press.

Del Llano, L. 2013. *Percepción del poder en cuentapropistas habaneros*, Facultad de Psicología, Universidad de la Habana, La Habana.

Del Real, Patricio, and Anna Cristina Pertierra. 2008. Inventar: Recent Struggles and Inventions in Housing in Two Cuban Cities.

Domingo Cuadriello, Jorge. 2008. "40 años despues: 1968." *Espacio Laical* no. 4 (28):52–55.

Domínguez García, María Isabel and María del Rosario Díaz. 1997a. Reproducción social y acceso a la educación en Cuba. Informe de investigación. In *Fondos del CIPS*. La Habana: CIPS.

Domínguez García, María Isabel; MR Díaz. 1997b. Reproducción social y acceso a la educación en Cuba. Havana: CIPS.

Domínguez, María Isabel, Claudia Castilla, Idania Rego. 2013. Políticas públicas de juventud e inclusión social: el caso de Cuba. edited by GT CLACSO Juventud – UNESCO. Havana, Cuba: Grupo de Estudios sobre Juventud del Centro de Investigaciones Psicológicas y Sociológicas (CIPS).

Domínguez, Jorge I., Omar Everleny Pérez Villanueva, and Lorena Barberia. 2004. *The Cuban economy at the start of the twenty-first century*. Cambridge: Harvard University, David Rockefeller center for Latin American Studies.

Dubinsky, Karen. 2016. *Cuba Beyond the Beach: Stories of Life in Havana.* Toronto: Between the Lines.

Dujarric, G, and M Vázquez. 2015. *Identidades sociales en grupos de altos ingresos económicos* Facultad de Psicología, Universidad de la Habana, La Habana.

Economist, The. 2012. "The deal's off:Inequalities are growing as the paternalistic state is becoming ever less affordable." *The Economist.*

———. 2016. "Cuban migrants The last wave: The urge to leave is strong, but the opportunity is diminishing " *The Economist,* January 14, 2016.

———. 2017. Special no more: An end to wet foot, dry foot. *The Economist,* http://www.economist.com/news/americas/21714600-outgoing-american-president -makes-it-harder-donald-trump-undo-rapprochement.

Emirbayer, Mustafa, and Eva M. Williams 2005. "Bourdieu and Social Work." *Social Service Review* no. 79 (4):690–724.

Erisman, H Michael, and John M Kirk. 2009. Cuban Medical Internationalism: Origins, Evolution, and Goals. New York: Palgrave Macmillan.

Escobar, Luz. 2016. "La escuela de los otros." *14 y Medio,* 2 de febrero del 2016.

Espina Prieto, Mayra , Lilia Núñez Moreno, Lucy Martín Posada, and Gisela Angel Sierra. 2003. Componentes socioestructurales y distancias sociales en la ciudad. In *Efectos sociales de las medidas del reajuste económico sobre la ciudad. Diagnóstico y perspectiva.* La Habana: Centro de Investigaciones Psicológicas y Sociológicas.

Espina Prieto, Mayra Paula. 2015. "Reforma Económica y política social de equidad en Cuba." In *Cuba: los correlatos socioculturales del cambio económico,* edited by Mayra Paula Espina and Dayma Echevarría, 197–223. La Habana: Ruth Casa Editorial, Ciencias Sociales.

Espina Prieto, Mayra, Lilia Núñez Moreno, Lucy Martín Posada, Laritza Vega Quintana, Adrián Rodríguez Chailloux, and Gisela Ángel Sierra. 2004. Heterogenización y desigualdades en la ciudad: Diagnóstico y perspectivas. Equipo de Estructura Social y Desigualdades, CIPS.

Fernández Estrada, Juliette 2012. "Protestantismo y migración en Cuba: Algunas pistas históricas de este nexo." La Habana, Cuba: CIPS.

Ferriol, Ángela, D Quintana, and V Pérez. 1999. "Política social en el ajuste y su adecuación a las nuevas condiciones." *Cuba: investigación económica* no. 5 (1).

Ferriol, Angela;Goran Therborn;Rita Castinneiras. 2004. *Política Social: El mundo contemporáneo y las experiencias de Cuba y Suecia.* Havana: INIE.

Frank, Marc. 2010a. "Cuba announces mass layoffs in bid to spur private sector." *Reuters.*

———. 2013. *Cuban Relevations: Behind the Scenes in Havana.* Gainesville, FL: University of Florida Press.

Frank, Marc 2010b. "Factbox: Cimex, Cuba's largest commercial corporation." *Reuters,* September 27, 2010.

Frederik, Laurie A. 2012. *Trumpets in the Mountains: Theater and the Politics of National Culture in Cuba.* Durham, NC: Duke University Press.

Galbraith, J, L Spagnolo, and D Munevar. 2006. "Pay Inequality in Cuba: the Special Period and After." *Society for the Study of Economic Inequality.* http://www.ecineq. org/milano/WP/ECINEQ2006–52.pdf.

García Espinosa, Julio. 1959. La vivienda. ICAIC.

Garth, Hanna. 2009. "Things Became Scarce: Food Availability and Accessibility in Santiago De Cuba Then and Now." *NAPA Bulletin* no. 32 (1):178–192. doi: 10.1111/j.1556-4797.2009.01034.x.

Gómez Yera, Sara. 1974. De cierta manera. ICAIC.

González-Corzo, Mario A. . 2010. The Reduction of State-Sector Workers in Cuba. http://rigofa2010.blogdiario.com/1286916964/the-reduction-of-state-sector-work ers-in-cuba-by-mario-a.-gonzalez-corzo/.

González, N 2006. *Familia, racialidad y educación*, Department of Sociology, Universidad de la Habana, La Habana.

Gordy, K. 2006. "Sales plus economy plus efficiency = revolution"? Dollarization, consumer capitalism, and popular responses in special period Cuba." *Public Culture* no. 18 (2):383–412. doi: 10.1215/08992363-2006-009.

Granma. 2008. "Official information on preliminary data of damages caused by Hurricanes Gustav and Ike." *Granma*.

Grogg, Patricia. 2009. "Ser o no ser de la libreta de abastecimiento." In *Fotos de Cuba.* , edited by IPS. Havana: InterPress Service.

Grusky, David B. 2001. "The Past, Present and Future of Social Inequality." In *Social Stratification: Class, Race and Gender in a Sociological Perspective*, edited by David B. Grusky. Boulder: Westview Press.

Gutiérrez Alea, Tomás and Juan Carlos Tabío 1995. Guantanamera.

Hamilton, Carrie. 2012. *Sexual Revolution in Cuba: Passions Politics and Memory*. Chapel Hill: University Of North Carolina Press.

Haney, Lynne. 1999. "But We Are Still Mothers': Gender, the State, and the Construction of Need in Postsocialist Hungary." In *Uncertain transition: ethnographies of change in the postsocialist world*, edited by Katherine Verdery and Michael Burawoy, 151–187. Lanham: Rowman & Littlefield.

Hansing, Katrin and Manuel Orozco. 2014. The Role and Impact of Remittances on Small Business Development during Cuba's Current Economic Reforms. In *desiguaALidades.net* Research Network on Inter-Dependent Inequalities in Latin America.

Härkönen, Heidi. 2014. *To not Die Alone: Kinship, Love and Life Cycle in Contemporary Havana, Cuba*, Anthropology, University of Helinski, Helinski, Finland.

Havane, Lycée Français de La. 2017. *Lycée Français de La Havane* Lycée Français de La Havane 2017 [cited May 31 2017]. Available from http://www.ecolehavane.org/.

Henken, Ted. 2004. "Between Ideology and Pragmatism: the Revolution and the Private Sector before the Special Period, 1959–1990." *Cuba in Transition* no. 13.

Hernández, Rafael. 2015. La hora de las UMAP: Notas para un tema de investigación. Catalejo, el blog de Temas: Temas.

Hernández, Rafael and Jorge Domínguez. 2013. Cuba, Updating the Model. Washington, D.C. and Havana, Cuba: Ediciones Temas and David Rockefeller Center For Latin American Studies.

Hsu, Carolyn L. 2007. *Creating Market Socialism: How Ordinary People Are Shaping Class and Status in China*. Durham, NC: Duker University Press.

IPS. 2008. *CUBA: "Few Deaths Do not Mean Storm Damages Were not Massive." Interview with Susan McDade, UN Resident Coordinator in Cuba* 2008 [cited September 21, 2008 2008]. Available from http://www.ipsnews.net/news.asp?idnews=43900.

———. 2009. "Eliminating Subsidies in Cuba." *Inter Press Service*, September 9.

ISH. 2017. *About the International School of Havana* 2017 [cited May 31 2017]. Available from http://www.ishavana.org/index.php/about.

ITU. 2015. Mobile-cellular telephone subscriptions. edited by International Telecommunications Union.

Jatar-Hausmann, AJ. 1999. *The Cuban way: Capitalism, communism, and confrontation*: Kumarian Press.

Juventud Rebelde. 2012. "Los cambios al detalle." *Juventud Rebelde*, December 1, 2012.

Karl, Terry 1975. "Work Incentives in Cuba." *Latin American Perspectives* no. 2 (4 Supplement Issue Cuba: La Revolucion en Marcha):21–41.

Kirk, John M. 2015. "Cuban Medial Internationalism under Raúl Castro." In *The Revoluion under Raúl Castro: A Contemporary Cuba Reader*, edited by Marguerite Rose Jimenez Philip Brenner, John M. Kirk, William M. LeoGrande, 251–260. Lanham: Rowman & Littlefield Publishers.

Klepak, Hal. 2004. "The Armed Forces Today and Tomorrow." In *Cuban Society in a New Century*, 279.

Lamrani, Salim. 2014. Conversations with Eusebio Leal Spengler. In *Huffington Post*.

Landau, Saul. 2010. Will the Real Terrorist Please Stand Up?

Leal, Eusebio. 2015. Curriculum Vitae. Oficina del Historiador de la Ciudad de La Habana.

Ledeneva, A.V. 1998. *Russia's economy of favours: blat, networking, and informal exchange*. Vol. 102: Cambridge Univ Pr.

Leogrande, William. 2015. "A New Crisis of Cuban Migration." *New York Times*, December 4.

Lewis, Oscar, Ruth M. Lewis, and Susan M. Rigdon. 1978. *Neighbors: Living the Revolution. An Oral History of Contemporary Cuba*. Urbana: University Of Illinois Press.

Leyva Martínez, Ivette. 2010. *Gastos en pensiones ponen en jaque al sistema de seguridad social* 2010 [cited 2016. Available from http://cafefuerte.com/csociedad/467-gastos-en-pensiones-ponen-en-jaque-al-sistema-de-seguridad-social/.

Liebow, Elliot. 1967. *Tally's corner: a study of Negro streetcorner men*. Vol. 1st. Boston: Little, Brown.

Lumsden, Ian. 1996. *Machos, Maricones and gave: Cuba and homosexuality*. Philadelphia: Temple University Press.

Martín Fernández, C., Perera Pérez, M., & Díaz Pérez, M. . 1996. "La vida cotidiana en Cuba. Una mirada psicosocial. ." *Temas* no. 7:92–9.

Martín Posada, Lucy, and Lilia Núñez Moreno. 2013. "Geografía y Hábitat: Dimensiones de equidad y movilidad social en Cuba." In *Desarollo económico y social en Cuba: Reformas emprendidas y desafíos en el siglo XXI*, edited by Omar Everleny Pérez Villanueva Jorge I. Domínguez, Mayra Espina Prieto and Lorena Barberia. México: Fondo de Cultura Económica.

Martin, Randy. 1994. *Socialist Ensembles: Theater and State in Cuba and Nicaragua.* Minneapolis: Minnesota Press.

Martín Romero, José Luis , and José Luis Nicolau Cruz. N.D. "Trabajo y vida cotidiana en el reajuste cubano."

Martín Romero, José Luis, Armando Capote González, Arnaldo Pérez García, Isabel Candelé Porro, Juan Carlos Campos Carrera, José Luís Nicolau Cruz, and Niubes Montes De Oca Pernas. 2000. Informe Ejecutivo: Reajuste y trabajo en los '90. La Habana: Grupo de Estudios Sociales del Trabajo, Centro de Investigaciones Psicológicas y Sociológicas (CIPS).

Mederos Anido, Anagret, and María del Carmen Zabala Argüelles. 2015. "Las percepciones de las desigualdades sociales de los actores locales del desarollo." In *Cuba: los correlatos socioculturales del cambio económico*, edited by Mayra Paula Espina and Dayma Echevarría, 183–196. La Habana: Ruth Casa Editorial, Ciencias Sociales.

Mesa-Lago, Carmelo. 2005. "Social and economic problems in Cuba during the crisis and subsequent recovery." *CEPAL Review* no. 86:177.

Mesa-Lago, Carmelo and Pavel Vidal-Alejandro. 2010. "The Impact of the Global Crisis on Cuba's Economy and Social Welfare." *Journal of Latin American Studies* no. 42:689–717 doi: doi:10.1017/S0022216X10001331.

Mesa-Lago, Carmelo. 2002. Growing economic and social disparities in Cuba: impact and recommendations for change. In *Cuba Transition Project (CTP)*. Miami: Institute for Cuban and Cuban-American Studies, University of Miami.

Miller, Nicola. 2003. "The absolution of history: Uses of the past in Castro's Cuba." *Journal of Contemporary History*:147–162.

Miroff, Nick. 2015. *Washington Post*, December 5, 2015.

Molina Diaz, E. 2007. "Cuba: Economic restructuring, recent trends and main challenges." *Centre for Researches on International Economics. Havana University, Cuba. www.ideaswebsite.org/ideasact/jun07/Beijing_Conference_07/Elda_Molina.pdf.*

Morris, Emily. 2014. "Unexpected Cuba." *New Left Review* no. 88:5–45.

Nerey, Boris, and Nivia Brismart. 1999. Estructura social y estructura salarial en Cuba: encuentros y desencuentros. La Habana: la Universidad de la Habana.

Núñez Sarmiento, Marta. 2010. "Cuban Development Strategies and Gender Relations." *Socialism and Democracy* no. 24 (1):127–125.

ONE. 2012. Anuario Estadistico de Cuba.

———. 2015. 7.2 Ocupados en la economía según su situación del empleo. La Habana: ONEI.

ONEI. 2010. Población proyectada por grupos de edades seleccionados, 2010–2030. Havana.

———. 2011. Anuario Demográfico de Cuba 2010. La Habana: Oficina Nacional de Estadísticas.

———. 2012. 7.15 Main indicators of the social welfare system: Anuario Estadístico de Cuba 2012. La Habana: Ministerio de Trabajo y Seguridad Social.

———. 2013. Salario Medio en Cifras, 2012. Havana Cuba: ONEI.

———. 2014a. Salario medio en Cifras 2014. La Habana.

————. 2014b. Turismo: Llegada de Visitantes Internacionales, Enero-Marzo 2014. edited by Dirección de Industria y Medio Ambiente. Havana: ONEI.

Padrón Hernández, Maria. 2012. *Beans and Roses: Everyday Economies and Morality in Contemporary Havana, Cuba*, School of Global Studies, University of Gothenburg, Gothenburg, Sweden.

Palmer, Brian. 2010. Vivia la Revolucion? How has Cuba's socialist economy weathered the recession? *Slate*.

Pañellas Álvarez, Daybel. 2013. "¿Será posible el cambio de mentalidades? ." *Temas: Cultura, Ideología y Sociedad.* no. 73 (enero-marzo):91–99.

————. 2015. "Impactos subjectivos de las reformas económicas: Grupos e identidades sociales en la estructura social cubana." In *Cuba: los correlatos socioculturales del cambio económico*, edited by Mayra Paula Espina and Dayma Echevarría, 164–182. La Habana: Ruth Casa Editorial, Ciencias Sociales.

Pearson, Ruth. 1997. "Renegotiating the reproductive bargain: Gender analysis of economic transition in Cuba in the 1990s." *Development and Change* no. 28 (4):671–705. doi: 10.1111/1467-7660.00060.

Pérez Dueñas, Yaineris, Armando Rangel Rivero. 2012. "Quince años: impacto social y familia." In *Cuba etnografica*, 141–160. La Habana: Fundación Fernando Ortiz.

Pérez Izquierdo, V., Oberto Calderón, F., & González Rodríguez, M. . 2004. "Los trabajadores por cuenta propia en Cuba. ." *Cuba Siglo XXI(XLVII)*.

Pérez, Louis. 1998. *Cuba: between reform and revolution, 3rd edition.*

————. 2006. *Cuba: between reform and revolution.*

Pertierra, Anna Cristina. 2008. "En Casa: Women and Households in Post-Soviet Cuba." *Journal of Latin American Studies* no. 40:743–767. doi: 10.1017/s0022216x08004744.

————. 2011. *Cuba: the Struggle for Consumption.* Coconut Creek, FL: Caribbean Studies Press.

————. 2015 "Cuban girls and visual media: bodies and practices of (still-) socialist consumerism." *Continuum* no. 29 (221–11).

Peters, Philip 2000. *The Farmers Market: Crossroads of Cuba's New Economy.* Arlington, VA: Lexington Institute.

Phillips, EF. 2007. "Maybe Tomorrow I'll Turn Capitalist": Cuentapropismo in a Workers' State." *Law & Society Review* no. 41 (2):305–342.

Population Reference Bureau. 2016. *Glossary of Demographic Terms.* Population Reference Bureau [cited June 9, 2016 2016]. Available from http://www.prb.org/Publications/Lesson-Plans/Glossary.aspx.

Porter, Amy L. 2008. "Fleeting Dreams and Flowing Goods: Citizenship and Consumption in Havana Cuba." *PoLAR: Political and Legal Anthropology Review* no. 31 (1):134–149.

Portes, Alejandro. 1998. "Social Capital: Its Origins and Applications in Modern Sociology." *Annual Review of Sociology* no. 24:1–24.

Powell, Kathy. 2008. "Neoliberalism, the Special Period and Solidarity in Cuba." *Critique of Anthropology* no. 28 (2):177–197.

Ratilainen, Saara. 2012. "Business for Pleasure: Elite Women in the Russian Media." In *Rethinking Class in Russia*, edited by Suvi Salmenniemi, 45–66. London: Ashgate.

Redacción Café Fuerte. 2012a. "Cuba autoriza visitas de balseros, médicos y deportistas desertores." *Café Fuerte*, October 25, 2012.

Redacción Café Fuerte. 2012b. "Cuba: Mil emigrados retornan cada año para quedarse en el país." *Café Fuerte*, October 24, 2012.

Reuters. 1995. "Self-Employment May be Answer to Cuba's Problems." *LA Times*, February 23, 1995.

Ritter, Archibald 2005. "Survival Strategies and Economic Illegalities in Cuba." *Cuba in Transition* no. 15:342–359.

Ritter, ARM, and N Rowe. 2002. "Cuba: From" Dollarization" to" Euroization" or" Peso Reconsolidation"?" *Latin American Politics and Society* no. 44 (2):99–123.

Rivkin-Fish, M. 2009. "Tracing landscapes of the past in class subjectivity: Practics of memory and distinction in marketizing Russia." *American Ethnologist* no. 36 (1).

Rodríguez Alemañy, Daylén , and Jorge E. Torralbas. 2011. "Con el catalejo al revés": Identidad social de los grupos de la estructura socioclasista cubana. La Habana: Facultad de Psicología.

Rosendahl, Mona. 1997. *Inside the Revolution:Everyday Life in Socialist Cuba*. Ithaca, NY: Cornell University Press.

Round, John. 2012. "The Excluded Class: Russia's Forgotten Middle-aged Men." In *Rethinking Class in Russia*, edited by Suvi Salmenniemi, 241–256. London: Ashgate.

Sacchetti, Elena. 2009. "You Wanna Live, You've got to be Creative" the Experience of Microenterprise in Cuba." *Aibr-Revista De Antropologia Iberoamericana* no. 4 (2):173–203.

Salmenniemi, Suvi. 2012. "Introduction." In *Rethinking Class in Russia*, edited by Suvi Salmenniemi. London: Ashgate.

Sánchez Egozcue, Jorge Mario. 2012. "Challenges of Economic Restructuring in Cuba." *Socialism and Democracy* no. 60 (26).

1998. Cuba, inflación y estabilización.

Schmidt-Colinet, Lisa, Alex Schmoeger, and Florian Zeyfang. 2016. "Microbrigades – Variations of a Story and related projects." *Public* no. 52:195–201.

Segre, Roberto, Mario Coyula and Joseph Scarpaci. 1997. *Havana: Two Faces of the Antillean Metropolis*. Edited by RJ Johnston and P Knox, *World Cities Series*. Chichester, England: John Wiley & Sons.

Smith, B. 1999. "The Self-Employed in Cuba: A Street Level View." *Cuba in transition* no. 9:49–59.

Smith, Lois M., and Alfred Padula. 1996. *Sex and revolution : women in socialist Cuba*. New York: Oxford University Press.

Solberg, M. 1996. *Liten by, stort helvete: mangfoldige overlevelsestrategier i 90-årenes Cuba*. Universitetet i Oslo, Oslo.

Sorolla Fernández, Ileana. 2011. Apuntes de un cuaderno de bitácora: continuidades y cambios en el patrón migratorio externo cubano (2000–2010). In *III Seminario Permanente de Migración*. la Universidad de Quintana Roo, México.

Sorolla, Ileana and Rebeca Oroza 2011. Comportamiento previsible de las migraciones externas cubanas en el periodo 2010–2015. Actualización en el año 2011. La Habana: Centro de Estudios de Migraciones Internacionales, Universidad de La Habana.

Spetalnick, Matt, Alexander, David and Trotta, Daniel 2016. "U.S. eases Cuba trade and travel rules ahead of Obama visit." *Reuters*, March 15, 2016.

Stenning, Alison. 2005. "Where is the Post-socialist Working Class?: Working-Class Lives in the Spaces of (Post-)Socialism." *Sociology* no. 39 (5):983–999.

Tabío, Juan Carlos. 2008. El cuerno de la abundancia.

Tamayo, René. 2015. "¿En qué actividad y en qué provincia se gana más?" *Juventud Rebelde*, September 1, 2015.

Taylor, Henry Louis. 2009. *Inside el barrio: a bottom-up view of neighborhood life in Castro's Cuba*. Sterling, VA: Kumarian Press.

The Economist. 2004. Small business just got smaller; Life in Cuba. *The Economist*, October 16.

Togores González, Vivian. 2007. The Changes in the Socio-Economic Structure of Cuba: Income, Labor Markets and Consumption. In *International Seminar Equity and Social Mobility: Theory and Methodology with Applications to Bolivia, Brazil, Cuba, and South Africa*. Brasilia, Brazil: UNDP/IPC.

Togores González, Viviana. 1999. Cuba: efectos sociales de la crisis y el ajuste económico de los 90's. In *Balance de la economía cubana en los noventa*: Universidad de La Habana, Centro de Estudios de la Economía Cubana.

———. 2003. "Ingresos monetarios de la población, cambios en la distribución y efectos sobre el nivel de vida." In *15 Años: Centro de Estudios de la Economía Cubana*. . La Habana: Editorial Félix Varela.

Torralbas, Jorge Enrique, and Daylén Rodríguez Alemañy. 2011. *Con el catalejo al revés. Grupos e identidades en la estructura social cubana*, Facultad de Psicología, Universidad de la Habana, La Habana.

Trotta, Daniel. 2016. "Cuba's tourism boom is starting to slow down." *Business Insider*.

Uriarte, Mirén. 2008. "Social Impact of the Economic Measures." In *A contemporary Cuba reader: reinventing the Revolution*, edited by Philip Brenner, Marguerite Rose Jimenez, John M. Kirk, William M. LeoGrande, 285–291. Lanham: Rowman & Littlefield.

Valdés Carranza, Julio, Juan Valdés Paz, and Raúl J. Rosales. 2004. "Institutional Development and Social Policy in Cuba: "The Special Period." *Journal of International Affairs* no. 58 (1):175–188.

Valdés Paz, Juan 2005. Cuba in the "Special Period": From Equality to Equity. In *Report on the Americas #15 Changes in Cuban Society since the 90s*, edited by Lilian Bobea Joseph S. Tulchin, Mayra P. Espina Prieto, Rafael Hernández. Washington DC: Woodrow Wilson Center for International Scholars.

Vidal Alejandro, Pavel 2010. Cuban Economic Policy under the Raul Castro Government. Institute of Developing Economies of the Japan External Trade Organization.

Weinreb, Amelia Rosenberg. 2009. *Cuba in the shadow of change: daily life in the twilight of the revolution, Contemporary Cuba.* Gainesville: University Press of Florida.

Wilson, Marisa. 2014. *Everyday Moral Economies: Food, Politics and Scale in Cuba.* Edited by Niel Coe and Joanna Bullard, *RGS-IBG*: John Wiley and Sons.

Wilson, Marissa L. 2009a. "Ideas and ironies of food scarcity and consumption in the moral economy of Tuta, Cuba." *JASO-online* no. 228.

———. 2009b. "'¡ No tenemos viandas!'Cultural ideas of scarcity and need." *International Journal of Cuban Studies* no. 2 (1):1.

Yurchak, Alexei. 2003. "Russian Neoliberal: The Entrepreneurial Ethic and the Spirit of "True Careerism." *Russian Review* no. 62 (1):72–90.

Index

Page references for figures are italicized.

About the Author

Hope Bastian is a professor at San Geronimo College, University of Havana, and Associate Director of the Consortium for Advanced Studies Abroad (CASA) in Havana, Cuba. She has worked with educational programs in Havana since 2004 through the Martin Luther King Center, Casa de las Américas and other Cuban institutions. In addition to her teaching and research, she frequently lectures for visiting academic groups and consults for faculty members and administrators organizing academic programs in Cuba. Her website is www.hopebastian.com.

Made in the USA
Middletown, DE
27 January 2024

48536476R00128